THE CHATTER BOX

An Insider's Account of the Irrelevance of Parliament in the Making of Canadian Foreign and Defence Policy

Benson & Hedges

BY
ROY REMPEL

BREAKOUT EDUCATIONAL NETWORK

BREAKOUT EDUCATIONAL NETWORK
IN ASSOCIATION WITH
DUNDURN PRESS
TORONTO · OXFORD

Publisher: Inta D. Erwin
Copy-editors: Debbie Smith and Amanda Stewart, First Folio Resource Group
Designer: Bruna Brunelli, Brunelli Designs
Printer: Webcom

National Library of Canada Cataloguing in Publication Data

Rempel Roy, 1962–
    The chatter box: an insider's account of the increasing irrelevance
of parliament in the making of Canadian foreign and defence policy/by Roy Rempel

One of the 16 vols. and 14 hours of video which make up the
    underground royal commission report
Includes bibliographical references and index.
ISBN 1-55002-425-6

1. Canada. Parliament. 2. Paliamentary practice — Canada.
3. Canada. Parliament — Reform. I. Title. II. Title: underground royal
commission report.

JL136.R44 2002   328.71   C2002-902305-X

1   2   3   4   5   06   05   04   03   02

Printed and bound in Canada.
Printed on recycled paper. ❂
www.dundurn.com

Exclusive Canadian broadcast rights for the *underground royal commission* report

intelligent television

Check your cable or satellite listings for telecast times

Visit the *urc* Web site link at:
www.ichanneltv.com

THE CHATTER BOX

About the *underground royal commission* Report

Since September 11, 2001, there has been an uneasy dialogue among Canadians as we ponder our position in the world, especially vis à vis the United States. Critically and painfully, we are re-examining ourselves and our government. We are even questioning our nation's ability to retain its sovereignty.

The questions we are asking ourselves are not new. Over the last 30 years, and especially in the dreadful period of the early 1990s, leading up to the Quebec referendum of 1995, inquiries and Royal commissions, one after another, studied the state of the country. What *is* new is that eight years ago, a group of citizens looked at this parade of inquiries and commissions and said, "These don't deal with the real issues." They wondered how it was possible for a nation that was so promising and prosperous in the early 60s to end up so confused, divided, and troubled. And they decided that what was needed was a different kind of investigation — driven from the grassroots 'bottom,' and not from the top. Almost as a provocation, this group of people, most of whom were affiliated with the award winning documentary-maker, Stornoway Productions, decided to do it themselves — and so was born the *underground royal commission!*

What began as a television documentary soon evolved into much more. Seven young, novice researchers, hired right out of university, along with a television crew and producer, conducted interviews with people in government, business, the military and in all walks of life, across the country. What they discovered went beyond anything they had expected. The more they learned, the larger the implications grew. The project continued to evolve and has expanded to include a total of 23 researchers over the last several years. The results are the 14 hours of video and 16 books that make up the first interim report of the *underground royal commission.*

So what *are* the issues? The report of the *underground royal commission* clearly shows us that regardless of region, level of government, or political party, we are operating under a wasteful system ubiquitously lacking in accountability. An ever-weakening connection between the electors and the elected means that we are slowly and irrevocably losing our right to know our government. The researchers' experiences demonstrate that it is almost impossible for a member of the public, or in most cases, even for a member of Parliament, to actually trace how our tax dollars are spent. Most disturbing is the fact that our young people have been stuck with a crippling IOU that has effectively hamstrung their future. No wonder, then, that Canada is not poised for reaching its potential in the 21st century.

The *underground royal commission* report, prepared in large part by and for the youth of Canada, provides the hard evidence of the problems you and I may long have suspected. Some of that evidence makes it clear that, as ordinary Canadians, we are every bit as culpable as our politicians — for our failure to demand accountability, for our easy acceptance of government subsidies and services established without proper funding in place, and for the disservice we have done to our young people through the debt we have so blithely passed on to them. But the real purpose of the *underground royal commission* is to ensure that we better understand how government processes work and what role we play in them. Public policy issues must be understandable and accessible to the public if they are ever to be truly addressed and resolved. The *underground royal commission* intends to continue pointing the way for bringing about constructive change in Canada.

— Stornoway Productions

Books in the *underground royal commission* Report

"Just Trust Us"

The Chatter Box
The Chance of War
Talking Heads Talking Arms: (3 volumes)
No Life Jackets
Whistling Past the Graveyard
Playing the Ostrich

Days of Reckoning
Taking or Making Wealth
Guardians on Trial
Goodbye Canada?
Down the Road Never Travelled
Secrets in High Places
On the Money Trail

Does Your Vote Count?
A Call to Account
Reflections on Canadian Character

14 hours of videos also available with the *underground royal commission* report.
Visit Stornoway Productions at www.stornoway.com for a list of titles.

For Rebecca,
whose assistance in editing and helping organize this manuscript
was invaluable!

TABLE OF CONTENTS

FOREWORD

There is a great deal of literature dealing with the public policy process of Canadian national defence. The memories and reminiscences of a few politicians add detail to our understanding of how Canada decides its national defence policy, though few soldiers or officials offer much to the chronicle. What is missing from the record is information about how political leaders and parties actually consider these central national matters behind closed doors. Roy Rempel has carefully, and at times passionately, pried open many doors to allow us a peek at the partisan politics of national defence in Parliament and in the political parties over the last 10 years.

The view is not always pleasant. One encounters an establishment of members of Parliament who seem unable to comprehend national defence policy except in partisan terms. MPs typically hunt through the daily headlines, "the clips," seeking ways to embarrass the government or, from the government benches, ways to deflect criticism on to the opposition. On the one hand we see opposition parties bereft of information on what may be happening to defence dollars and members of the Canadian Armed Forces. On the other hand we witness Cabinet ministers who have access to critical information using it not to enlighten debate but to obfuscate meaning and confuse the opposition — and by extension every Canadian. The defence of Canada is treated as a political weapon, not a matter of urgent concern.

It is not easy for "an ordinary member of Parliament" to understand the intricacies of defence policy making, and there are real obstacles before those who try. Members of Parliament have many duties that consume much of their time. Interests vary and it would be unreasonable to expect every member in every party to be absorbed in defence policy and the Canadian Forces. Yet Parliament does not provide much assistance to members who might wish to become informed or to build on experiences gained outside Parliament. Even members of parliamentary committees who deal routinely with security, defence and foreign policy matters have little support. They depend on open sources, a small committee staff and a few experts inside and outside their parties for advice on and explanations of the issues of the day.

These revelations are not entirely new, but what is particularly disturbing is the evident tendency across Parliament to see national defence policy as merely a partisan tool. From Roy Rempel's perspective as an insider who worked on the Hill, hired specifically to research defence issues, one sees party leaders who concoct questions and policy options from thin air and fashion crude interpretations of facts to suit their political interests. Researchers are routinely dismissed or ignored. Questions are prepared for Parliament not as a means to hold ministers to account, but to hold the attention of the media. The purpose for asking questions is most often to "take a position" in order to look sincere and decisive. For the opposition, once the question is asked the answer can be ignored. On the government side, once the answer is given the issue can be neglected. What matters in Parliament — and to the media — is the politics of national defence policy, not the policy itself.

Governments have, over the years, and not just in regards to defence policy, recruited the public service to their cause — to stay in power come what may. The Defence and Foreign Affairs department bureaucracies, as Rempel explains in painful detail, have come to see themselves as partisan supporters of the government. Bureaucrats treat members of the opposition — and backbenchers besides — if not as the enemy, then at best as their ministers' personal foes, to be avoided at all cost. The recent truthful, apolitical testimony before Parliament by the chief of the defence staff and his senior officers concerning the "Eggleton affair" was a sensation only because it was so unusual to see any government official or military officer give blunt, nonpartisan responses to highly political questions.

Rempel records instances in which back-bench members of the governing party, though seemingly speaking their own minds in Parliament, were in fact merely reading texts loaded with political purpose, provided to them by officials working at the behest of their ministers. There are many ways besides deceitfulness and artful dodging to mislead Parliament and the public. Asking members to present to Parliament not their views, but the views of the very bureaucratic ghost writers they are supposed to be overseeing, seems the nadir of political skulduggery; but there are apparently no end of willing participants to this charade.

Both sides of the House play games in Parliament to win public support by their show of decisiveness. Rempel notes the constant changing of seats during Question Period and debates as members attempt to fill the space around speakers to give the impression, through the House of Commons television network, that members are actively discussing the great issues of the day, even though the House may be practically empty. It is, in Rempel's view, yet another attempt to mislead Canadians. Though this tactic is so common as to be unremarkable, it becomes a serious matter when Parliament is asked to debate national defence issues, and none as important as the deployment of Canadians to war zones around the world. Here scornful mockery reaches grand proportions.

Canadians have come to expect that Parliament will be called to debate war and peace because few matters are more important when national security is threatened and the lives of members of the Canadian Forces may be on the line. Moreover, politicians, especially while in opposition, have often rightly made an enormous fuss over military failures in good order and discipline. Duty to Canada and the critical requirements of civil control over the military demand — as the commissioner of the inquiry into the deployment of the Canadian Forces to Somalia so eloquently wrote — "a vigilant Parliament."

But what do Canadians get in moments of crisis? Most often they see a near empty House where a few members of Parliament, detailed for duty by their whips, deliver dreary dribble in sombre, self-righteous tones. Ministers, even the principal ministers, often leave the Commons

13

immediately after delivering their required remarks. The debates, if that is what they are meant to be, become a rehearsed repetition of positions rather than a search for a national point of view. No greater disservice has ever been provided by so few to so many.

Rempel brings to life this central failure of Parliament and parliamentarians of all ranks as he describes "sleepwalking to war." He records the dearth of debate about Canadian strategies in the war in Kosovo as the most recent example of the failure of Parliament to guide and control national defence. The failure was not, however, merely a failure to consider if and how Canada would participate in the war. Rather, he describes a jumble of political confusion, as ministers and members of Parliament, both in the opposition and in the government back benches, focused primarily on "the news story of the week," seemingly oblivious to the significance of these events and stories for Canada.

Overseeing the defence of Canada is Parliament's most important duty. Yet most observers and scholars would say that it is the least understood and most neglected subject before the House. Some argue that Parliament is increasingly irrelevant in most fields of government, but especially so in defence and foreign policy. But the fault is not with Parliament, the system or the grand buildings on the Hill. If Parliament is irrelevant, then the fault is not in our institutions, but in ourselves. One can blame citizens and urge them to direct their representatives to act responsibly, but this is a faint hope when people are consumed with their personal lives. Indeed, it is because of this circumstance that Canadians elect their peers to go to Parliament to represent their interests, not their member's party's interests.

Canadians should not be expected to have to watch suspiciously the behaviour of their members of Parliament to ensure that they will act in the public interest. Yet this important book argues otherwise. Every Canadian, therefore, should confront the facts presented here and then demand an explanation for why the political establishment and Parliament in its present form are failing Canada, and failing the members of the Canadian Armed Forces especially.

Dr. Douglas Bland
Chair of Defence Management Studies
Queen's University, Kingston, Ontario
2002

INTRODUCTION

During the German Empire (1871–1918) a national parliament was established in that country. This parliament, or *Reichstag*, was the first in Germany to be elected by universal (albeit male) suffrage. While the *Reichstag* was powerful in theory it soon became known as the *Quasselbude* or "Chatter Box." Elected legislators hotly debated national issues, but their power remained largely fictional. Real power was instead concentrated in the hands of the aristocratic national elite.

This book is about my own experience in Canada's "Chatter Box" — our House of Commons. Most Canadians may believe that Parliament is the centrepiece of our democracy. Indeed, in theory our Parliament is supreme. If one were to examine the official job description for MPs, one might find references to functions such as debating; passing and amending federal legislation; raising and approving the expenditure of federal tax revenue; and overseeing the activities and conduct of government.

The reality, however, is quite different. In truth MPs do none of these things. To the extent that real "debating" occurs in the House of Commons, it almost never influences the outcome of proposed legislation. Every piece of legislation passed by Parliament originates outside of Parliament — in the bureaucracy. Furthermore, it is rare for any bill introduced in the House of Commons actually to be amended by the House itself. Legislative outcomes in Canada are always predetermined and MPs play almost no role in the process beyond acting as rubber stamps for whatever the government wants to do.

MPs have no role with regard to the raising or spending of public money. The Estimates (or the government's annual budgetary proposals) are always passed exactly as introduced.

And as I found during my three years on the Hill, MPs are also not playing an effective role in overseeing the activities of government in any area — particularly, I found, in the area of foreign policy and national defence. The only power that parliamentarians have is to try and attract media attention. This results in a Parliament in which debates are superficial and melodramatic and in which discussions are rarely relevant or serious. In essence the Canadian Parliament has become a modern, 21st century "Chatter Box" from which the real interests of ordinary Canadians are largely excluded.

The absence of any serious debate in our national legislature has profound implications for the ability of Canada to shape international events, to respond to internal crises and emergencies and even for our capacity to protect our national sovereignty. It is my view that unless Canadians are able make our national institutions relevant to addressing the problems that confront us as a nation, our national sovereignty will continue to erode and could even disappear.

CHAPTER ONE

Parliament and the War on Terror

I first heard the news of the attack on the World Trade Center when I walked into the office of the leader of the Opposition in Centre Block on Parliament Hill. I was on my way to a meeting with the Opposition's foreign affairs spokesperson, Brian Pallister. Brian had planned a meeting with officials from the Leader's research and communications staff to go over preparations for the coming fall session of Parliament. Parliament was on its three-month summer break, with the fall session set to resume on September 17, less than a week away. As the scope of the day's tragedy unfolded, it became readily apparent that the entire agenda for the fall session of Parliament had just changed.

All of us will remember where we were on Tuesday, September 11, 2001. Like the attack on Pearl Harbor, the attacks of September 11 awakened America in a stark fashion to the clear and present danger posed to the security of the United States. However, this time the enemy was not striking just at military targets — indeed the preferred targets were unarmed civilians.

I was certainly convinced that had the terrorists been able to, they would have sought to kill three million people on September 11 rather than 3,000. With the proliferation of nuclear, bacteriological and chemical weapons around the world and given the existence of states and regimes willing to support terrorist objectives, such a tragedy is not beyond the realm of possibility.

It was clear to me at that time, as it was to many others, that Canada should be in the forefront of the coming battle against the terrorist threat. For one thing, 24 Canadians had died in the World Trade Center on September 11. The terrorists had certainly made no distinction between American citizens and those of other nationalities in their attack. They obviously could not be expected to make any such distinctions in the future. For another, the attack on the World Trade Center represented an attack on the North American economy. Nearly 80 percent of Canadian trade is with the United States, and one in four Canadian jobs is linked to Canada–U.S. trade. Therefore these attacks represented a serious threat to Canada's economy as well. It was obvious that with $1.7 billion in cross-border trade with the United States every day, Canada had to be on the inside of any U.S. security perimeter and not on the outside looking in. Lastly, it had been apparent since the arrest of convicted terrorist Ahmed Ressam on the Canada–U.S. border in December 1999 that terrorists were using Canada as a staging ground for operations being carried out in the United States. Canada simply could not afford to be a transitway for such attacks and would have to take all necessary measures to prevent this.

But on September 11 all that parliamentarians knew was what the public knew — that a major and co-ordinated terrorist attack had been launched against the very heart of the United States; that terrorists had, seemingly with relative ease, hijacked four planes and crashed three of them into the World Trade Center and the Pentagon.

On September 11 few members of Parliament (MPs) likely knew who Osama bin Laden was, what al-Qaeda was, who the Taliban were, what the political/military situation was in Afghanistan or how the terrorist crisis was potentially linked to other Middle East problems. There had been little or no serious discussion of such issues in Parliament in the past and this made most MPs uninformed. There was a steep learning curve to go through after September 11; however, after three years experience on the Hill I knew that most MPs could expect to have no input on the crisis confronting Canada, even if they made the most concerted of efforts to come up to speed on the issues.

"Where is the News?"

I came to work on Parliament Hill in September 1998. In my studies at university I specialized in international relations, strategic studies and Canadian defence policy. Although I worked for the executive council of the Newfoundland government for a time, my principal expertise is in the area of Canadian defence and foreign policy. I graduated with a Ph.D. in international relations from Queen's University in 1993 and taught international relations and Canadian foreign and defence policy at Memorial University in Newfoundland from 1994 to 1998.

It was on the strength of this background that I was hired in 1998 by the office of the leader of the Opposition, primarily to work on Canadian defence policy issues. When I was hired Paul Wilson was the director of the research office and, like me, he had graduated with a Ph.D. from Queen's University, though his was in history. I had not known Paul at Queen's, but I soon found that he was most interested in increasing the policy expertise of the Leader's research office in several areas, including defence. Foreign affairs and defence had not really been a strong point of the Reform Party platform until after the 1997 election. Preston Manning, the leader at that time, had preferred to focus his interest primarily on domestic, and especially constitutional, issues.

When I arrived in Ottawa I was introduced to the rest of the research staff. The staff includes a director of research and about six to 10 policy analysts, or "researchers." Each researcher is normally assigned several areas of responsibility, or files, and I was no exception. The duties of a researcher are first to examine those news stories that touch on the file areas he or she is responsible for and to determine where questions in Question Period should be focused. Secondly, researchers prepare background notes on current issues and write policy papers and proposals. They also write speeches and occasional articles for the Leader and members, and they do background research for House debates. Given the number of file areas one researcher covers, it is simply impossible to stay on top of all the issues in all policy areas at all times. As a result, researchers tend to focus a great deal of their attention on the issues of the day, as highlighted in the newspapers and on TV. This is also the focus of most MPs.

Many who have worked on the Hill, both MPs and staff, have long wanted to change this reactive approach. Certainly one of my own objectives was to help MPs ask questions to bring about realistic and more substantive debate in a way that might influence national policy and better advance Canadian interests. I believe that more reasoned and realistic discussions in Parliament are an essential prerequisite to establishing a longer-term consensus to effectively advance Canada's interests abroad. However, I gradually learned that this is not what Parliament is all about. Parliament is simply too theatrical and devoid of any real authority or power to allow for such discussions.

When I arrived on the Hill I had thought that perhaps there might be some contact between researchers of different parties in order to discuss issues and develop co-ordinated strategies for MPs, both in the House and especially in committee. But the relationship between political parties on the Hill is far too partisan and there is virtually no professional contact or communication between staff of different parties except on rare and discrete issues.

Parliament is used by government not as a source for new ideas but rather to legitimize policy decisions that the prime minister and Cabinet have already made. I began to awaken to this reality almost immediately, when in the fall of 1998 the House of Commons Standing Foreign Affairs Committee produced a report on the subject of NATO's nuclear policy. In drafting that report the government simply used its majority on the committee to rubber stamp the policy that Foreign Minister Lloyd Axworthy had already decided to pursue. The report suggested that Canada work for the elimination of nuclear weapons and push NATO to alter its nuclear strategy.

Based on my experience I knew that these objectives were completely unrealistic given Canada's modest international influence. NATO's major powers had repeatedly rejected the Canadian initiative, with Britain's minister of state for the armed forces calling it "completely unacceptable."[1] How could a country that had no nuclear capability itself and that was part of a nuclear-armed alliance hope to persuade other nuclear powers to relinquish weapons that they regarded as essential for their own security? How could one seriously expect to de-invent a technology that had existed for 50 years?

After some discussion the Reform Party caucus came to the conclusion that the official Opposition should write a more realistic dissenting opinion, calling on Canada to work for arms control and judicious arms reductions, but emphasizing the importance of keeping Canadian foreign policy firmly planted in the real world. Fellow researcher Chris Champion and I wrote the dissenting opinion. It was my hope that the adoption of a more realistic position by our party would raise the level of debate.

The committee members were furious when Reform members announced that they would dissent from the majority report. The committee then arbitrarily limited the Reform minority report to no more than two pages. Even so, the entire issue received only limited media attention. After a day or two it disappeared from the pages of the newspapers.

Because issues in the news are here today and gone tomorrow, after an issue is no longer topical many MPs simply forget about it. It is not uncommon for some MPs, having completely forgotten a stance that was taken a few months previously, to take exactly the opposite position later. In such an environment it is very difficult to address issues in anything but the most superficial manner.

The melodramatic nature of Question Period further encourages superficiality. Questions and answers are limited to 35 seconds each. Both government and opposition seek to get the best sound bite that they can out of those 35 seconds. As a result, Question Period has come to follow a predictable pattern. Opposition questions seek to embarrass the government; government answers rarely answer the questions posed and instead spin whatever message the government is seeking to convey while making the opposition's approach appear silly. There is little real debate in such an environment.

The partisan nature of Question Period sets the tone for all House activities, and even committee sessions are usually conflictual. In this atmosphere it becomes virtually impossible for Parliament to fulfill any meaningful policy-related function. "Where is the news?" is the single most important criterion for any question asked and for most Parliament Hill activity. "If the point won't make it into the media," I was often told, "there is almost no reason for making it."

In Canada Parliament is not an institution from which new and serious ideas are usually allowed to emerge. The government has its own agenda and it always gets its own way if it is determined to push a measure through. The partisan nature of the political system also means that the government is extremely reluctant to accept (at least overtly) any suggestion from the opposition, no matter how sensible it may be. The fact that opposition proposals are usually designed to embarrass the government in some way does not help matters.

Working on the Hill, I have found that Parliament has little effective function beyond acting as a "theatre" to expose government shortcomings. It is almost totally irrelevant in influencing government policy and in representing the interests of the Canadian people. This, I have to say, has been the single most frustrating aspect of my own job. More importantly, it was in this atmosphere that Parliament tried to "respond" to the attacks of September 11.

Parliament Confronts the War on Terror

Prior to the events of September 11 and in my capacity as a defence researcher, I had been looking at some of the past actions committed by the al-Qaeda terrorist network against the United States. Those actions included the bombing of the Khobar towers in Saudi Arabia in 1996, the attacks against the U.S. embassies in Tanzania and Kenya in 1998 (which actually killed more local Muslims than they did Americans) and the bombing of the USS *Cole* in Aden in 2000.

Chris Champion followed a different connection in his capacity as immigration researcher. He looked in some detail at the activities of the Ahmed Ressam terrorist cell which had operated in Canada prior to 1999. Ressam, an Algerian national, had entered Canada in 1994 and immediately began to plan attacks against both American targets and the Jewish community in Montreal. Despite links to unsavoury groups and a conviction for break and enter, he had been able to stay in Canada and was even able to leave the country for terrorist training in Afghanistan and return under an assumed name. He was finally arrested, not by Canadian authorities, but by U.S. customs officials at the Canada–U.S. border in December 1999 as he attempted to enter the United States to carry out bomb attacks to coincide with the start of the new millennium. This and other cases pointed to serious problems in the Canadian refugee determination system. In light of our research, neither Chris nor I found ourselves totally uninformed regarding the background of the September 11 events or of the sorts of concerns these events could and should raise. That, of course, was our job.

On September 12, the day after the attacks, I was called to leader Stockwell Day's office to discuss the position that the official

Opposition should take to the horrifying events of the previous day. It was agreed that the most important message should be sympathy for the victims and their families. It was also decided to stand with the prime minister and show a united front. However, serious steps were required to shore up Canada's security, and it was clear that the opposition would have to call for strong measures to protect Canadians.

The same day, in a separate meeting, all the Alliance spokespeople, or "critics," responsible for national security files were brought together in a pan-Canadian conference call. Party policy critics are those MPs who are responsible for following government policy in particular areas, questioning particular initiatives of the government and hopefully advancing policy alternatives.

The critics on the call that day included our solicitor general and our defence, transport, justice and immigration critics. No commercial aircraft was yet flying anywhere in North America, so it wasn't even clear at that time if the MPs could make it back to Ottawa for September 17. But it was immediately apparent that all of our MPs were convinced that however Canada reacted, the response would have to be a strong one.

After each MP provided an overview of what he or she saw as the main issues in his or her particular portfolio area, it was agreed that each critic would draft a list of three priorities for action in each portfolio, which we would then seek to put forward in Parliament.

It was already evident that the United States was undertaking a complete review of its internal security measures. Within days of the attack Congress appropriated $40 billion in emergency funding. It passed a resolution authorizing the president to take all necessary measures to protect the United States. The president ordered the mobilization of 50,000 U.S. military reservists and national guardsmen. New security measures were ordered at all U.S. airports and it was announced that sky marshals would henceforth be flying on domestic American flights. Additional legislation was passed within weeks to complement an anti-terrorism act that had already been passed in 1996.

Shortly after September 11 a briefing was provided to Stockwell Day by Mel Capp, Ottawa's senior civil servant. Mr. Capp was accompanied by the commissioner of the RCMP, Giuliano Zaccardelli. The briefing did not provide any classified information, but was nevertheless remarkably frank on the situation confronting the country. Brian Pallister, Jim MacEachern (the leader's chief of staff), Ted Morton (the director of research), Mark Cameron (Day's senior policy advisor) and I were in attendance. These are all very talented people. Ted Morton, for instance, is a University of Calgary professor who has published extensively on constitutional and judicial issues. He was also elected to the Senate from Alberta in 1998, in a provincial process that the prime minister had refused to recognize.

Mr. Capp initially reported that it was feared that up to 100 Canadians, and perhaps even as many as 500, might have been killed at the World Trade Center. This information shocked everyone in the room and was based on the number of missing person reports that the Canadian consulate in New York had initially received. Fortunately most of these people were later accounted for and the actual Canadian death toll was smaller than originally forecast — around two dozen people. But the scope of the danger was clear. Both Canada and the United States faced a grave threat.

After Capp's briefing it was agreed that the government should be pressed harder to take a firm position. I argued that, with the Canadian death toll potentially high, we had to emphasize that this was clearly not just an attack on Americans and America. Day agreed and borrowed a line suggested by Brian Pallister, that there could be "no rear-guard positions in the war on terrorism." Everyone believed that Canadians would be expecting a resolute response and we had to assume that the events in New York and Washington would be the only item on the House agenda once Parliament reconvened on September 17.

The official Opposition made the war on terrorism its top priority in the new session of Parliament. Other parties did the same. Since MPs are elected to represent the views of Canadians, many might expect that the House of Commons would actually have been involved in shaping the nature of the Canadian response. But it was not. Indeed, every initiative coming from the opposition, no matter what the content, was rejected.

Theoretically all opposition parties have the means to bring proposals before the House for consideration. They all receive a certain number of so-called "supply days" to introduce issues for discussion. After September 11 those supply days were used by the opposition parties to address the terrorism issue. The Alliance decided to use its first supply day, on September 18, to press for new Canadian anti-terrorist legislation.

The supply day motion that the Canadian Alliance proposed on September 18 suggested that the Justice Committee of the House of

Commons study several proposals to serve as the basis for a new anti-terrorism act. These proposals were based on similar legislative provisions incorporated in Britain's Anti-Terrorism Act, adopted in 2000, and consisted of measures such as the naming and banning of terrorist groups; prohibiting fundraising by such groups in Canada and stripping them of charitable status; the power to freeze and seize their assets; increased resources for law enforcement agencies; and the power to extradite terrorists from Canada if wanted for crimes abroad, even when they were being sought for capital offences.

These proposals were relatively straightforward. The last was the most controversial since in February 2001 the Supreme Court had ruled that the minister of justice had to seek assurance, except in exceptional cases, that the death penalty would not be imposed on any person extradited from Canada. The Court had not actually defined what it meant by "exceptional cases," but since the government maintained that it had the ability to extradite individuals from Canada even in capital cases, the Alliance proposal to study options for clarifying what was meant by "exceptional cases" should not have been a problem.

Even so, the government had its members vote down the motion. The vote was 199 to 70. In subsequent weeks the government took other steps that signaled it would move entirely at its own pace and was not interested in any real parliamentary input. Later in that first week, as committees began to meet, opposition members tried to call witnesses who could discuss issues related to the terrorist crisis to appear before those committees. When government whips learned that efforts were being made to call the minister and commissioner responsible for Canada Customs before the Finance Committee, Liberal members were called out of committee one by one to deny the committee quorum, that is, the minimum number of members required to be present for a committee to meet. The result was that the Finance Committee could not meet.

For the most part, debates and discussions were limited and superficial. On November 5 members of the Standing Committee on National Defence were simply told by the chair of the committee, David Pratt, that they would be considering an interim report that same day — contents unknown. That evening they were finally shown the report, which turned out to be on the terrorism crisis and military readiness. They were then given less than an hour to read it before commenting on its contents. The report was approved that same evening. Only the

Alliance dissented, partly because of the shotgun process and partly to argue for more specific recommendations.

The national media devoted almost no attention to these issues. The fact that an anti-terrorist proposal was voted down in Parliament on the second day of its sitting got almost no play. Despite all the efforts by MPs and opposition staff to better understand the consequences and implications of September 11 and to draft policy proposals, the media was actually waiting for word from the only person who really counted in determining Canada's response. Political power in Canada is concentrated in the hands of the prime minister, certain key ministers and very senior advisors. On an issue like the war on terrorism, that means that there is ultimately only one point of view that really counts — that of the prime minister.

When Parliament resumed on September 17 the opposition had hoped that the government would immediately take the opportunity to outline some of the measures that it planned to take in response to the attacks. But those who were looking for this were disappointed. There was no sign that the government was ready to do anything specific.

The government had called a "take-note" debate — where members are able to express their views on a given issue — for the first day that the House was sitting. Take-note debates centre on a government-proposed motion on which members are able to speak. No specific proposals are usually made in such debates and there is no voting.

The motion for the September 17 take-note debate expressed condolences to the American people. It also reaffirmed Canada's commitment "to the humane values of free and democratic society and its determination to bring to justice the perpetrators of this attack on these values and to defend civilization from any future terrorist attack."[2]

The prime minister kept his message vague and general when he spoke to this motion. He expressed his support for the United States, but without announcing any specific measures. Nor did the speech announce any initiatives for reinforcing Canadian security. Despite the fact that the prime minister declared that everything changed as a result of September 11, it was clear that he was in no rush to be thrown off the agenda that he had already set for the fall term in Parliament.

This left most of his ministers in limbo. No minister can take a major policy initiative without the prime minister's go ahead, so most ministers were put in the uncomfortable position of defending the status quo. This remained the case well into October, when just $250 million was finally allocated for new security measures, warships were dispatched to the Indian Ocean and a new anti-terrorist bill was introduced in the House.

Most ministers could get away with uttering platitudes in response to serious questions. For instance, the minister of transport, David Collenette, initially refused even to consider the idea of putting sky marshals on commercial aircraft, saying that this idea simply wasn't "the Canadian way."[3] He later relented in the face of American insistence that any aircraft flying into Washington D.C.'s Reagan airport would be required to have armed security personnel on board. The Alliance's transport critic, James Moore, had also been very successful in making the issue of sky marshals a major public relations issue.

But the government's proposed terrorism bill was in a different, more familiar category. Instead of reflecting the views of MPs who actually represented Canadians, the anti-terrorism bill was entirely the creation of lawyers in the Justice Department. Like all legislation, it may have reflected the priorities of the legal community, but it had no input from the representatives of ordinary Canadians. While it is right and proper for government to lead in initiating policy, there should at least be real opportunity for serious parliamentary input.

There were many opposition parliamentarians who could make substantive contributions if allowed to: Vic Toews, the Alliance justice critic, was a former Manitoba attorney general as well as a former Crown prosecutor; Peter McKay of the PCs was also a former Crown attorney. But the legislation had no such input. Opposition proposals to address the ease with which terrorists had been able to enter Canada were rejected. The legislation failed to address Canada's inability to deport many suspected terrorists, and it still allowed terrorists convicted of mass murder to apply for parole after 25 years. It also largely ignored the concerns of civil libertarians that some of the provisions granted the government sweeping new powers which might become permanent instead of sunsetting when the terrorist crisis passed.

Parliament was unable to force the government to address these issues. The prime minister stated that he alone would make all decisions on changes. In responding to a question from the NDP's Bill Blaikie on November 5, he simply stated, "I will listen to members first and I might say yes or no."[4]

"I might say yes or no" — Such concentrated power characterizes the nature of Canadian parliamentary government as I have experienced it. Every issue of any importance and even issues of limited significance that are raised in the House are entirely micromanaged by the Prime Minister's Office (PMO). This reality has made a sham out of debates in the House of Commons and rendered the views of MPs irrelevant.

The review of the terrorist legislation by the House Justice Committee was largely a formality. The only amendments permitted were those that were suggested by outside legal groups close to officials in the Justice Department, like the Canadian Bar Association. While 77 percent of ordinary Canadians thought that the government did "too little" or "far too little" to make sure that Canada does not act as a base for terrorists, and 76 percent even agreed with capital punishment for terrorists, these views were simply ignored in the nature of the legislation that was adopted.[5]

Similarly, the dispatch of Canadian ships to the Indian Ocean and the later decision to commit ground troops to Afghanistan were both announced by the minister of national defence in the break weeks of the fall session, when Parliament was not sitting. Despite the support of a majority of members of Parliament for military measures, no serious debate, let alone a vote, was permitted on these decisions.

Majority governments, which are the norm in Canada, are immune to domestic political pressure whenever they choose to be so — and increasingly the concentration of power in Canada has allowed governments to govern in that manner. The most significant influence on the prime minister during the terrorist crisis emanated from outside the country. Ironically for a government that constantly preached a strong sovereignty theme, the views of the United States were perhaps most dominant in determining the positions that Canada took both with regard to continental security and the deployment of the Canadian Forces. In this sense, the discussions that Jean Chrétien had with President Bush at the White House on September 24, more than anything that was said in Parliament, governed the decisions taken by the Canadian government after that date.

While there were those who pleaded for Parliament to be given a significant role, these requests largely fell on deaf ears. One such plea came from Joe Clark in his opening address on September 17:

Parliament should be told what changes the government is now contemplating, what reviews of policy it plans, what military, intelligence or other role Canada can play in a campaign against the terrorists. If some of that information is confidential then let the government give that information to parliamentary leaders on a confidential basis. This is a Canadian concern. This is Parliament's concern. This is not a matter reserved to those who sit in the secrecy of the Privy Council Office. To rebuild the trust of the public, to rebuild the trust of our allies, to rebuild the trust of financial markets, Parliament must be fully informed and advised.[6]

But that oversight function is simply not one that Parliament is able to perform in the Canadian political system, nor was it permitted 10 years previously when Clark was minister for external affairs.

I can think of very few occasions in my time on the Hill when the House of Commons played the role for which it was intended — either legislating, controlling spending or providing real oversight over the activities of government. The terrorist crisis of 2001 was no exception.

"Punching Above Our Weight":
Parliament and the Decline of Canada's International Influence

I was watching the CBC nightly news one evening, shortly after Canada made its decision to deploy ships to the Indian Ocean. This particular broadcast included a piece by Brian Stewart on the military commitment that Canada had just announced. After his report Stewart sat down with CBC anchor Peter Mansbridge and commented that the size of the commitment showed how Canada was "punching above its weight" in the current conflict. How the deployment, by a so-called G8 country, of just five ships — which within just six months would have to be reduced to only three or four ships because neither personnel nor ships were there in sufficient numbers to sustain anything more — could be said to constitute punching above the country's weight was left unexplained.

The myth that is believed by much of the Canadian establishment is that Canada is a country with significant influence internationally. The government's 1995 foreign policy statement *Canada in the World* claims:

Canada occupies a position of leadership among the open, advanced societies which are becoming increasingly influential as world power is dispersing and becoming more defined in economic terms ... Canada can further its global interests better than any other country through its active membership in key international groupings ... Canada, thus, is in a privileged position to influence change and to benefit from opportunities as we move toward the end of the 20th century.[7]

The claim is made not only by the government; it is made by many MPs speaking in Parliament and it is a view supported by some in the academic community and the media. Unfortunately, however, it is not a view that is shared by our major allies who know that we bring too little in terms of hard-power resources — whether military, financial or intelligence — to the table.

President Bush's omission of Canada in his speech to Congress on September 19, as he thanked various foreign countries for their support of the United States, seemed to shock many Canadians. But the speech merely confirmed the fact that Canada does not rank very high among America's foreign policy concerns. It is not seen as a particularly influential country. This perspective is shared by other major powers.

In 2000 French foreign minister Hubert Védrine ranked Canada below states like Nigeria, Egypt, Australia, Poland, Spain, South Africa, Mexico, Brazil and Iran in terms of global and regional influence. Védrine noted that Canada could only be considered part of this middle-ranking group of countries by virtue of its membership in organizations like the G8 and NATO.[8] This corresponds with what I was told by officials at the German embassy in 1990. Of six ranking levels for German missions abroad, the mission in Ottawa was ranked by the German Foreign Office at the third level from the bottom.

In October 2001 Foreign Minister John Manley admitted publicly what had been known by informed observers for years, that Canada is "still trading on a reputation that was built up two generations and more ago — but that we haven't continued to live up to." He also said that "you can't just sit at the G8 table and then, when the bill comes, go to the washroom."[9]

I believe that there is a direct link between the decline of Canada's influence internationally and the irrelevance of Parliament in the making of Canadian foreign and defence policy. The views, perspectives and foreign policy proposals of Canadian political leaders and bureaucrats are neither effectively questioned nor properly critiqued in the national legislature. The absence of serious oversight makes it easier for government to ignore issues with which it is uncomfortable or which it has little interest in. Without serious oversight, ad hoc and ill-thought policy making becomes the norm.

In spring 2001 I was able to meet with some visiting Australian officers who were in Ottawa for defence meetings. While talking about their country's defence policy review one year earlier, they referred to several day-long Cabinet briefings/discussions which were held on specific defence issues (such as amphibious lift requirements) as the Australia white paper was drafted.

The contrast with Canada is striking. Based on the general neglect of defence that I have witnessed both through my academic studies and in person on the Hill, I find it difficult to imagine Canadian Cabinet ministers sitting through even an hour of rudimentary defence discussions, let alone devoting an entire day to them. Certainly truly substantive defence discussions almost never take place in Parliament. The lack of any serious focus on defence issues by politicians is a principal reason for the unprepared condition that the Canadian Forces find themselves in today.

Parliament has been left totally out of the loop in the decisions made to deploy Canadian Forces to help fight the war on terror. This is partly because the government knows that the Canadian Forces are seriously ill-equipped for the operations that they might be asked to perform. In December 2001 the auditor general noted that the Forces face about a $1 billion to $2 billion annual shortfall in the equipment and operations budgets.[10] This means that Canadian military capability is eroding every year as old equipment is not replaced and the Forces are not permitted to train to the extent that is required to maintain combat effectiveness. In an extraordinary comment, the auditor general said that government claims that the Forces are combat-capable should be "taken with a grain of salt."[11]

Small wonder that the government strongly resists any serious public discussion on defence issues that might further expose the state to which the Canadian Forces have been allowed to decline. Although in 2001 both Senate and House of Commons committees had been studying operational readiness issues for several months, these hearings and the damning conclusions of independent experts and the interim report of the House Committee in November 2001 generated only spotty media coverage. The media knew that no decisions of any import could be taken by a parliamentary committee.

In the first two months of the war the military commitments that Canada made were largely symbolic — the deployment of a navy task group, which of course had no ability to participate in military operations in landlocked Afghanistan, and the commitment of 40 troops from the secretive Joint Task Force (JTF) 2 for an undisclosed role in Afghanistan. However, I and others were concerned that with Parliament totally out of the picture, the government might be tempted to make ill-advised commitments simply to show that it could still do so.

It became evident just how far both the minister of national defence, Art Eggleton, and the prime minister were out of the picture in January and February when the minister made inconsistent statements to the House about when he knew that prisoners had been handed over to American forces by JTF-2 troops. The Minister revealed that briefings to him about JTF-2 operations in Afghanistan were only verbal. The prime minister, in turn, was only briefed on such operations when Eggleton felt it necessary — a process which left the prime minister totally unaware for eight days that Canadian troops in Afghanistan had even taken prisoners. This confirmed the extent to which Canada's political leaders were entirely detached from what Canadian troops were doing or from the challenges they faced.

In November the government announced that it was planning to deploy 1,000 Canadian troops to Afghanistan as part of a peacekeeping force. At first the prime minister commented that Canadian troops would not be going if it meant waging war. This did not inspire confidence that the prime minister was at all familiar with the political situation in Afghanistan. If Western troops were going to be deployed in Afghanistan in any capacity in the middle of a war, one had to expect that it was very likely that some faction or other was going to be shooting at them at some point.

As if this were not disconcerting enough, through a military source we learned that two-thirds of the air force's 32 main transport aircraft (the C-130 Hercules) were unavailable due to required maintenance and breakdowns. Nineteen of these aircraft were more than 35 years old and because of budget cuts had not been replaced. Military sources informed us that it would take about 400 C-130 flights to deploy the battalion to Afghanistan and support it, making the entire proposal dubious to say the least.

Brian Pallister proposed to ask a question in the House on this incredible situation. He did so on November 19. But although he clearly indicated that two-thirds of the air force's C-130s might not be operational, the media showed little interest. As the defence researcher I lobbied to get the question bumped up to the "leader's round" for the next day. The leader's round refers to the first round of questioning in Question Period, where the leaders or other senior MPs from the four opposition parties ask their first questions of government ministers. The leader's round usually generates the most media attention of any of the questions asked in the House on a given day, but in this case the key issue was lost in the telling. Once the media had ignored the story twice, the matter was dropped from the Question Period line-up.

The opposition parties might have had better luck in holding the government to account had they co-ordinated their attack and focused on issues of real substance and import. But the intense competition between the parties for media attention mostly killed such co-operation. Moreover, caught up in the theatre of Question Period, parties have a real difficulty in selecting issues that are actually relevant to Canadians. While many might regard the well-being of Canadian soldiers whom the government proposes to drop into the middle of a war zone 10,000 kilometres away is such an issue, many parliamentarians appear not to attach a great deal of importance to such matters.

In the fall of 2001 I cannot recall a single question asked in the House by Liberal, NDP or Bloc Québécois members on military readiness issues. Instead, Bloc and NDP members tried to suggest that the Government of Canada could get the United States to "stop the bombing" or even to change the types of weapons the Americans were using. "Will the prime minister intervene and call on the Americans to stop dropping cluster bombs on Afghanistan?" the Bloc's Gilles Duceppe asked in the House on November 8.[12] The treatment of prisoners by the Americans then consumed much of the parliamentary debate in January and February.

Day after day Bloc and NDP members would ask the same type of largely irrelevant questions even as they ignored practical matters such as Canadian military readiness. While most parliamentarians inside the House seemed incapable of pinning down Defence Minister Eggleton on issues over which he actually had some influence or control, I at least hoped that reporters outside the House would be able to do so. But because of the limited interest and/or defence expertise in the parliamentary press corps, this simply did not happen.

In early January, despite the prime minister's initial reluctance, it was announced (again while the House wasn't sitting) that 750 Canadian troops would be deployed to Afghanistan for six months to serve with U.S. forces. These troops would be reliant on American air transport to get there and would be entirely dependent on American support while in the theatre of operations.

A joint sitting of the House of Commons Foreign Affairs and Defence committees was called only two weeks after the decision to deploy had already been made. The advance team of Canadian troops had already departed! Serious issues were raised in that committee session concerning the dependence of that small contingent of Canadian troops on U.S. forces; the hurried way in which the mission appeared to have been taken on; the fact that the rules of engagement were still being drafted; the way in which potential prisoners would be treated given the U.S. view that the Geneva Convention did not apply; and the constraints imposed on Canadian soldiers as a result of the ill-considered land mines treaty. Canadian soldiers would be legally obligated to refrain from planning or participating in planning any operations involving the use of antipersonnel land mines, but could nevertheless be put in the awkward position of having to shelter behind U.S. mines while deployed on the mission. There was great unease among members of all parties represented on the committee over the many unanswered questions and the circumstances into which Canadian soldiers were being deployed.

The standard take-note debate was finally held on January 28 even as the main body of Canadian soldiers was leaving for Afghanistan. No vote on the deployment would be permitted. The motion placed on the order paper for discussion was bland in the extreme — merely calling on parliamentarians to "take note of the deployment of Canadian Forces personnel in Afghanistan."[13] Of the five party leaders, only Alexa McDonough briefly participated in the debate.

Despite the fact that the debate concerned the deployment of Canadian soldiers into a war zone, only Canadian Alliance members, led by the senior defence critic, Leon Benoit, focused their questions on military preparedness issues. To this the government's response was by and large contemptuous. For instance, when Alliance MPs quoted General (Ret.) Lewis MacKenzie's concerns about the state of Canadian military preparedness, the parliamentary secretary for defence, John O'Reilly, retorted:

> When Lewis MacKenzie wanted to run for parliament, he came to the prime minister and asked him for what party he should run. The prime minister advised him to run as a Liberal. Lewis MacKenzie decided he would run for the Conservative Party, which won two seats, and the prime minister won 182. I do not know that I would want to follow Lewis MacKenzie into battle with that kind of judgment.[14]

As will be illustrated in the chapters that follow, in such debates, which the government always seeks to manage as carefully as possible, there is always a group of back-bench government MPs who are provided with speeches written for them by officials in the departments of National Defence and Foreign Affairs. Many of the other MPs who participate focus their comments entirely on issues most likely to capture media attention.

On this occasion most opposition MPs and some rebellious Liberal backbenchers commented on the handling of prisoners by the Americans. That issue was hot in the press and had already provoked more anti-American comments from MPs than it did support for our neighbours to the south. Liberal MP John Bryden even noted:

> [I am] not frightened because international terrorists will attack Ottawa or that biological terrorism will appear in Montreal, Ottawa, Toronto or ... the United States. I am frightened because I am afraid that the United States ... might lose its commitments to the protection of our democratic values and, more important, our respect for the rule of law.[15]

Some MPs had lost all sense of what the real threat to Canada was. The only House debate on the deployment of Canadian troops to Afghanistan was largely wasted since the focus was on an issue over which the government had virtually no influence and which was totally irrelevant to the dangers that would soon be confronting Canadian troops deployed in the field.

Just over three months later, the House debated defence issues yet again. By now four Canadian soldiers had been killed in Afghanistan and more had been wounded in a so-called "friendly-fire" incident with their American allies. Soon after this tragic event the leader of the Opposition called the minister of national defence to appear before the House and discuss his department's budget plans for the coming year. This revived a practice that had been dormant since the 1960s. Under brand new rules, the leader of the Opposition was now able to designate two ministers to appear before the whole House for up to five hours to discuss their planned budgets. It was far from real oversight, but at least it seemed to be a step in the right direction.

Mr. Eggleton had certainly not been pleased when informed that he would have to appear for five hours of questioning on his department's spending plans. According to a Liberal Cabinet minister who spoke with an Alliance official, the defence minister had reportedly exclaimed, "Who the f--- came up with that idea?"

Although a few weeks later he would be forced from office on another issue, on this occasion he needn't really have worried. The House proved to be largely empty when it met on May 7, with perhaps 10 percent of members present. Bloc and NDP questions for the minister did not get into any detail. Behind the House chamber, in the lobby, each party is provided with television sets to monitor the debates. But NDP and Bloc staffers in the lobby soon turned their television sets from the debate to the hockey game.

While the Canadian Alliance prepared quite detailed questions, it had less than two hours of questioning time; this included time available to the minister to provide answers. The rest of the five hours was divided between the other opposition parties and government members — and Liberal members took up more than half of that remaining time. Whether by design or neglect, no Liberal members of the House of Commons defence committee, who were arguably the most knowledgeable on defence issues in that caucus, asked any questions. Questions from Liberal MPs were "soft balls" related to the Canadian Rangers, the cadet program, private–public sector partnerships in military housing and so on. Despite the war, there were no probing questions from Liberal members on military equipment or readiness issues.

The Parliament Hill press corps was wholly uninterested in any debate that occurred after 6:00 p.m. — war or no war. Alliance staff members talked to several reporters who occasionally covered defence issues. All indicated that they would not attend an evening debate. When the debate began there was only one journalist in the press gallery and he left long before the halfway mark of the five-hour debate, after pronouncing it "boring" to an Alliance staff member.

This meant that all the important questions asked that evening went unreported in the press the next day. The Alliance's Monte Solberg, one of the best parliamentarians in the House, cornered the minister on the government's decision to purchase $100 million worth of Challenger executive jets to transport the prime minister and Cabinet at a time when Canada was at war and the Forces were facing a $1.3-billion annual deficit in their operations budget. Leon Benoit was able to get the minister to acknowledge that despite this annual deficit, only $700 million would be added to the budget base of the defence department over the next five years. Joe Clark had a good exchange with the minister on the implications for Canada of the new U.S. Northern Command. And Jason Kenney exposed the hollow nature of the government's claim, in the budget, that it had invested more in "education and training," when in fact the army had not conducted a brigade-level exercise for 10 years and, for instance, flying hours for the Aurora maritime patrol aircraft had been reduced by more than half in the nine years that the government had been in office.[16]

But all this was irrelevant to the government, which had already decided exactly what it would spend on defence, the war on terror and on particular equipment projects — whether they were needed operationally or not. Once again, Parliament simply had no influence at all over what the government did. Even so, the prime minister's earlier glib comment that "our soldiers have been just about everywhere in the world ... they have always performed well. They have always been properly equipped"[17] wasn't fooling the men and women of the Canadian Forces or our allies.

The situation confronted by Canadian troops in the war on terrorism is similar to what they confronted in Kosovo just two years before. In fact, over the past 10 years Canadian soldiers have repeatedly been deployed into situations for which they were both ill-prepared and ill-equipped. Canadian soldiers know better than any that due to the chronic neglect of the Armed Forces by successive Canadian governments, they have been asked to do too much with far too little support. All the while Parliament has stood on the sidelines, entirely irrelevant.

NOTES

1. Mike Blanchfield, "Canada Wasting NATO's time," *Ottawa Citizen*, February 7, 2000, p. A3.
2. Canada, Parliament, House of Commons, *Debates*, Vol. 137, no. 79 (September 17, 2001) p. 5115.
3. House of Commons, *Debates*, Vol. 137, no. 87 (September 27, 2001) p. 5663.
4. House of Commons, *Debates*, Vol. 137, no. 109 (November 5, 2001) p. 6932.
5. COMPAS Inc., *Canadians' Anti-Terrorist Mindset: Foreign Policy after the World Trade Center Calamity* (September 19, 2001).
6. House of Commons, *Debates*, Vol. 137, no. 79 (September 17, 2001) p. 5125.
7. Canada, Department of Foreign Affairs and International Trade, *Canada in the World* (Ottawa: Public Works and Government Services Canada, 1995) p. i.
8. Hubert Védrine, dialogue with Dominique Moisi, *Les cartes de la France a l'heure de la mondialisation* (Paris: Librarie Artheme Fayard, 2000) pp. 14–15.
9. Paul Wells, "We Don't Pull Our Weight," *National Post*, October 5, 2001, p. A1.
10. "National Defence In-Service Equipment" (Chapter 10) in Canada, Auditor General of Canada, *Auditor General's Report* (Ottawa: Office of the Auditor General, December 2001) paragraphs 10.11–10.12.
11. *National Defence In-Service Equipment* [media release], Office of the Auditor General, December 4, 2001.
12. House of Commons, *Debates*, Vol. 137, no. 112 (November 8, 2001) p. 7160.
13. House of Commons, *Debates*, Vol. 137, no. 133 (January 28, 2002) p. 8359.

14. House of Commons, *Debates*, Vol. 137, no. 133 (January 28, 2002) p. 8384.

15. House of Commons, *Debates*, Vol. 137, no. 133 (January 28, 2002) p. 8393.

16. House of Commons, *Debates*, Vol. 137, no. 184 (May, 7, 2002) pp. 11; 333–371. See also Minister Eggleton's reference to enhanced investment in "education and training" in: Canada, Department of National Defence, *Estimates, 2002–2003: Part III — Report on Plans and Priorities* (Ottawa: Public Works and Government Services, 2002) p. ii.

17. House of Commons. *Debates*, Vol. 137, no. 114 (November 19, 2001) p. 7259.

CHAPTER TWO

Sleepwalking to War: Parliament and the Kosovo Crisis

When the war broke out in Kosovo in March 1999 most parliamentarians probably could not have found the province on a blank map of Europe. I remember a conversation that I had with one senior parliamentarian shortly after war erupted. I happened to mention that I had heard that a British aircraft carrier had just been dispatched to join the coalition forces. He expressed some surprise that Kosovo was near a body of water. One might have expected that since the Kosovo crisis had been brewing for years and Canadians had been in the Balkans since 1992, parliamentarians, especially parliamentary leaders or those charged with responsibility for foreign policy, might be reasonably well informed about events. But this was simply not the case. Indeed, I found that some MPs tended to develop a glazed look if policy discussions lasted longer than about five minutes.

Knowledge is power and the lack of knowledge on the Hill is one of the most serious impediments to having a truly effective Parliament. This meant that Parliament, which in theory is supposed to represent the views of Canadians by debating issues in a serious manner, was ineffective in exercising any meaningful oversight as Canada moved toward war. This allowed the government to completely control the agenda for discussion. It created circumstances in which it was easy to mislead Parliament and the public. Once the war in Kosovo broke out, the need to show solidarity predominated, for the sake of our soldiers.

Shades of Grey: The Conflict in Kosovo

For most people the Kosovo crisis erupted in March 1998 when Serb forces initiated a crackdown on the forces of the Kosovo Liberation Army (KLA). Very soon thereafter, in June 1998, NATO began preparations to intervene in Kosovo. At that time air operations were already being rehearsed. This was covered in all the major media and reported on the front pages of Canadian newspapers.[1] Yet the issue remained one that was external to Parliament. There were no investigations by parliamentary committees; no questions were even asked in the House as the crisis heated up.

Prior to 1998 Kosovo had been in the news for years as a future potential flash point in the Balkans. Although the territory was an integral part of Yugoslavia, Kosovo's population mix was 90 percent Albanian and just 10 percent Serb. Events in the province were closely linked to the civil war that had erupted in Yugoslavia in 1991. The dispute between Serbs and Muslim Albanians over Kosovo stretched back centuries.

The territory is of great historical significance to Serbs. The original Serbian monarchy emerged in Kosovo in the 12th century. The seminal event in Serbian history also occurred in Kosovo — namely the Serb defeat at the Battle of Kosovo at the hands of the Turks in 1389. That event led to the subordination of Orthodox Serbia to the Islamic Ottoman Empire. Indeed, Serbia was completely overrun in 1459 and ceased to exist as an independent entity.

Serbian autonomy within the Ottoman Empire was won in 1815 after armed revolts. More fighting later in the century led to Serbia's full independence in 1878. The fighting in this period involved large scale "ethnic cleansing" as 250,000 Serbs were driven from Kosovo by ethnic (and predominantly Muslim) Albanians. This process was reversed during the Balkan wars of 1912–14, when the Serbs drove many Albanians from the province.

During World War II Yugoslavia was occupied by the Axis powers. Kosovo was assigned to Italian occupation and the Italians turned the

Albanian population loose on the Serbs. Later in the war the Germans recruited an Albanian SS Division from the Kosovo region. By 1948 many Serbs had left the territory, which was then two-thirds Albanian and one-third Serb. The Serb population continued to decline in the following years. Yugoslavia's ruler, Josip Broz Tito, granted Kosovo new autonomy within Yugoslavia between 1974 and 1989. Serbs felt persecuted during this period, and this contributed to a further exodus.

In 1989 Slobodan Milosevic used the 600th anniversary of the Serb defeat at the Battle of Kosovo to enflame nationalist sentiment in Yugoslavia. He revoked Kosovo's autonomy and began to rule the territory with a heavy hand. This ignited the territory's Albanian nationalist movement. Albanians began to agitate for independence in the face of Serb domination of public institutions.

By 1993, in the midst of the civil war in Bosnia, the Kosovo Liberation Army was formed. Based on Albanian clans, it was financed through various means, including the Albanian diaspora, but also through drug- and gun-running and by receiving funds from radical Islamic states. It was at this time that alleged links were established between the KLA and Osama bin Laden's al-Qaeda terrorist network. The KLA's illegal activities were so successful, it was said that the organization soon muscled Turks out of the European heroin trade.

In 1996 the KLA began a campaign of intimidation and assassination inside Kosovo. The targets were both Serbs of the ruling elite as well as those Albanians who "collaborated" with the authorities. Eighty-six people were murdered by the end of 1997. In that same year unrest inside Albania itself was widespread. Armouries in the country were looted, and guns and ammunition soon started flooding into Kosovo.

In the first two months of 1998 alone, 66 people were killed as a result of KLA terrorism. Faced with this escalation, the Milosevic regime responded brutally. In March a Serb offensive led to the deaths of up to 1,500 Albanians — not only KLA fighters, but also many civilians — and the destruction of villages.[2]

Slobodan Milosevic was certainly fanning the flames of Serb nationalism and war for his own gain, but then so too were other leaders in the former Yugoslavia. One of the most noted experts on Yugoslavia, Misha Glenny, writes, "Inside Serbia and Croatia, the two presidents [Franjo Tudjman and Milosevic] were playing the same game — consolidating control over the machinery of state through purges and intimidation."[3] Both individuals constantly evoked images of the Second World War to shore up their popularity and whip up support for war.[4] According to Major-General Lewis MacKenzie, the UN commander in 1992, Bosnia's Muslim president, Ali Izetbegovic, consistently engaged in blocking efforts to find a negotiated settlement. Prior to the war President Izetbegovic had promoted a political agenda every bit as radical as that of both Tudjman and Milosevic.

Although all sides were responsible for failing to make peace in Yugoslavia after 1992, most of the blame was placed on the Serbs due to their dominant position. The United States and the West became anxious to contain the escalating conflict. Kosovo was seen as the linchpin in this regard. If fighting erupted there, it was feared that it might spread to Macedonia which was also about 25 percent ethnic Albanian. A war that grew to include Macedonia might draw in yet more powers — possibly the Greeks on the Serb side and the Turks on the Albanian side. It might even lead to Russian intervention on the Serb side. At least, this was the great fear.

It was then that the first Bush administration, in one of its last acts in office, laid the groundwork for NATO intervention in Kosovo. In December 1992 it warned that "in the event of conflict in Kosovo caused by Serbian action, the United States will be prepared to employ military force against the Serbs in Kosovo and in Serbia proper."[5] The Americans wanted to contain violence to the former Yugoslavia and saw extension of fighting into Kosovo as the danger point where violence might spill over Yugoslavia's borders. They were probably right in fearing that Milosevic might well use the cover of a war in Bosnia to settle scores in Kosovo while world attention was focused elsewhere.

At the same time, however, the U.S. warning had the effect of further identifying the Serbs and Milosevic as the primary, and even the sole, villains in the former Yugoslavia. This tendency would only grow in the coming years. The effect was to simplify the conflict. Arguably, the simplification of the conflict drew in the American media. Americans loved underdogs and hated bullies. The Serbs were increasingly identified as the latter.

The Clinton administration began America's more interventionist role innocently enough by beginning air drops of supplies to refugees in Bosnia. But this limited intervention was soon judged to be unsatisfactory. The killing did not stop. The American role began to escalate. The

U.S. began to provide clandestine aid to both the Croats and the Bosnian Muslims.

By 1995 the Croats were ready to initiate a decisive offensive against the Serbs. In August they launched their main attack against the Serb-held Krajina region. Canadian troops, situated in the UN buffer zone, were quickly overrun and the Serbs routed. In the days that followed, between 150,000 and 300,000 Serbs were expelled in the biggest single ethnic-cleansing operation that had taken place in Europe since World War II.[6] Despite the obvious atrocities committed against the local civilian population, President Clinton welcomed the Croat offensive as opening the way to the solution of the Yugoslav conflict.[7] That was true as far as it went — but at what cost?

Meanwhile in neighbouring Bosnia, the Serbs had been pushing for a definitive victory all through the summer of 1995, prior to Croatian or NATO intervention. They took two of the so-called UN safe areas — Zepa and Srebrenica. In the latter city, the Serbs murdered many of the Muslim men captured there. The world justly condemned these actions but said nothing about the attacks that had continuously been launched against Serb forces from these same "safe zones" or about the expulsion of hundreds of thousands of Serb civilians from the Krajina just one month later.

Finally, in the fall of 1995, NATO intervened in Bosnia with large-scale air strikes against the Serbs. With Croat and Bosnian Muslim forces poised to make major gains of their own, the Serbs sued for peace. Bosnia became a de facto NATO protectorate and would likely remain at peace only as long as allied forces remained there. Meanwhile, however, the violence did not end in Kosovo, and instead appeared to be escalating.

Following fighting between the KLA and the Serbs in March 1998, U.S. secretary of state Madeleine Albright urged that immediate action be taken to punish Belgrade. Despite the increases in KLA guerrilla activity, the Serbs were labelled as the instigators of the fighting.[8] That the Serbs conducted themselves in a brutal fashion, there could be no doubt. However, while Serb actions were consistently singled out for condemnation, KLA atrocities were ignored. So too were links between the KLA and international terrorist groups such as al-Qaeda — which provided both money and fighters to support the KLA campaign.[9]

As NATO involved itself more deeply in Kosovo, Canada found itself totally out of the loop. On June 11–12 NATO defence ministers, under American urging, ordered their military chiefs to prepare options for intervention. Air exercises were held on June 15 over Macedonia (Exercise Determined Falcon) to back up the call by the international contact group (Britain, the United States, Italy, Germany, Russia and France) for a cease-fire. But Canada wasn't part of the contact group, despite years of lobbying to get on, and it was the only NATO nation with an air force to not participate in the air exercises. The air force, having just retired the last of its air-refuelling 707s, couldn't get its CF-18s to Italy in time.[10]

During the Bosnian war Canada had resisted NATO's military intervention in that conflict. In November 1994, during the war in Bosnia, Prime Minister Chrétien commented in the House of Commons:

> I have always made it very clear to the president of the United States ... that we do not think that there should be a lifting of the arms embargo and that no one from the outside should participate in this war. We always made it clear that if everybody from the outside were to mind their own business and the [UN] troops there handle the search for peace as best they can, it would be so much the better.[11]

However, as American policy became increasingly bellicose, Canadian policy was "adjusted." And the Americans continued to turn up the pressure. On September 23, 1998, the UN Security Council, again under American pressure, passed Resolution 1199, demanding an immediate end to the fighting in Kosovo. But the KLA had no interest in stopping the fighting since every military action undertaken by the Serbs would be condemned as aggression.[12]

On September 24 NATO defence ministers met in Portugal while NATO ambassadors approved an activation warning for the alliance's armed forces. A phased air campaign was being planned. But NATO had some political challenges of its own. For one, the North Atlantic Treaty made no provision for offensive military action by the alliance. Yugoslavia was clearly not threatening NATO.

There was another dilemma. The Russian veto on the UN Security Council closed the possibility of getting approval for military action from the UN. Many would question how NATO could attack a sovereign state without UN authorization. The response by NATO was to claim that the prospect of an "immediate and overwhelming catastrophe" existed for the civilian population in Kosovo unless the conflict was resolved. This was dubious to say the least. Certainly the war in Kosovo was a serious matter, but in comparison to other conflicts around the world, it was hardly the most serious humanitarian problem —at least not until NATO began bombing.

Nevertheless, this rationale would be used as the dominant justification for intervention. A key meeting at Heathrow Airport was held on October 8. It involved both Madeleine Albright and U.S. negotiator Richard Holbrooke; the British foreign secretary, Robin Cook; the French foreign minister, Hubert Védrine; the German foreign minister, Klaus Kinkel; and the Russian foreign minister, Igor Ivanov.

Kinkel and Cook reportedly pressed the Russians to allow them to pass a resolution through the UN Security Council authorizing the use of force. But Ivanov reportedly refused, saying the Russians could never take such a stand publicly. In a cynical piece of Realpolitik, Ivanov pointed out that if the Western allies acted through NATO, Russia would "just make a lot of noise" but would do nothing. This was what the Americans had wanted all along, with Albright arguing that the UN was unnecessary. In her view NATO had the legitimacy to act entirely on its own. In the next few days NATO prepared for action on this basis.[13]

Even so, Milosevic was able to slip the trap prepared for him. In last-minute meetings with Richard Holbrooke on October 12, Milosevic agreed to a deal. The Organization for Security and Co-operation in Europe (OSCE) would deploy unarmed verifiers in Kosovo, and both the KLA and the Serbs would agree to a cease-fire while a political settlement was reached.

From the beginning the Clinton administration was unhappy with this compromise deal. It had backed itself into a corner by giving Milosevic the opportunity to accept the compromise. But this didn't bring an end to the fighting. The KLA had no incentive to stop fighting and Yugoslav security forces were determined not to lose control of Kosovo by default. Madeleine Albright was soon looking for ways to move beyond the October agreement. "We are nothing more than gerbils running on a wheel," she is reported to have said in reference to the inconclusive nature of the deal.[14]

The Racak massacre on January 15, 1999, provided a rationale to pressure the Serbs to make further sweeping concessions. The evidence as to who was responsible for this massacre of 45 people has been mixed. Most, including the International War Crimes Tribunal in the Hague, placed the blame on the Serb security forces. Others charged that the dead were KLA fighters and that the Serbs had been set up to make it look as though they had killed innocent civilians. A team of Finnish forensic experts published a report in February 2001 indicating that neither the identity of the killers nor their motives could be proved on the basis of the forensic evidence.

However, in the charged atmosphere after Racak, the Serbs were quickly held by most observers and the media (including most Canadian parliamentarians) to be responsible for the murder of civilians. Nobody seriously questioned this conclusion. Most parliamentarians believed that opposition to taking military action would not play well with the public or, more particularly, the national media. In the first days of the war all the main parties generally gave their support to Canadian involvement. Like the public at large, they simply bought into the media's vilification of Slobodan Milosevic and the Serbian side. There was also a recognition that since war was being initiated by the United States, Canada did not have the weight or credibility to stand aside.

Gabriel Keller, the French co-head of the Kosovo Verification Mission, noted his suspicions about the events at Racak almost immediately, finding the event far too convenient to be believed at face value. However, William Walker, his American counterpart, immediately blamed the Serbs for the massacre.[15] On January 30 the North Atlantic Council described the events in Kosovo as a "threat to peace and international security." It said:

> NATO's strategy is to halt the violence and support the completion of negotiations on an interim political settlement for Kosovo, thus averting a humanitarian catastrophe. Steps to this end must include acceptance by both parties of the summons to begin negotiations … on an interim political settlement within the specified time frame …
>
> If these steps are not taken, NATO is prepared to take whatever measures are necessary … The Council has therefore agreed today that the NATO secretary general may authorize air strikes against targets on FRY [Federal Republic of Yugoslavia] territory.[16]

Both representatives of the Yugoslav government and Kosovar representatives were summoned to Rambouillet, in France. Although the talks were chaired by Robin Cook and Hubert Védrine, the Americans were the key behind-the-scenes force at the talks. Christopher Hill, the U.S. ambassador to Macedonia, played the leading role on the negotiating team, while Jim O'Brien from the U.S. Department of State headed up the legal team. Americans also played a central role in advising the Kosovar delegation at Rambouillet.

Although the Americans sought to convince the KLA negotiators that the presence of a NATO-led force would be their insurance, the representatives were unmoved. They wanted full independence. In response, Madeleine Albright gave them a letter on February 22 which stated, "This letter concerns the formulation (attached) proposed for Chapter 8, Article 1 (3) of the interim Framework Agreement. We will regard this proposal, or any other formulation of that article that may be agreed at Rambouillet, as confirming the right for the people of Kosovo to hold a referendum on the final status of Kosovo after three years."[17]

In the meantime no carrots were offered to the Serbs. NATO was demanding that it be allowed to deploy a military force in Kosovo and that Yugoslav forces be reduced to a token level. In effect, NATO was demanding that the Yugoslavs surrender the province to make it an alliance protectorate. Given the cultural and historic significance of the province to the Serb people, they refused. No Yugoslav government could have agreed to surrender such a historic portion of the national territory to foreign control without a fight. The text of the proposed agreement also gave NATO troops free reign to enter the rest of Yugoslavia.[18]

These were not so much negotiations as they were a *diktat* — an agreement forced on one of the parties through the threat of military action. The KLA was never under threat of military action. Only the Serbs were in that position — one in which they had been before. In 1941 Germany, backed by its satellites, had demanded that Yugoslavia join the Axis camp or face military intervention. They had refused then against hopeless odds. They would do so again.

On February 22 both the Serbs and the Kosovars were sent back to consult with their leaders. Kosovar negotiators found that their leaders were amenable to the agreement. All the pressure would then be placed on Milosevic to agree. When the talks resumed the Kosovars signed the agreement — an event that the chief Russian negotiator refused to witness. The Serbs, under instructions from Milosevic, but also with the backing of the whole Yugoslav parliament, refused.

Richard Holbrooke was then sent on one last mission to Belgrade. He was not offering any compromises this time. As Milosevic was bluntly told, it was take it, or we'll make you take it! Many Americans were convinced that, faced with imminent bombing, Milosevic would yield. But he did not. On March 24 the bombing began. NATO expected an immediate Serb capitulation.

Shades of Grey Discussed in Black and White Terms

Within three weeks of my arrival on the Hill in September 1998, Parliament became involved in the Kosovo crisis. A key part of my job in Ottawa between September and March was to try to make Reform members of Parliament familiar with the situation in Kosovo and Yugoslavia so as to enable them to participate in parliamentary discussions and debates. I compiled background material on the specifics of the conflict, on the nature of Canadian involvement and the position of the Government of Canada, on Canadian military units most likely to be involved in actions in the Balkans, on the shortcomings in Canadian military capability and on the likely goals of American and NATO strategy in the war.

What is interesting in hindsight is that at no time was I asked to analyze what Canada's interests actually were in this crisis. Why were we there? What did we have at stake? Potentially, was this an issue over which Canadians should be killed? To be sure, I provided some of this information in my briefing materials, but unfortunately I soon found that most MPs in all parties were not particularly interested in asking questions about the complexities of the issue or about Canadian involvement. Many were more interested in taking positions that made them look decisive.

When the war broke out Parliament's focus was primarily in terms of it being the news story of the week — little more. For the most part, this meant that the discussion in Parliament about events was simplistic. Parliamentarians, like the media, participated in painting events in the Balkans in black and white terms — the Serbs being the bad guys and the others (Croats, Bosnian Muslims and Kosovars) the good guys.

To a large extent our serving diplomats appearing before parliamentary committees did the same. Milosevic and the Serbs were always described as the key problem in the Balkans. Given many of the thuggish practices of Milosevic's troops in Kosovo, they were an easy target. But their actions weren't the whole story. Many of the actions of Kosovo guerrilla groups were equally appalling. However, this was rarely the story told to parliamentarians. Parliamentarians simply ended up parroting the overly simplistic rhetoric of the diplomats.

The result was that by the time war was imminent in March 1999, the consistent trumpeting of a particular line had made it impossible to suddenly look at the problems in Kosovo and the former Yugoslavia in a more balanced and realistic fashion. This was tragic because the real experts, those who had been on the ground in the Balkans, did know better. Our troops had been in Bosnia and Croatia for seven years. They knew that there were no good guys in this conflict. They knew that choosing sides in these conflicts in the hopes of righting the terrible wrongs being committed was futile. But somehow, in all the years that Canadians were in the Balkans, that message never got through to Parliament.

The decision-making process in the Reform Party during the period leading up to and during the war was to a large extent governed by Bob Mills, our lead foreign affairs critic, and Art Hanger, the chief defence critic. It was only later that Preston Manning became engaged in the issue.

I found that if I had the opportunity to brief Bob Mills on issues, he would listen and take my views into account. However, those opportunities usually did not arise. As best we could, we had to try to anticipate what the key issues might be and when they might arise. Bob took many initiatives on his own. There was little obligation for Bob to consult with either Preston Manning or caucus, though if an initiative went wrong or rubbed some in caucus the wrong way, Bob, like any other critic, would be quick to hear about it.

As the party's defence researcher I worked very closely with Art Hanger. Art takes a no-nonsense approach to issues, which he seeks to tackle honestly. As the defence critic he always placed a great emphasis on the interests of our serving personnel and he had no desire to become part of the "old boys' club" of MPs. In this regard, he was very frustrated with the Liberal government's neglect of defence.

Very soon after I arrived on the Hill I went to work with Art's office in drafting a minority report to the government's planned review of quality-of-life issues in the Canadian Forces. When Art became convinced that the Liberals and the other opposition members were going to ignore the real reason for low morale in the Canadian Forces, he decided to oppose the majority report.

Art never hesitated in carving out a minority position on this issue. Low morale had less to do with quality-of-life issues than it did with the fact that the government had ignored the real equipment needs of the Forces for years. Through an Access to Information request, we also confirmed how social engineering was lowering training standards in the Forces in order to correct what was perceived to be a gender imbalance in the Canadian military. These factors combined to sap morale in the Forces. They contributed to the high numbers of soldiers seeking early retirement. Art wanted no part of a report that would whitewash these facts and pretend that the solutions were simply grounded in more pay and more quality-of-life programs run by Ottawa bureaucrats.

But Kosovo was, of course, a different sort of issue. It required a more co-ordinated approach between critics who were used to taking positions on their own. Because of a somewhat disjointed and ad hoc decision-making process, it proved to be difficult to discuss many of the issues at stake in Kosovo. While both critics had been in their posts for some time, they had not focused on the details of problems in the Balkans or on the issue of Kosovo to any great extent. This meant that as the crisis developed, the formulation of perspectives and positions had to begin virtually from scratch.

Initial Take-Note Debates

"Canadians expect the House of Commons to ... advance solutions."

From the 1993 Liberal policy document
Reviving Parliamentary Democracy

Take-note debates on foreign policy issues were introduced by the Liberals soon after they took office in 1993. In a Liberal policy document entitled *Reviving Parliamentary Democracy*, published just before the 1993 federal election, Liberal MPs, including Don Boudria, Alfonso Gagliano and Peter Milliken (the present Speaker), called for action to address "the continuing failure of Parliament to address effectively the problems that face us." "Canadians," they wrote, "expect the House of

Commons not merely to discuss openly the problems of the nation, but also to advance solutions. They expect the Commons to explore Canada's problems rationally and to establish policies for resolving them. These expectations are not being met." With regard to foreign policy, they said:

> At present, reports to the House and debates are at the whim of the government, leading to a lack of coherence and public involvement in the discussion of these important issues ... The House of Commons and its relevant committee should have regular opportunities for full debate on Canada's foreign policy pertaining to its economic, social and political relationships.[19]

But after the Liberals were elected this pledge was quickly forgotten. On the surface the Liberals claimed to have implemented their promise by instituting the take-note debates on foreign policy questions. In practical terms, however, these debates did nothing to implement the pledge to "explore Canada's problems rationally and establish policies for resolving them."

The debates, in fact, became an additional tool for enhancing the government's control of the agenda. Few events are more choreographed to support government policy than these take-note debates. From start to finish the government is in complete control of events. Nothing is left to chance.

First, as little notice as possible is given for the opposition to prepare for the debate. The government proposes these debates to the House leaders of all the parties with usually no more than 24 to 48 hours' notice. Sometimes opposition parties are told that a debate will take place in a few days, but are not informed of the subject matter until just before the debate. This process always works to the government's advantage since departmental officials may already have been preparing for weeks.

Second, the motion being debated is usually worded as softly as possible to encourage all-party support. During the Kosovo crisis, for instance, when military action was clearly imminent, or even when the war had already begun, the motions themselves never referred to military action. Instead, the House was usually asked to take note of the humanitarian situation and Canada's efforts to help resolve it.

Third, there is never any voting associated with the take-note debate. Voting requires a precise motion in which the specifics of government policy would be more thoroughly explored. This is unacceptable to a government that wants to retain total control of the agenda and limit discussion to the most basic level.

Fourth, government ministers always set the tone for the discussion. While ministers' speeches may have been in preparation for weeks, opposition members usually only speak on the basis of hastily drafted talking points. Expert input is limited to the staff available in the opposition research offices and to the few, if any, additional experts who may be consulted, often by phone, in the limited time available.

Fifth, the government always has a ready pool of yes-men and yes-women in the back benches, available to do its bidding. With a few exceptions, Liberal MPs have been notoriously compliant with the wishes of the government.

Sixth, and probably most important, the focus of the media is usually elsewhere. Take-note debates do not make for exciting television. As well, most debates usually take place later in the day when most journalists have gone home. There is no time to include excerpts from the debates in the next day's papers. If it doesn't make the news, it isn't particularly important to most people in the Ottawa elite. The generally accepted view of Ottawa elites is that nothing that happens in the House is actually of relevance to any policy decision being made by government. In public everybody pretends that the views of Parliament are extremely important, but few actually believe it.

This is probably the most important factor undermining the seriousness with which MPs take the debate process. When nothing one says is of relevance to the decision taken, it tends to reduce the enthusiasm with which one prepares for a debate.

The First Debate: October 7, 1998

The debate in the House on October 7, 1998, was provoked by the seeming imminence of military action. With Canada having already moved six of its CF-18s to Italy, assisted by American tanker aircraft, the Canadian government thought it time to go through the motions of "consulting" Parliament.

We received notice of the debate about 24 hours beforehand. Although Chris Champion and I immediately set to work writing talking points and background notes, we also had to try to brief MPs on the key issues. As usual, the duty schedules of MPs did not permit much time for meetings and discussions, so talking points and background information were compiled and then simply forwarded by e-mail to the MPs' offices.

In the few hours we had prior to the debate, Chris and I jointly drafted briefing material for MPs based on both the particulars of the Kosovo crisis and the issues the party had raised in the past on military intervention issues. In February 1998 Preston Manning had spoken in the House of Commons on possible military action in the Gulf and had outlined several criteria "which should be satisfied before Canada commits itself to responding to requests for participation in multilateral initiatives to prevent and remove threats to peace."[20] These included satisfying Parliament that a serious international threat existed; ensuring that there was a workable plan and strategy for military action, a well-defined mission and a clear definition of Canada's role; and making certain that the expected role was within Canada's fiscal and military capabilities.

Our note reflected these criteria and warned of some of the possible consequences associated with NATO military action, particularly actions that the Serbs might take in retaliation — including the mass expulsion of Kosovars from the territory. We warned that given the centrality of Kosovo to the Serbs, the Milosevic government would likely resist NATO military action. We further suggested that NATO intervention might encourage the Kosovars to push for complete independence, a development likely to be extremely damaging for regional stability.

Chris and I thought it important to try to meet with Bob Mills in advance of the crisis since his office would take the lead in issuing talking points and setting the tone for the debate. Bob was busy with other meetings when Chris and I arrived at his office on the morning of October 7, so Chris and I met with Rob Norris, Bob's executive assistant. Rob made it clear at the outset that Bob was going to call for aggressive military action by NATO in Kosovo and was planning to throw his whole support behind the government. Rob's view was that the public and the press were strongly in favour of military action and Reform couldn't afford to be on the wrong side of the issue.

When I drew attention to Mr. Manning's criteria prepared for an earlier crisis, Rob simply responded, "OK, let's go through them." He began to go down the list: "Does a serious international threat exist, and have diplomatic efforts failed? Yup, that's the case. Is there multinational support for military action? Yes there is!" I interrupted and pointed out that it was up to Parliament to decide these issues after a full discussion. Rob then revealed that Bob had already decided to endorse bombing by NATO. He had drafted his Members' Statement, which he was to deliver in just a few minutes and which would call for "strategic strikes" by NATO.

Bob's statement set the tone with which the official Opposition approached the Kosovo issue on that day. Although the statement was never discussed outside his own office, other MPs who were scheduled to speak and who knew little about Kosovo took their lead from it and followed the same theme.

This was my first exposure to the time pressures involved in formulating positions on foreign policy issues. Bob was certainly trying to do the right thing. He believed that something had to be done about the human rights abuses he saw in Kosovo. But, in my view, that initial position could have been better considered.

Like Bob and most other MPs, Art Hanger was strongly of the view that something should be done to force Slobodan Milosevic to the table. Art was also confident that American and NATO military action would be quick and decisive. However, after he reviewed the briefing material provided and considered the implications of NATO military action and Canadian involvement, he decided that it was important to pose tough questions to the government, especially concerning the equipment and readiness of the Canadian Forces. Given Art's general predisposition to support military action, he was in somewhat of a difficult position. He would be supporting military action in principle, but raising serious questions about the nature of the mission and the preparedness of the Canadian Forces to participate.

But his difficulties accurately reflected the dilemma of the Canadian position. Canada's influence in NATO was now so weak that, politically, Canada did not have the ability to either influence or opt out of NATO actions. Canada would almost inevitably be dragged along by whatever the alliance decided. At the same time, the Canadian Forces had been so badly neglected over the years that Canada's ability to participate effectively was severely limited.

The Debate Begins

The motion presented by the government read as follows: "That this House take note of the dire humanitarian situation confronting the people of Kosovo and the government's intention to take measures in co-operation with the international community to resolve the conflict, promote a political settlement for Kosovo and facilitate the provision of humanitarian assistance to refugees."[21]

The motion naturally said very little. It certainly made no mention of the imminence of military action. Lloyd Axworthy's opening remarks were in the same vein. Axworthy began by expressing his thanks to members of the House "for granting the opportunity for this special debate on the situation in Kosovo."[22] This was nonsense, of course, since the government had called the debate with its usual few hours' notice. Many of the points made by Axworthy raised serious questions. For one, he stated that the required solution was to support Kosovo's independence within Yugoslavia. What that meant exactly was unclear. Could one speak about Quebec's independence within Canada? Since Kosovo was an integral part of Yugoslavia, force would clearly have to be used to carve this province out of its parent state. This went considerably beyond what NATO was saying at the time.

Furthermore, the idea that Kosovo would be independent within Yugoslavia would require a more or less permanent NATO presence in the territory, both to prevent the Serbs from retaking the province and to prevent the Kosovars from seeking full independence. In essence, Kosovo would become a NATO protectorate and Canada would be directly involved. For Canada this represented unprecedented intervention in the internal affairs of a sovereign state and clearly required serious parliamentary discussion.

Axworthy then went through a list of alleged Serb atrocities being cited by NATO spokespeople. Although there was no question that the Serbs had committed atrocities, many of the specific allegations were debatable. Moreover, no mention was ever made of the unsavoury actions of the KLA, who were known to have provoked Serbian security forces and murdered their moderate Albanian opponents.

The minister also attempted to trumpet the measures Canada was taking. "Canada," he said, "has attempted to mobilize and energize international action."[23] In this regard he talked about the letter he had sent to the Russian foreign minister in an effort to find a solution.

Of course, the reality was that the Russian foreign minister probably had only a vague idea of who Lloyd Axworthy was. Moreover, neither the Russians nor Canada's allies had much interest in Canadian views on the Kosovo crisis. All the important decision making on the NATO crisis had been made by others up to that point.

Few of Mr. Axworthy's comments were actually challenged by opposition members. Daniel Turp of the Bloc did raise the issue of the justification for intervening in the internal affairs of a sovereign nation. He suggested that NATO would be acting illegally if it entered into military action without the approval of the Security Council. In an exchange with Liberal MP Ted McWhinney, Turp said, "I think it is difficult to claim under international law as it currently stands that the use of force, even in this case, would be consistent with the charter without prior authorization of the Security Council."[24] Despite these reservations, which were put as delicately as possible, all the opposition MPs spoke in favour of military intervention.

Bob Mills began his statement with the obligatory reference to the "obvious atrocities" being committed by the Serbs. "We all believe that we must respond," he said. Speaking for the Reform Party he stated that "we would support the ultimate decision to use military force if dealing with someone like Mr. Milosevic." Later he said, "the bombing will bring Milosevic to the table because he understands a plank over the head."

Bob believed that Canada had the ability to play a unique and effective role on the world stage. "We can show some leadership," he said. "We could become mediators in the world … We have a reputation which would allow us to be there and do things that the Americans cannot do, the Russians cannot do, the French cannot do and the British cannot do. No one can do it but a country like Canada, which is a middle power." I have found that many Canadians have understood only too little about the realities of power in international affairs. Real influence only comes from real capability.

Bob did raise some questions related to the implications of military action. He wondered why we were choosing to intervene in Kosovo when there were so many other areas where human rights were being abused and nothing was being done. "What about Rwanda? What about Nigeria?" he asked.

Having already endorsed bombing he added:

> Canadians want to know a number of things. They want to know what we will bomb if we have to bomb something. They want to be assured that we are not just going to create more

victims ... We need to be assured by our defence minister about the readiness of our troops and equipment. We are concerned about Russia ... we are concerned about Macedonia and Albania and a potential flare-up. We are also concerned about Greece and Turkey, two NATO partners that may come into conflict in terms of this decision. We need to ask those questions and need to be sure we have looked at them before we get too far into any kind of military action.[25]

But these questions, like the legal doubts raised by Turp, were posed after he had already endorsed military intervention. Other MPs did the same. They included the Bloc's René Laurin and the NDP's Svend Robinson. Their speeches were generally along the lines of Reform's Gary Lunn, who commented that "the only thing Mr. Milosevic understands is being clubbed over the head. ...Canada and the rest of the world have been more than patient with Mr. Milosevic. ... These are fascinating debates when we look at the details. However, at the end of the day I would like to offer my encouragement to both ministers [Axworthy and Eggleton] who were present tonight. I hope there will be a long-term commitment on the part of Canada."[26]

Keith Martin of Reform, who was one of the most active and free-thinking MPs on the Hill, supported the near universal call for strong action. He stated that "[Milosevic] is not withdrawing his troops and we must bomb." But he also suggested that despite the bombing, Canada should play a mediation role — a role he thought was possible due to "its enormous diplomatic ability and international respect." He noted that he had already "introduced a private members' motion ... asking the minister of foreign affairs to bring together like-minded nations to have a common foreign policy in certain areas and particularly the area of conflict prevention."[27]

Gordon Earle, the NDP's defence critic, somewhat bizarrely spoke of the United Nations as comprised of individuals: "The Security Council is comprised of individuals. In reality it comes down to what each and every one of us individuals feels in our hearts in terms of how to deal with our fellow human beings and whether we allow these atrocities to exist."[28] The sentiment was certainly admirable, but it revealed a rather naive understanding about not only the nature of the United Nations, but also about the complexity of the crisis in the Balkans and how it could be resolved.

Gurmant Grewal, who was Reform's deputy foreign affairs critic, was always very sincere in the sentiments he expressed, although some of his analogies were on occasion difficult to follow. He said:

> Perhaps I can tell a story about a donkey that was sick. The farmer who owned the donkey was giving it medicine that was very bitter. The farmer's son was helping him by holding the donkey by the ears. They were forcing medicine into the donkey's nostrils because they wanted to cure it, but the donkey thought that they were pulling his ears. We have to do that; we have to pull the ears. When diplomacy fails we have to take military action.[29]

In the midst of all the wisdom of the evening, Bill Graham of the Liberals pointed to the "tremendous unanimity in the House … The need to act is clear."[30] That was the essence of what the government was after in holding the debate at all. It wanted to point to the support of Canadians as represented through their "well-informed" members of Parliament.

I was quite surprised when I was told that many government MPs simply pick up their speeches from a table as they enter the House. Those speeches have been drafted by officials in the very departments which, as legislators, they are supposed to oversee. The drafting of government members' speeches begins in the departments of Foreign Affairs and Defence as far in advance of the debate date as possible. The tone of the speeches is carefully prepared to correspond to the message that the government is trying to put across.

While nearly every speech delivered in the House of Commons receives varying degrees of input from staff members, opposition speeches or statements are always drafted by party officials who are there to assist in the preparation of their party's policy. It should not be the job of civil servants to tell parliamentarians what to say. This turns democratic government on its head. It makes Parliament into nothing more than a rubber stamp for what the bureaucrats want done. But that is what happens.

Liberal MP Aileen Carroll's speech was written for her by Axworthy's officials and concluded with the words: "While Canada and our partners in the international community do not seek to impose our own solutions, we cannot be neutral to the suffering being experienced and to the threat to international peace and security that is posed by this current crisis. Through the United Nations and through NATO we must act to help end the suffering and bring about a lasting answer to these very complex problems. Time is running out."[31]

Stirring perhaps, except that every word had been written for her. After Carroll finished speaking, Bill Graham felt the need to add to the farce by saying, "I would like to thank the member for Barrie–Simcoe–Bradford for her very thoughtful and sensitive appreciation of the situation."[32] Jean Augustine, another Liberal MP, devoted a considerable segment of her speech to condemning the Milosevic government for its actions in Kosovo. Much of her speech had also been written by foreign affairs officials. (See Appendix comparing speeches drafted by government officials with the addresses actually delivered in the House by MPs.)

During this entire debate, which lasted several hours, only two members had anything substantive to say about the preparedness of the Canadian Forces for military action, about actual military objectives and about exit strategies. For most members, these questions seemed to be almost too mundane to consider. For instance, after reading her speech, Jean Augustine was asked by Gurmant Grewal how well she thought Canadian troops were prepared for the mission they were being asked to undertake. Augustine replied that she had not participated in the debate as an accountant. She blandly noted that the defence minister had already outlined "the number of aircraft we have."[33] That for her was sufficient.

In the end, only David Price, at that time a Progressive Conservative, and Art Hanger raised military-related questions. Price strongly condemned the government for its refusal to allow a real debate and vote on the issue of military action. He commented at length on the pitiful condition of the Canadian Forces. He then lamented that the minister of defence had already left the House and therefore had not heard any of these concerns.

Naturally, government ministers weren't in the House to hear most of the speeches. They left the House soon after completing their remarks to do more important things. Nor was Art Eggleton present for the comments by the Reform Party's defence critic. In his speech, Art Hanger asked a number of the questions that I had discussed with him earlier in the day.

Art felt that he had little choice but to join other members in saying that if NATO took military action, Canada could not stand aside. At the same time, however, he was clearly uneasy about the way in which the government was moving and by the blank cheque which Parliament appeared to be giving them.

While this opening debate on the Kosovo crisis was irrelevant to Canadian policy making, it nevertheless had the effect of setting the tone for each of the political parties related to the Kosovo crisis. Until this point there had been no reason for any of the parties to commit themselves enthusiastically to military action, the parameters of which were clearly unknown and for which the Canadian Forces were largely unprepared. Yet that is exactly what they did on October 7. A course had been set from which it would be difficult to turn aside later on.

Parliamentary "Oversight": October 1998 to February 1999

"I should first point out that under no circumstances are we talking about a force that would be going in as an active intervention."

Lloyd Axworthy, House of Commons, February 17, 1999

After the October discussion in Parliament a compromise deal was reached between Richard Holbrooke and Milosevic which delayed a confrontation for a few more months. The Kosovo issue moved off the front pages of the newspapers. As if by reflex it also immediately moved off the parliamentary agenda. However, there should have been no issue of greater importance. Surely if our troops were to be asked to participate in a war, they should be properly equipped. This was Parliament's responsibility — at least in theory. But very few MPs seemed concerned about it.

Between October 7, 1998, and the next take-note debate on February 17, 1999, only seven questions related to Kosovo were asked of the government during Question Period. One of these was asked by Bob Mills (October 28) on the potential dangers which awaited unarmed Canadian observers deploying to Kosovo. He touched on the whole question of the difficulties and complexities associated with long-term involvement in Kosovo. The issue deserved greater attention from the opposition, but it ended up being raised only once in Question Period.

To his credit, I know that Bob pushed to raise this and other matters, but there was consistent skepticism from those who ran Question Period about whether these matters were "newsworthy."

The three other questions were asked by Liberal MPs (October 23 and 30 and February 8). These questions were entirely pre-planned with government. They allowed a minister to talk about events in a given area, highlighting the government's policy approach. Such questions are almost never picked up by the media but they do assist the government in killing time during Question Period.

The January 15 massacre at Racak put Kosovo back on the international agenda. Parliament resumed sitting on February 1, 1999, after its Christmas break. However, even though Kosovo was on the international agenda, it wasn't a serious issue for Parliament. Few parliamentarians probably believed that the crisis would develop into a war. NATO, equally confident that Yugoslavia would break under international pressure, was looking at the deployment of a military force of 28,000 troops from member states to replace the unarmed international observers who had been deployed under the auspices of the October agreement.

Canada was asked to participate in this force and it was under these circumstances that the government found it desirable again to bring the matter before Parliament. On February 16 Parliament was given 24 hours' notice that the issue would be debated the next day. This no-notice debate corresponded with the usual practice, but what added to the shallowness of the discussion was that the House Foreign Affairs Committee had been scheduled to receive a briefing on the Kosovo situation on February 18 — one day *after* the debate in Parliament. In other words, MPs would be asked for their views in the House prior to hearing from departmental experts on the nature of the current crisis.

To his credit, Daniel Turp of the Bloc confronted Lloyd Axworthy on this matter in committee on February 17. Axworthy just happened to be appearing before committee that day on other matters, and it afforded some opportunity to focus on the new crisis in Kosovo. Turp took the opportunity to note his strong disapproval of the timing of the take-note debate. He spoke in English (very rare for Bloc members while participating in parliamentary duties) to ensure that his concerns would be clearly heard by Axworthy. He said that in the past he had informed Axworthy's officials that the take-note debates in Parliament were "not well prepared, well orchestrated. ... If you want to have

Parliament involved in this, if you want to have meaningful debates in Parliament, as you've said you do, this is not the way to do things."[34]

The Committee chair, Bill Graham, immediately leaped to Mr. Axworthy's defence, claiming that the agenda for the House was set by House leaders, not the minister. But this argument was specious. Everybody knew that the government set the parameters for these debates and only brought them to the attention of House leaders at the last possible moment. Of course, this wasn't the way to do things — if, that is, you actually wanted real debate. But if you didn't want real debate, it was exactly the way to do things.

In preparing for the debate with only 24 hours' notice, Chris Champion and I again did our best to draft talking points and provide an analysis of the situation. As usual we could only work on the basis of open sources of information. Members of Parliament generally have access to no more information than does the general public. Briefings provided by foreign affairs and defence officials to MPs in committee only include information that could generally be obtained from media sources. Even on those rare occasions when briefings are "in-camera," or "secret," no information that is not already available in the media is shared with parliamentarians.

Be that as it may, Chris and I were faced with the usual scramble to get material ready and see who would be on the speaking list. Of course, this had less to do with who might know something about the issue at hand than it did with who was available to speak on a given evening. The process was that the talking points were drafted by us in research and then sent by the critics' offices to those MPs who were on the speakers' list. Occasionally Chris and I could lobby to get more knowledgeable MPs to put themselves on the list, but most of the time that matter was out of our hands.

For this debate, in addition to our foreign affairs and defence critics, Bob Mills and Art Hanger, Reform had three other MPs on the speaking list — Gurmant Grewal, the deputy foreign affairs critic, Jim Abbott, member for Kootenay Columbia, and Rob Anders, member for Calgary West. Neither Abbott nor Anders had spoken in the October 7 debate.

When the debate was held, the government lumped in two totally different issues in an effort to kill two birds with one stone. In addition to Kosovo, it also decided that the House should simultaneously discuss the deployment of 38 Canadian personnel to support a UN peacekeeping mission in the Central African Republic.

The government's intent was clear. It was trying to signal that Kosovo was just another peacekeeping venture — no different than the missions that Canadians had previously been involved in. It was a poor attempt to dilute substantive discussion of the Kosovo question. The motion for the debate read: "That this House take note of possible Canadian peacekeeping activities in Kosovo and the possible changes in peacekeeping activities in the Central African Republic."[35]

A total of 21 MPs from all parties showed up to discuss the Kosovo and Central African Republic missions that evening. Twenty-two MPs had spoken during the earlier debate on October 7. Fourteen members spoke in both debates. Thus, since this was the last debate in Parliament prior to the outbreak of the war, only 29 of the entire complement of about 301 MPs in the House of Commons spoke in one debate or the other — amounting to less than 10 percent of all the members of the House of Commons. Given the fact that the lives of hundreds of Canadians would later be put at risk, this was very surprising to a novice researcher like me.

But the House is very rarely full for such debates. MPs speaking in the Chamber during both Kosovo debates were speaking to an empty room. Few if any MPs were there just to listen. MPs on the duty roster have to be there no matter what the topic. In order to make the House look full on TV, the other MPs, those who are on House duty or who may be awaiting their turn to speak, crowd around the member who happens to be speaking.

On February 17, as during every take-note debate, Mr. Axworthy went through the motions of pretending that it mattered. He began by justifying the discussion of Kosovo and the Central African Republic in the same debate by saying that it "demonstrates the range and extent of Canada's worldwide interest." He said that the reason for giving the House such short notice was that, in case of an agreement at Rambouillet that weekend, the government would have the "full opportunity to hear from members of Parliament from all regions what they think the best judgment should be of Canadians on this very crucial issue."[36]

This was laughable since every take-note debate was held on short notice. Moreover, the very idea that the government really cared what members of Parliament thought and would wait for their input was patently absurd. Decisions on the scope and nature of Canadian involvement had already been made. Canadian CF-18s were already in Italy and the minister of national defence had already announced that 800 Canadian troops would be deployed as part of the NATO intervention force. And once again Liberal members were about to read word-for-word speeches that government bureaucrats had already written for them.

Axworthy downplayed the prospect that Canada would participate in any military action: "I should first point out that under no circumstances are we talking about a force that would be going in as an active intervention."[37] This was wishful thinking since the Serbs had already explicitly rejected the deployment of any armed international force on their territory.

Axworthy also repeated the pretence that NATO was an impartial mediator in the conflict between two warring parties. If the parties didn't come to an agreement, he warned, NATO would be forced to take action. Everyone knew that no military action would ever be taken against the KLA. Only the Serbs were being threatened with military action.

Defence Minister Eggleton, clearly the junior of the two ministers, entered the debate to provide the Defence Department's perspective. He also stated that ground troops would not be deployed "in some warlike conditions," but rather in a "permissive environment." Canadian military units would only be deployed under Canadian command. They would go with the "best equipment," he said at one point. Moreover, even though Canada would be deploying only 500 to 800 troops, Eggleton claimed that they would be "viable units" deployed under Canadian command.[38]

The statements by the two ministers left the usual legion of unanswered questions with regard to the nature of the mission, Canada's role and our ability to carry it out. Our token contingent of 500 to 800 troops could hardly be a viable independent unit. It would be totally reliant on allied logistics and other support. Moreover, contrary to Mr. Eggleton's claim, it would have to be placed under the command and control of a larger allied unit.

As usual, after the two ministers made their introductory remarks the main spokespeople for the opposition parties took their turn. Over the previous four months Bob Mills had been one of the few MPs who had become increasingly wary of NATO's policy in Kosovo. In October he had said that bombing would bring Milosevic to the table. Now, having looked at the issue more closely, he was skeptical. His comments drew on the talking points that Chris and I had prepared, but the words were almost entirely his own. He said that the government was, in effect, asking for a "blank cheque" from Parliament. He was especially incensed about the lack of information that had been provided by the departments of National Defence and Foreign Affairs and about the short notice prior to the debate.

Bob's comments immediately drew fire from other members of the House. When Bob was finished, Julian Reed, the parliamentary secretary to Lloyd Axworthy, jumped up and protested, "I remind the House that this debate is not about whether we bomb anybody. It is not about whether we send troops into a conflagration. It is a debate about peace-keeping forces and whether they should go into the Central African Republic and into Kosovo. It has nothing to do with bombing. It has nothing to do with striking."

Reed's comments were ridiculous, given the *diktat* then being imposed at Rambouillet. This would be proven within weeks, but on this day Bob's speech clashed with the message that the government was trying to convey.

Somewhat surprisingly, Daniel Turp of the Bloc joined in the attacks against Bob. "The Reform Party critic is not acting as a respon-sible member of the official Opposition should," he said.[39] Because of Bob's comments, Bloc and government members both accused the Reform Party of having changed its position on Kosovo, backing away from the military action the party had supported in October. The real-ity was that there was little likelihood that Reform would withdraw its support for the government in the event of military action. But taking Bob's lead, Reform members were at least willing to ask critical ques-tions of the government in advance.

Reform members focused many of their comments on the plight of the Canadian Forces. On the previous day the government had unveiled its budget for the coming fiscal year, which had included nothing to address the equipment crisis of the Canadian Forces. This despite the fact that another commitment was again being prepared for the Canadian Forces and even though active planning for military opera-tions in Kosovo was at an advanced stage.

Under the circumstances, I was pleased that Art Hanger and Rob Anders both drew attention to some of the real problems faced by the Canadian Forces. Rob, drawing on some of the points I had made in my briefs, commented on some of the key equipment deficiencies confronted by the army. He noted the well-known shortcomings of the Griffon heli-copters which were then already identified for deployment to Kosovo.

Rob also asked this key question: "Should Canadians die to ensure stability in the Balkans?" Were these vital interests for Canada? He noted that Canadians had already died in Bosnia: "How big a sacrifice can Canada be expected to make if our vital interests are not at stake and especially if this government is not willing to give the Forces the supplies, material and equipment they need to be able to make sure they are not putting their lives at any more risk than they absolutely need to?"[40]

Surely these were questions that in these circumstances should have been at the crux of parliamentary oversight responsibilities on Kosovo. They focused on both the ability of Canada to carry out any role asked of it and on the risks to Canadian troops. However, aside from the Reform MPs, only then-PC David Price focused on questions related to the equipment of the Canadian Forces. Most of the parliamentarians who spoke discussed the issue of Kosovo in general terms, with few specifics.

During his speech NDP defence critic Gordon Earle simply asked, "How well equipped are our troops?"[41] During the previous six years the NDP never criticized cutbacks in defence spending. Now it was calling for aggressive action and leadership on Canada's part. How this was to be done in the absence of adequate funding for the military and declining influence in NATO was left to the imagination.

The Bloc's defence critic, René Laurin, was similarly oriented, stating that "the Bloc Québécois is in favour of Canada sending troops to this interposition and peacekeeping operation … We also agree with the use of force to put an end to atrocities occurring anywhere in the world."[42]

Ted McWhinney of the Liberals, who had been an international law professor before being elected to Parliament, talked about the legalities and theories of military intervention in the affairs of sovereign states. This was certainly important, but the issues of the mechanics of intervention and whether the Canadian Forces were actually able to carry out the task at hand were completely ignored. No other Liberal MP raised the issue either.

For government MPs this was probably understandable. Asking hard questions about capability might be a career-breaking move. But what was the excuse for many of the other opposition members from the Bloc and the NDP? Certainly it is true that time constraints and debates held at short notice just didn't allow for much preparation and background research. However, some MPs are always better prepared than others despite these constraints. Some might point to the fact that the third, fourth and fifth place opposition parties don't have the research resources that the official Opposition has. While this is true, MPs who do a little reading and who know their brief can make a reasonable showing of themselves even with limited staff resources. When David Price was with the PCs (he crossed to the Liberals in 2000), he was able to generate quite effective comments for the Kosovo debates. Unfortunately most MPs simply don't feel that there are political rewards if they prepare analytical comments or questions.

Six Liberal backbenchers spoke that evening. Of these six, four certainly had their speeches written by Axworthy's and Eggleton's officials even though they passed these views off as their own. It was perhaps justifiable in the case of two of the members, the foreign affairs and defence parliamentary secretaries, Julian Reed and Robert Bertrand. When they speak in the House, they speak on behalf of the government and it seems acceptable that their statements be fully in keeping with government policy. However, there is no reason why backbenchers, who are supposed to be exercising oversight on government policy, should have their remarks completely choreographed by government bureaucrats.

And choreographed they certainly are. For example, in the advance preparation for one of the speeches to be delivered in the February 17 debate by the Department of National Defence (DND), the first draft began with the words: "Mr. Speaker, today we are facing an increasingly intractable conflict in an increasingly fragile world. Over the past few weeks we have seen the renewal of violence in Kosovo ..."

These and subsequent sentences were then stroked out by a more senior DND official after reviewing this first draft. The senior official advised that "this is a 'good news' address. It should focus on the positive outcome of Rambouillet and why we ought to support a peace agreement by sending CF personnel if such a 'beast' is struck."[43] The wording in the speech was changed accordingly.

Liberal MPs David Pratt and Paul Szabo both read speeches they had been given that evening (see Appendix). As chairman of the House of Commons standing defence committee, David Pratt would later make a positive contribution to raising awareness of many of the problems confronting the Canadian Forces. But when it came to Canadian policy on Kosovo, he simply read the government line he had been given, using phrases like, "*As I conceive it*, there are four key reasons why we should favourably consider a role in any NATO-led operation in Kosovo." Perhaps he should have said, "*As conceived by the Department*

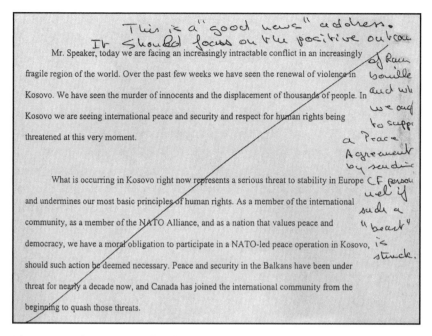

The process of writing speeches for MPs involves considerable effort on the part of government bureaucrats to "stage manage" what legislators actually say. In the above example, an early Defence Department speech for MPs, prepared for the February 17 debate, is changed to make the message more "up beat".

of National Defence, there are four key reasons ..." since it was department personnel who wrote those words.

Paul Szabo devoted all but the last four paragraphs of his speech to the situation in the Central African Republic. That wasn't surprising since that happened to be the topic of the DND-written speech that he happened to pick up when he went into the House. But since he had a bit of time left at the end of his speech, he threw in a few thoughts of his own about the Kosovo mission, concluding with the statement, "I am pleased to support the minister's call for parliamentarians to support our participation in Kosovo as well as in the Central African Republic."[44]

Cynically, Lloyd Axworthy lauded these spoon-fed comments two months later before the Foreign Affairs Committee when he said, "I have read those transcripts [of the parliamentary debate], and I have found them to be extremely helpful. They have given good advice. They have indicated support for what the government has done so far. When a member of Parliament gets up on his or her feet to speak, I respect what he or she has to say and I listen carefully to it."[45] I had to stop myself from openly laughing.

Despite ongoing talks at Rambouillet in February and March, after the February 17 debate the House went back to sleep on the Kosovo issue. In the five weeks between February 17 and the outbreak of the war on March 24, just one question was asked in Question Period related to the negotiations at Rambouillet. That question was asked by Reform member Jim Hart on February 18 — the day after the take-note debate. In those same five weeks no meetings of the House of Commons Foreign Affairs or Defence committees were devoted to the Kosovo situation. It is also instructive that neither the prime minister nor any of the four opposition party leaders had participated in either the take-note debates or in committee sessions related to Kosovo.

When the war broke out on March 24, Parliament was suddenly confronted with a war for which Canada was unprepared. Having failed to focus on Kosovo in the months preceding the war because the issue wasn't newsworthy, after March 24 parliamentarians suddenly had a very newsworthy issue but now felt themselves restricted in what they could say because of the need to show solidarity with Canadian troops.

NOTES

1. Paul Koring, "Warplanes Await NATO's Call," *The Globe and Mail*, June 12, 1998, p. A1; Paul Koring, "NATO Rehearses Air Raids on Kosovo," *The Globe and Mail*, June 16, 1998, p. A1.

2. Bob Allen, *Why Kosovo? Anatomy of a Needless War* (Ottawa: Canadian Centre for Policy Alternatives, July 1999) pp. 15–16.

3. Misha Glenny, *The Balkans, 1804–1999* (London: Granta Books, 1999) p. 630.

4. In Croatia this gave ethnic Serbs good reason to fear for their safety. Hundreds of thousands of Serbs had been murdered during the Second World War at the hands of the Nazis and their allies, the Croatian Ustashe.

5. Mark Danner, "Endgame in Kosovo: Ethnic Cleansing and American Amnesia," in *Kosovo: Contending Voices on Balkan*

Interventions, William Joseph Buckley, ed. (Grand Rapids, MI: William Erdmans Publishing, 2000) p. 63.

6. Doug Bandow, "Hypocritical Humanitarianism" in Ted Galen Carpenter, ed., *NATO's Empty Victory* (Washington, D.C.: CATO Institute, 2000) p. 38; Glenny, p. 650.

7. Glenny, p. 650.

8. Christopher Layne, "Miscalculations and Blunders Lead to War," in Ted Galen Carpenter, ed., *NATO's Empty Victory* (Washington, D.C.: Cato Institute, 2000) pp. 11–20.

9. Jerry Seper, "KLA Rebels Train in Terrorist Camps; Bin Laden Offers Financing Too," *Washington Times*, May 4, 1999, p. A1.

10. Paul Koring, "Warplanes Await NATO's Call," *The Globe and Mail*, June 12, 1998, p. A1. The last Canadian 707 tankers were retired in 1997.

11. Canada, Parliament, House of Commons, *Debates*, Vol. 7 (November 28, 1994) p. 8349.

12. Tim Judah, *Kosovo: War and Revenge* (New Haven, CT: Yale University Press, 2000) p. 178.

13. Judah, pp. 182–183.

14. Judah, p. 192.

15. Judah, p. 194.

16. *Statement of the North Atlantic Council on Kosovo* [media release], Brussels: North Atlantic Treaty Organization, North Atlantic Council, January 30, 1999.

17. Judah, p. 215.

18. Annex B of the agreement stated that NATO troops would receive "together with their vehicles, vessels, aircraft, free and unrestricted passage throughout the FRY including associated air space and territorial waters. This shall include, but not be limited to, the right of bivouac, manoeuvre, billet and utilization of areas or facilities as required for support, training and operations." Judah, p. 210.

19. David Dingwall, Alfonso Gagliano, Peter Milliken and Don Boudria, *Reviving Parliamentary Democracy: The Liberal Plan for House of Commons and Electoral Reform* (Liberal Party document, January 1993).

20. House of Commons, *Debates*, Vol. 5 (February 9, 1998) p. 3590.

21. House of Commons, *Debates*, Vol. 10 (October 7, 1998) p. 8914.

22. House of Commons, *Debates*, Vol. 10 (October 7, 1998) p. 8914.

23. House of Commons, *Debates*, Vol. 10 (October 7, 1998) p. 8915.

24. House of Commons, *Debates*, Vol. 10 (October 7, 1998) p. 8925.

25. House of Commons, *Debates*, Vol. 10 (October 7, 1998) pp. 8918–8920.

26. House of Commons, *Debates*, Vol. 10 (October 7, 1998) p. 8933–8934.

27. House of Commons, *Debates*, Vol. 10 (October 7, 1998) p. 8938.

28. House of Commons, *Debates*, Vol. 10 (October 7, 1998) p. 8929.

29. House of Commons, *Debates*, Vol. 10 (October 7, 1998) p. 8949.

30. House of Commons, *Debates*, Vol. 10 (October 7, 1998) p. 8939.

31. House of Commons, *Debates*, Vol. 10 (October 7, 1998) pp. 8943–8944. Actual speech was compared with drafts of speeches obtained from the Department of Foreign Affairs and International Trade through an Access to Information request.

32. House of Commons, *Debates*, Vol. 10 (October 7, 1998) p. 8944. Actual speech was compared with drafts of speeches obtained from the Department of Foreign Affairs and International Trade through an Access to Information request.

33. House of Commons, *Debates*, Vol. 10 (October 7, 1998) pp. 8950–8951.

34. Canada, Parliament, House of Commons, Standing Committee on Foreign Affairs and International Trade, *Minutes of Proceedings and Evidence*, Meeting 92 (February 17, 1999). Sections 15:45–15:50.

35. House of Commons, *Debates*, Vol. 14 (February 17, 1999) p. 12038.

36. House of Commons, *Debates*, Vol. 14 (February 17, 1999) pp. 12038–12039.

37. House of Commons, *Debates*, Vol. 14 (February 17, 1999) p. 12042.

38. House of Commons, *Debates*, Vol. 14 (February 17, 1999) pp. 12041, 12043.

39. House of Commons, *Debates*, Vol. 14 (February 17, 1999) p. 12045.

40. House of Commons, *Debates*, Vol. 14 (February 17, 1999) pp. 12072–12075.

41. House of Commons, *Debates*, Vol. 14 (February 17, 1999) p. 12051.

42. House of Commons, *Debates*, Vol. 14 (February 17, 1999) p. 12049.

43. Speeches prepared for parliamentarians on Kosovo (February 1999) by the Department of National Defence. Drafts obtained through Access to Information request.

44. House of Commons, Debates, Vol. 14 (February 17, 1999) p. 12066.

45. House of Commons, Standing Committee on Foreign Affairs and International Trade, *Minutes of Proceedings and Evidence*, Meeting 113 (April 15, 1999). Sections 1605–1610.

CHAPTER THREE

Parliament During the War

"Since Canada is a member of NATO, the G8 and the Security Council, why is it not the one showing leadership and innovation on the diplomatic front?"

Bloc MP René Laurin, House of Commons, April 23, 1999

Prior to the outbreak of the war on March 24 almost no questions had been asked in the House about the Kosovo crisis. Discussions in committee had been shallow and involved less than 10 percent of MPs. Only about 10 percent participated in the take-note debates. Many government MPs simply read the speeches prepared for them by bureaucrats.

When the war broke out on March 24, most MPs were therefore confronted with the Kosovo issue for the first time. Many had never given anything more than the most cursory attention to foreign policy issues. Most MPs simply had no sense of how limited Canada's role in the world really was and how little influence Canada actually had.

This contributed to incredibly naive assumptions about Canada's role and about the opportunities for Canada to show leadership in order to end the war. I even heard one senior MP privately suggest that perhaps NATO could stop the atrocities by dropping camcorders to Kosovar civilians to allow them to film their attackers and provide the necessary proof. While some MPs pressed for simple solutions, most neglected the basic reality of Canadian military preparedness.

On March 24 it was clear that Kosovo was finally the story of the day. However, news that the war had broken out came only minutes before Question Period. Preston Manning was the only leader who asked all his questions on the Kosovo issue on the first day — a tribute to his ability to think on his feet as neither he, nor any of the other party leaders, had participated in any of the previous take-note debates on Kosovo.

Instead of asking about Kosovo, the Bloc's first question was on the decision to award a contract to build a new Canadian embassy in Berlin to a consortium that included a company based in Lloyd Axworthy's home riding. After being roundly condemned by Axworthy for their choice of questions, the Bloc members devoted two later questions to Kosovo. No further questions were asked by any other member on the first day.

Preston Manning and Gilles Duceppe were the only leaders to ask questions about Kosovo on Day Two. NDP leader Alexa McDonough asked about growing American ownership in Canada's high-tech industry, while the PCs devoted their leader's round to asking questions about federal funding for homelessness. Both the NDP and the PCs put their Kosovo questions near the bottom of the order paper on Day Two. With the end of business on March 25, Parliament recessed for two weeks.

The parties generally believed that the war would be a short one, and many MPs had difficulty believing that the war was of much relevance to Canada. Yes, Canadians were involved, but any sense that what was happening was of potentially great significance to the future of NATO and its role in Western security was almost completely absent.

In the two weeks that Parliament was recessed, this perspective changed entirely. In that time it became obvious that the war in Kosovo was a major news story. Since the government had encouraged the idea of a short and easy war and since the war was not over, the opportunity now existed to potentially hurt Liberal credibility. It was then that Kosovo became an issue of high importance. Focusing on Kosovo from this angle — as a means to damage Liberal credibility — actually served to undermine Parliament. Discussions inevitably became simplistic and melodramatic. Prescriptions became unrealistic, with calls for the government to "show diplomatic leadership" and "solve the crisis."

Most of these suggestions were based on the day's newspaper stories. As such, they lacked any real understanding for the realities of the situation on the ground. MPs from all parties succumbed to the tendency to oversimplify.

When the House resumed, a virtual flood of questions was directed at the government. On the first day back — April 12 — every opposition question was on Kosovo; on April 13 and 14 there were 25 questions each day; on April 15, 21 questions.

The purpose of the questions was two-fold: first, to allow party leaders to appear "statesmanlike" by asking relevant questions about Canadian policy and, second, to score political points and expose, if possible, any shortcomings in government policy. There was little expectation that the opposition could actually influence government policy, especially when its position was largely supportive of that taken by the government.

Within Reform, suggestions for daily questions generally came from whatever angle people thought might be the most newsworthy. Since there was no requirement to consult with the research department on the nature of questions asked, I was often not aware of the content of the questions until I heard them in the House.

I thought questions concerning the equipment and preparedness of the Canadian Forces were among the most relevant that we could ask because the lives of Canadians were directly involved. But there was resistance to the idea of questions with too many facts. Detailed questions about military equipment and hardware were only rarely considered. I was told that none of the parliamentary press would know what the particular pieces of equipment under discussion were, and there was little use in trying to clarify the matter. Questions about the nature of NATO policy or about Canadian input into NATO decision making were seen as dull and unlikely to catch media attention. Such questions did not lend themselves to being summarized in five- or 10-second sound bites.

Another problem with the nature of the questions asked was that many MPs didn't know why particular questions might be important. Within Reform, there were no detailed policy discussions on the nature of the conflict, on possible pitfalls in NATO strategy or on the shortcomings in Canadian capability. Preston Manning raised the idea of hosting a few Balkan experts at his home in Stornoway to discuss various aspects of the crisis. This was an excellent idea but unfortunately it never went forward.

Chris and I and the rest of the research staff were fortunate to have been joined by Dr. Ben Lombardi who only a few weeks before had taken up his new role as Bob Mill's executive assistant. Until March Ben had been working at the Department of National Defence in the Directorate of Strategic Analysis, where he had been responsible for Eastern Europe. He was, of course, a specialist on the Balkans. When the Kosovo war erupted Ben was immediately involved in working with Bob to formulate the party's position on the crisis. Ben's expertise was potentially invaluable, but he was never utilized to his potential in an environment in which political posturing rather than substantive discussion is the name of the game. Attempts to arrange briefings for parliamentarians fell through due to lack of interest. Within a few months his frustration with the shallowness of much of the politics on the Hill would lead him to return to DND.

The Views of MPs: The April 12 Take-Note Debate

"I join this debate to say a number of things, but first and foremost to speak my mind."

Liberal MP Hec Clouthier,
reading a speech on Kosovo written by the
Department of National Defence, House of Commons,
April 12, 1999

Another take-note debate was scheduled for April 12, the day the House was to resume sitting after its two-week spring break. The government had not recalled Parliament during the break despite the distinct lack of an early victory in the Kosovo war.

Within the Reform Party, many viewed this as a mixed blessing: a conference call during the break period (March 26 to April 12) had revealed differences of opinion between those who believed that the party had to support the government and war effort almost unconditionally, and those who believed that Reform still had an obligation to raise serious questions. Our communications staff was pressing for a simple message that would appeal to the public. "I don't care whether we support the war or oppose it," one staff member said, "but let's have a clear message one way or the other."

Bob Mills was now in the "reluctant camp." He had become increasingly uneasy about NATO policy and was worried that the government was blindly sending our troops into a conflict for which they were unprepared. In this regard he expressed his strong opposition to any support for a ground campaign. He did not trust either the government or NATO to keep our ill-equipped soldiers out of harm's way. Others suggested that our support for NATO military action should not be diluted.

These differences of opinion were natural. Given the issues at stake, arguments were passionate and even heated at times. Parliamentarians had awoken to the Kosovo issue and were debating the merits of Canadian policy even though their role would be limited. It was a pity that such arguments had for so long been absent from the House itself.

Differences of opinion between critics could really only be smoothed by Preston Manning's intervention. Although he had not been active on the Kosovo file, now that the conflict was under way, he was engaged and his speech in the April 12 debate would set the parameters for party policy.

Fortunately, while Mr. Manning had already pledged to support the government, he favoured a more nuanced approach. He was working on his speech that weekend and called both Ben and me to consult on what we thought of his approach. He planned to argue that Canada's objectives in the war should be grounded in the moral objective of stopping the ethnic cleansing then under way; the political objective of achieving a negotiated settlement to the problem of Kosovo; and the military objective centred on forcing Milosevic and the Yugoslav government back to the negotiating table.

Canada, he suggested, should support all three objectives, and the Reform Party should, in turn, support the government in achieving those objectives. However, Reform's support for the use of force would be qualified by two conditions. First, the government would have to continue to demonstrate to the House that the level of military force being applied was directly linked to the moral and political objectives that we were prepared to endorse. And second, it would have to be shown to Parliament that the military contribution made by Canada was within the capabilities of the Canadian Forces.

For all the work that we put into preparing our position, the truth was that there was never any doubt that we would support NATO's war against Yugoslavia. It was simply too late to do anything else. The telephone conversation that I had with Mr. Manning on April 11 on the Kosovo crisis was our first on that matter. It occurred only one day prior to the debate. It was simply impossible for any MP, even the leader of the Opposition, to become engaged in this issue at such a late stage and expect to have any hope of affecting policy one way or the other.

The debate held in the House on April 12 occurred nearly 20 days after the war erupted. Only 77 MPs would speak during the course of the debate — about one-quarter of House members. The debate was in the usual format, which did not allow for any vote at the end of the process. The motion itself was as innocuous as possible. It set no parameters at all for Canadian involvement. It provided no hint about the government's view on Canada's future role. Reading the motion on its own would have given no clue to anyone that a war was even under way. It read: "That this House take note of the continuing human tragedy in Kosovo and the government's determination to work with the international community in order to resolve the conflict and promote a just political settlement for Kosovo that leads to the safe return of the refugees."[1]

For the first time since the crisis erupted, the prime minister addressed the issue in the House. For the most part Mr. Chrétien spoke in generalities. He explained Canada's involvement not on the basis of the vital interests that Canada had at stake in Kosovo, but rather by referring to Canada's obligations to its allies. He said:

> It is important to understand that Canada is not acting alone. No one country can decide alone on operations or tactics. We are members of a team. We are contributing to a collective effort. And decisions are made collectively …
>
> To be a bystander on Kosovo today would be to betray our basic values, our national interest and our international obligations. That is not how Canadians do things. We live up to our commitments and keep our word all the way down the line.[2]

I found it striking that the prime minister's comments underscored the degree to which Canada had become a follower of decisions that were made elsewhere.

Mr. Manning spoke next. He committed the official Opposition to supporting the commitment of Canadian ground forces to the war subject to the two conditions we had discussed: "if NATO can demonstrate that such a commitment is necessary to halt the ethnic cleansing in Kosovo and provide a safe home for Kosovars in the region ... [and] subject to the condition that the Canadian government demonstrate to the House that the commitments requested are within Canada's capability." With regard to the latter condition, he commented that the defence budget had sunk from $12 billion to $9.3 billion under the Liberals, and in some categories of equipment Canada was at least "a generation behind its NATO allies."[3]

Manning was firmly convinced that Parliament's role in this issue, as in all others, had to be more substantial. He strongly believed that Parliament should set the parameters of Canada's involvement. That could be done only through a free vote in the House.

This resulted in an instinctive and negative reaction from most Liberals. Liberal MP John Bryden said that if a vote were actually held, MPs would be subject to pressure and intimidation from their ridings — an amazing statement. Bryden was saying that MPs might actually have to listen to their constituents! Manning responded by asking Bryden under what circumstances that was not the case. Bryden's comments were indicative of MPs who were so used to voting the party line that they actually feared being responsible to their constituents.

Bob Mills's speech reflected a somewhat different perspective about the opposition's role. "At this point in time and without further information, I am not in favour of committing Canadian forces to a ground campaign in Kosovo," Bob said. This position was more skeptical of a ground campaign than Preston Manning's speech; however, I did not see this as a problem. No political party should pretend to be monolithic. In the Canadian Parliament there is a tendency to pretend that political parties are. The media are very quick to point out any differences of opinion and to suggest that the party has no idea what it is doing or that its leadership is weak. The media rarely question the implications of the fact that Canada's "democratic" system rarely has any public displays of major policy differences within political parties.

Bob was virtually alone among parliamentarians in talking about the circumstances that had led to the war. He suggested that NATO had backed itself into a corner. "Once NATO committed itself to the solution of the Kosovar civil war and once it got into the Rambouillet peace talks, its credibility was put on the line," he said.[4] War became the only option once the Serbs refused to yield.

Ben Lombardi's experience proved invaluable for Bob as he formulated his position. Bob stated that NATO operations in Yugoslavia did not seem to coincide with the defensive alliance that had been created in 1949. He quoted what was then NATO's most recent strategic concept document of 1991, which said that "the alliance is purely defensive in purpose. None of its weapons will ever be used except in self-defence, and it does not consider itself to be anyone's adversary." He commented, "I do not think that anyone in this House would argue that the civil war in Kosovo directly threatened any NATO member." The issues involved in going to war over Kosovo, he explained, "touch on the very purpose of the alliance in the post–cold war." The decision to go to war over Kosovo might have far-reaching implications for NATO's future role and for Canadian international commitments. Bob concluded powerfully by declaring, "I want to be able to look the Canadian people in the eye and say with total sincerity that I thought Canada's vital interests were best served by engaging in a ground war. I want to be able to tell Canadians that if some of their sons and daughters do not come back from such a mission, the sacrifice was worthwhile."[5]

But by then it was fairly clear that the military operation had probably provoked ethnic cleansing which only started, on a large scale, *after* the bombing began. Moreover, the purpose of military action was not really to force the Yugoslav government back to the negotiating table. Rather, it was to force that government to accept the creation of a NATO protectorate over Kosovo, as had been demanded at Rambouillet.

Parliament was exactly the place for honest and open discussion. Unfortunately this never took place. The limited emphasis placed by parliamentarians on foreign and defence policy issues was certainly a major reason. The inclination to reduce complex issues to the simplest talking points was another.

For the Bloc, those talking points were usually framed with the party's sovereignty aspirations in mind. On this occasion party leader Gilles Duceppe said that Canada could not stand by as Kosovars were stripped of their nation and territory. Predictably, he made a specific reference to the possible partitioning of Kosovo and rejected the idea as unacceptable.

Duceppe also committed the Bloc to supporting NATO ground troops and said that his party would support Canadian involvement in a logistics force. While the Bloc was also wary of a frontline role, this seemed to be less out of a recognition that Canadian troops were ill-prepared for such a role than it was the product of a desire simply to avoid any Canadian or Quebec casualties.

Bloc members like Daniel Turp had long been concerned about the extent to which Parliament was being sidelined in the crisis. In this regard Duceppe noted that "Parliament must be kept better informed of the military and diplomatic strategy of the government." He suggested that the parties be briefed each morning, as had been the case in the Gulf War, and that all party leaders be invited to become part of the Privy Council to give them better access to confidential information. Like all other parties, he expressed the view of the Bloc that "the consent of members of Parliament must be sought before Canadian troops take part in ground battles."[6] His suggestions, including the idea of Privy Council membership for party leaders, were ignored.

Twenty days into the war, the NDP was beginning to unravel as some members were now reversing their initial support for the war. Earlier in Question Period Alexa McDonough had called on the prime minister to "initiate a diplomatic offer to the Milosevic government that if it will stop the ethnic cleansing … and agree to come to the negotiating table, then NATO will suspend its bombing."[7]

The call was naive. The prime minister had no such power and many members in the House knew it. Like other parties, the NDP legitimately demanded a greater parliamentary role. McDonough stated that "should the issue of ground troops become one as an absolute last resort, then it is absolutely incumbent upon the government to come before Parliament to set out clearly the military objectives, the terms of engagement, what precisely it is the government is proposing and after a full debate in Parliament, that no such initiative be launched without there being a full vote in Parliament."[8]

Since Tory leader Joe Clark was not present in the House, André Bachand and David Price were the main spokespeople for their party on the Kosovo issue. The Tories had belatedly, and somewhat reluctantly, lined up behind military action after Mr. Clark cracked the whip back at the beginning of March.

However, Bachand was one of the few MPs still somewhat skeptical about what Canada and NATO were doing in Kosovo. "How can we be totally convinced of what is going on in Kosovo, in terms of the involvement of Canada and NATO?" he asked. "We cannot be convinced of anything because we do not have the necessary information."[9] He reiterated the need for a greater and more relevant parliamentary role.

David Price again strongly condemned Liberal defence policy. Using words he would undoubtedly regret a few months later when he crossed the floor to join the Liberal Party, he lamented the fact that the Liberals had pursued soft power instead of firm power in international affairs. He condemned the Liberal cancellation of the EH-101 helicopters. He said that the Liberals had sent troops to Bosnia who became hostages; that they took benefits away from women and children in military families; and that they had given Canada the military disasters of Dieppe and Hong Kong. While he did make some valid points concerning Canadian military capability, much of his rhetoric was purely theatrical.

After the party leaders and critics for foreign and defence policy spoke came the opportunity for the backbenchers. In an unusual move, the government did not place any time limits on this take-note debate. Any MPs who wished to could speak, and the House remained sitting until well into the morning. Even so, nearly three-quarters of MPs did not take advantage of the opportunity.

The MPs who did participate could be divided into several categories. The first were those who supported the war in principle, believing that military action was necessary to stop brutal Serb actions in Kosovo. They did not express any reservations with regard to the type of military action which NATO or Canada might undertake to achieve that end. MPs in this category included much of the Bloc Québécois caucus, led by their foreign policy spokesperson, Daniel Turp. As Turp stated, "It is true that military personnel from Quebec and Canada, your sons and daughters, will put their lives on the line if ground troops are sent in, but sometimes the lives of others must be put on the line to ensure the survival of a people."[10]

Keith Martin of Reform was one member of the official Opposition to offer strong support to the government during the debate. "I applaud the government's support of NATO's bombing in the federal republic of Yugoslavia," he said. He likened Milosevic to Hitler, and condemned him for mass murder in Yugoslavia.[11]

Many Liberal MPs were of similar mind. Beth Phinney of the Liberals supported the government but commented that "we need to give our soldiers every possible guarantee that the resources available to them will match their sense of duty. We owe it to them."[12] Not many government MPs were willing to say that, given the Chrétien government's official attitude, which opposed any more defence spending.

Likewise, MPs like Ted McWhinney supported the government from a legal perspective, believing that the military campaign was justified under international law. He was also under no illusions about the significance of Canada's military effort. In a comment that contradicted the central role which the government claimed that Canada was playing in the war, he admitted:

> Our role is necessarily limited by the size of our army ... There are only four planes, I think. Of course, we have no control over the rules of the game. Nonetheless, since we are members of NATO, we were asked to co-operate, and we did so for these reasons. Even though our contribution is more of a symbol than a display of military might, I think that our membership in the alliance created an obligation for us.[13]

McWhinney later reported that he refused to read the speeches prepared for him by the government, saying that while he would familiarize himself with government policy, "I give my own speeches."[14] Both Turp and McWhinney had participated in previous take-note debates. They took their oversight role seriously. Many other MPs clearly did not.

Government members such as Hec Clouthier and Raymonde Folco slavishly followed the official line with little thought, reading what had been written for them by government bureaucrats. Clouthier began his address by saying, "I join this debate to say a number of things, but first and foremost to speak my mind."[15] Since these lines were written by officials of the Department of National Defence, it was questionable whether it was "his mind" that he was speaking. Later, Clouthier had the nerve to take issue with one of the comments made by Bloc Québécois MP Rene Canuel, admonishing the Bloc MP that "if we are playing mere politics, that is wrong."[16] (See speech comparison in Appendix.)

Taking their lead from Mr. Manning, Reform MPs generally supported military action, while continuing to raise valid questions. Jay

Hill, for instance, stated, "I support the continuing of the air war, but there must be some strong conditions and there must be an open and honest debate if we ever go to the next step. We are probably going to have to look at the insertion of ground troops in Kosovo. We definitely must have a vote in the House of Commons if and when that takes place." He referred to the "terrible state of equipment for our armed forces" to justify his hesitation on a possible ground campaign.[17] Diane Ablonczy picked up on this theme as well.

A few Liberals also qualified their support for military action. Clifford Lincoln, an independent thinker in that caucus, said that he supported sending in troops only in a peacekeeping capacity and that the military operation should not be enlarged by sending troops of any kind into Yugoslavia. Jim Karygiannis, on the other hand, appeared undecided and unable to make up his mind about the war: "I am not saying that the policy of bombing military installations is right or wrong … I will support whatever action is needed to bring peace to the world."[18]

Other members seemed equally bewildered and issued desperate calls for peace. Aileen Carroll, who had simply read a bureaucrat's speech back in October, now seemed stunned by the war. She seemed to have a 1960s flashback and remembered her opposition to the Vietnam War, saying this had been predicated on ending "jingoistic ventures" forever. "As Dylan maintained," she said, "God was on no warrior's side."[19] Deepak Obhari of Reform, like many NDP members, echoed the view that Canada could take the lead in ending the war: "Canada is in a position to take a leadership role … Canada can start by sending our diplomats to world capitals. Canada can campaign to get world leaders to descend on Belgrade."[20]

These were all well-intentioned words, but they were naive. Virtually all of these MPs were approaching the issue of Kosovo for the first time and simply did not know where they really stood, so they resorted to largely empty rhetoric.

Lastly, there were those MPs who were mostly opposed to military action. The NDP had flip-flopped since the war began, and most of its members were now opposed to the war. Svend Robinson had been among the loudest in calling for action since the fall. On March 31 he had even suggested to a joint meeting of the House of Commons Foreign Affairs and Defence committees that he supported a ground campaign — not to directly engage the Yugoslavs, but to protect the

Kosovars. Although how this could be accomplished was unclear, Robinson explained:

> ... the brutal reality is that Milosevic is winning the war on the ground. He is achieving his objectives on the ground in Kosovo ... Should the horror of ethnic cleansing continue and accelerate, is the Government of Canada prepared to consider, as General Lewis MacKenzie and others have recommended, a limited ground intervention to create a safe haven in Kosovo?[21]

Now, less than two weeks later, he argued *against* NATO's leading role in Kosovo: "NATO is clearly not the answer ... Canada has to show leadership within NATO and within the United Nations for an immediate return to the negotiating table."[22]

Gordon Earle, the NDP's defence critic, reinforced this by saying that "we have to branch away from what NATO is doing and move beyond it because it certainly has not accomplished the goal we hoped would be accomplished."[23] Commenting with horror at the prospect of a possible escalation to a ground campaign, Bill Blaikie said, "I would certainly be skeptical if the same people, the same analysts, the same brain trust that gave me assurances three weeks ago were then to come back to the House and say that they would like us to make a decision in favour of ground troops in Kosovo."[24] MP Pat Martin went on to suggest that Canada ground its CF-18s and instead supply aid to the growing numbers of Kosovar refugees.[25]

Even though they had little basis for it, NDP members had really believed that the war would be a short one. When that didn't pan out, their enthusiasm quickly collapsed. Had they devoted greater attention to actually informing themselves about the issues related to a possible war prior to its outbreak, their whole approach might not have been so breathtakingly naive.

A few other MPs also openly opposed the war, including independent member John Nunziata and Reform's Paul Forseth. Mr. Nunziata even tried to stop discussion of the government motion because he said that any debate without a vote was "meaningless and undemocratic."[26] He was unsuccessful in doing so. When it came time for his turn to speak, Forseth commented that "NATO is an alliance that was formed solely to defend its members against aggression, not to launch attacks against others … We now need to say to our club members in NATO that we played our role but we are out for now, putting Canadian planes on the ground to exercise independent thought and prepare for our role of peacekeeper and honest broker when the dust settles."[27]

Liberal John McKay was alone on the government benches in criticizing the government for "deliberately" choosing "not to maintain the capability of the Canadian Armed Forces to live up to the roles we have traditionally played on the world stage." He criticized the government for refusing to recall Parliament when crucial decisions regarding the deployment of Canadian soldiers were being made. He forcefully concluded by saying:

> We are entering into another nation's civil war, which has been going on for centuries and from which we will not easily or gracefully extract ourselves. We are in a moral quagmire where there are no innocents. We are in a legal quagmire where the rule of law is a victim. We are in a military quagmire from which we cannot readily extract ourselves. This reflects very poorly on our values as a nation and compromises our standing among the nations.[28]

While some MPs were clearly willing to question Canada's role in Kosovo, their role was of course highly circumscribed. In the end the sad reality was that nothing said on April 12–13 had the slightest impact on government policy, nor did any of the discussion affect what Canadian pilots were being asked to do in Kosovo. On April 13 Canadian fighters flew their 100th mission since the start of the war.

The Issue of a Parliamentary Vote

In the weeks that followed much of the political attention and debate focused on the question of whether Parliament would be allowed to vote on Canada's participation in the conflict. It never was. The government's refusal to allow a vote on Canada's role, let alone permit MPs to freely debate the parameters of Canadian involvement in the war, caused exasperation in the opposition parties. While in the British parliamentary system the Crown has the sole power to declare war and make peace, the evolution of parliamentary convention suggests that Parliament should now have a greater say on a matter of such importance.

As early as 1939 Parliament did vote on Canada's entry into the Second World War. The Mulroney government also allowed Parliament to vote on Canada's participation in the Gulf War in 1991, albeit only after the war had begun and the Canadian Forces were already in action. At the time, Lloyd Axworthy condemned the government for using Parliament "to try to rubber-stamp or ratify decisions already taken … as opposed to letting Parliament be the forum in which those decisions are formulated."[29]

This notwithstanding, in 1999 the Chrétien government did not allow Parliament even a belated vote. I witnessed a rare and heated argument on this issue in committee between the Bloc's Daniel Turp and Lloyd Axworthy on April 15.

Turp argued his points in English, strongly questioning the sincerity of the government's pledge to keep opposition parties informed and involved. He noted that decisions to deploy additional aircraft were being made with no parliamentary input; that briefings to inform opposition critics of events were totally inadequate; and that Parliament was being denied the right to vote on the issue.

Axworthy rejected Turp's arguments, asserting, against all the evidence, that the government was being extremely open. He even said that what the government faced in "Question Period every day … is far more open than anything Mr. Clinton ever has to face, as he's often said, or Madam Albright." This was laughable, considering the extensive oversight powers of Congress and the ability of the U.S. legislature to set real limits on military action undertaken by the president.

The exchange then grew more heated.

Axworthy: We have now had three major debates on this issue: last October, last February and on Monday night …

Mr. Turp: No specifics, Mr. Minister, generalities all the time during Question Period and committees.

Mr. Axworthy: Mr. Turp, what do you mean by generalities? When you're talking about whether there will be six more planes [committed], the fact is the decision hasn't been made yet …

Mr. Turp: That's not very convincing.

Mr. Axworthy: What more can I say? That's the way it is.

Mr. Turp: Give more information. Share information, as other countries seem to be sharing with their populations, with their MPs ... Parliamentarians need to be better informed, in the House and elsewhere.

On the issue of a parliamentary vote, Axworthy was unbending. He claimed to have a strong interest in what MPs had to say but, despite his rhetoric in 1991, would not support a vote on this occasion.[30]

In frustration, two of the opposition parties devoted two of their own supply days to further debating the Kosovo issue. The first debate came on April 19, on a motion sponsored by the Bloc Québécois. It proposed that the House "demand that the government submit to a debate and a vote in the House [about] the possibility of sending Canadian soldiers to the Balkans who may be involved in military or peacekeeping operations on the ground in Kosovo and the Balkan region."[31]

The motion was supported by all parties except the Liberals. As a result of that whipped vote, the motion was defeated by a 146 to 119 margin. None of the Liberal MPs who had expressed concerns about the war on April 12, nor even John McKay who had openly opposed the war in his speech, voted in favour of the Bloc motion. It seemed that although McKay was prepared to oppose the war, he was not prepared to demand any right to check the government's ability to wage it unhindered.

The involvement by bureaucrats in the April 19 debate was extensive. Despite the highly political nature of the debate, the Department of Foreign Affairs prepared speeches for government members. Three of the speeches written by Foreign Affairs officials for the debate on April 19 contain the notation, "Notes for remarks by a government member." The speeches drafted were mutually supporting, in that Speeches Two and Three in the series contained remarks designed to support the comments made in Speech One of the series. For instance, Speech Two contained the phrase, "I wish to support the point made by the member of Parliament for [insert the riding of the other MP speaking on humanitarian assistance]." Although these particular speeches were not used by government members for the debate on April 19, what is revealing is that bureau-crats (in this case from Foreign Affairs) seem to have had no trouble preparing what amounted to a script for MPs to follow in this highly political debate.

Mr. Speaker,

I wish to support the point made by the Member of Parliament for *[insert the riding of the other MP speaking on humanitarian assistance]*. As we debate Canada's involvement in the Balkans, I believe this House should focus its attention on the good we can do in this terrible situation. And this is definitely to provide humanitarian assistance to the hundreds of thousands of refugees who so desperately need it.

These people fled Kosovo leaving almost everything behind. A great number of them know they have nothing to go back to. Families saw their homes ransacked and burned. Shopkeepers saw their stores looted and their inventory destroyed. And I'm not even talking about the horrors they have witnessed, losing friends and family members in arbitrary acts of violence.

As Canadians, we know how fortunate we are. Our history has spared us such horrors within our borders. Yet we do know how to pull together to help people in times of need. Whether this need arises from natural disasters or armed conflict, whether it arises here or abroad, Canada and Canadians feel a moral obligation to help. We've shown it right here in the National Capital Region, when friends and relatives took people in during the ice storm. We've shown it as recently as last November, when our own Government as well as Canadians from all walks of life reached out to the victims of Hurricane Mitch, looking for ways to help in both short and long term.

I am proud that my Government came through once again, in the last few weeks, by providing $15 million in humanitarian assistance and food aid, in order to give some hope to refugees pouring into Albania, Macedonia and other relative havens in this troubled area.

Mr. Speaker,

As proud as we can and should be of our humanitarian assistance tradition, we do recognize that our responsibility towards a more equitable and more secure world does not end when crises no longer make the front pages of our daily newspapers. As citizens of the world, we do our best to contribute to preventative efforts, as we did by providing some $3.85 million to the OSCE's Kosovo Verification Mission (KVM). We are proud of the Canadian men and women who brought their skills and expertise to this international effort. I want to thank them for the role they played in providing the world with information about this incredibly complex situation.

As Canadians, we also do what we can to help countries rebuild after the fighting has stopped. By rebuilding, I mean rebuilding their communities, their schools, their hospitals. I also mean rebuilding the fragile balance of trust and respect which allows people of different origins to live in peace as good neighbours.

First page for speeches written for government MPs (not used on this occasion) for the April 19 debate. Bureaucrats make considerable effort to choreograph what MPs will say. The reference in the speech to "Insert the riding of the other MP speaking on humanitarian assistance," attempts to ensure that one MP's statements will follow smoothly on what a previous legislator has said. MPs become irrelevant and anonymous drones in this process, reduced to the status of pawns, simply reciting whatever speeches they are given.

In effect, government members were given arguments by the bureaucracy with which to rebut the opposition's call for a vote in Parliament on the commitment of Canadian troops to the Balkans. One of the speeches written by Foreign Affairs officials included phrases such as, "This motion proposes little in the way of changes which would make Canada's Kosovo policy process more transparent. The simple reason is that the process is already extremely open. The honourable members who have suggested that unilateral decisions are made behind closed doors have ignored the facts."[32]

DND bureaucrats, like their Foreign Affairs counterparts, were also actively engaged in justifying the no-vote policy. A briefing note prepared by the Directorate of Parliamentary Affairs of the Department of National Defence contained the following talking point related to a possible question on a vote:

Question: Why is the government ignoring Parliament as it responds to the crisis in Kosovo? Will the prime minister allow a vote before committing ground troops?

Suggested answer: The government is not ignoring Parliament on the issue of Canada's involvement in the Kosovo crisis. Since the outset of Canada's involvement in Kosovo, the government has consulted Parliament extensively. The House of Commons has had three full debates, in which all parties gave their strong support for our participation in NATO air strikes as well as our participation in a NATO-led force to implement a peace agreement ... There have also been extensive briefings of members of Parliament by the minister of foreign affairs, the minister of national defence, the minister for international co-operation and their respective officials. Moreover, ministers and officials have also participated in daily technical briefings which have been well-attended by the public and the press.

If pressed: In making its decisions respecting Canada's involvement in Kosovo, the government recognizes the importance of the views of parliamentarians on this crucial issue.[33]

One really has to question why defence bureaucrats were preparing any talking points at all on questions that were exclusively political in nature. One would have thought it was the Cabinet, including the minister of defence, that had decided not to hold a vote on the war. Why then was it necessary for bureaucrats to tell the minister how to answer such questions?

The NDP also brought the Kosovo issue to the House on April 27. Although its motion could not be voted on, the intent was to promote the search for a political solution and to try to push the government to "urge NATO not to take actions that expand the conflict and stand in the way of a diplomatic solution."

By the end of April the government's refusal to hold any vote on the Kosovo issue, coupled with the fact that the war did not seem to be going well, led many MPs to become more critical of the war. The NDP's support evaporated entirely. This began to worry some in DND. For instance, in reviewing the comments made by MPs during the NDP-sponsored debate on April 27, Nancy MacKinnon of the Parliamentary Affairs Directorate commented that "in general, the overall support for tougher military measures such as ground troops appeared softer in this debate than in those held previously."[34]

In the end, however, it really didn't matter. The policy decisions being made on Canada's behalf were not affected by the chatter on the Hill one way or the other.

NOTES

1. Canada, Parliament, House of Commons, *Debates*, Vol. 16 (April 12, 1999) p. 13573.
2. House of Commons, *Debates*, Vol. 16 (April 12, 1999) p. 13575.
3. House of Commons, *Debates*, Vol. 16 (April 12, 1999) p. 13579.
4. House of Commons, *Debates*, Vol. 16 (April 12, 1999) p. 13632.
5. House of Commons, *Debates*, Vol. 16 (April 12, 1999) pp. 13631–13634.
6. House of Commons, *Debates*, Vol. 16 (April 12, 1999) p. 13582.
7. House of Commons, *Debates*, Vol. 16 (April 12, 1999) p. 13566.
8. House of Commons, *Debates*, Vol. 16 (April 12, 1999) p. 13588.
9. House of Commons, *Debates*, Vol. 16 (April 12, 1999) p. 13585.

10. House of Commons, *Debates*, Vol. 16 (April 12, 1999) p. 13609.

11. House of Commons, *Debates*, Vol. 16 (April 12, 1999) pp. 13648–13650.

12. House of Commons, *Debates*, Vol. 16 (April 12, 1999) p. 13645.

13. House of Commons, *Debates*, Vol. 16 (April 12, 1999) p. 13615.

14. Ted McWhinney [interview]. Interviewed by Robert Roy of Stornoway Productions, October 2001.

15. House of Commons, *Debates*, Vol. 16 (April 12, 1999) p. 13668; speech compared to speech written for members of Parliament by officials in the Department of National Defence.

16. House of Commons, *Debates*, Vol. 16 (April 12, 1999) p. 13670.

17. House of Commons, *Debates*, Vol. 16 (April 12, 1999) p. 13656.

18. House of Commons, *Debates*, Vol. 16 (April 12, 1999) p. 13628.

19. House of Commons, *Debates*, Vol. 16 (April 12, 1999) p. 13606.

20. House of Commons, *Debates*, Vol. 16 (April 12, 1999) p. 13706.

21. Canada, Parliament, House of Commons, Joint Meeting of the Standing Committees on Foreign Affairs and International Trade and National Defence and Veterans Affairs, *Minutes of Proceedings and Evidence* (March 31, 1999). Sections 11:50–12:00.

22. House of Commons, *Debates*, Vol. 16 (April 12, 1999) p. 13616.

23. House of Commons, *Debates*, Vol. 16 (April 12, 1999) p. 13619.

24. House of Commons, *Debates*, Vol. 16 (April 12, 1999) p. 13672.

25. House of Commons, *Debates*, Vol. 16 (April 12, 1999) pp. 13574–13577.

26. House of Commons, *Debates*, Vol. 16 (April 12, 1999) p. 13573.

27. House of Commons, *Debates*, Vol. 16 (April 12, 1999) p. 13703.

28. House of Commons, *Debates*, Vol. 16 (April 12, 1999) p. 13660.

29. House of Commons, *Debates*, Vol. 13 (January 15, 1991) pp. 16991–16992; Canadian Press Staff, "Opposition Denounces Increase in Gulf Force," *The Toronto Star*, January 12, 1991, p. A1.

30. Canada, Parliament, House of Commons, Standing Committee on Foreign Affairs and International Trade, *Minutes of Proceedings and Evidence* (April 15, 1999). Sections 15:55–16:10.

31. House of Commons, *Debates*, Vol. 16 (April 19, 1999) p. 13997.

32. Canada, Department of National Defence, [internal document]. Suggested Answer to Possible Question on the Issue of a Parliamentary Vote.

33. Department of National Defence, [internal document]. Directorate of Parliamentary Affairs. Suggested Answer Related to Parliamentary Vote.
34. Department of National Defence, [internal document]. Nancy MacKinnon. Comments Made by MPs in the House of Commons, April 27, 1999.

CHAPTER FOUR

The Canadian Forces Struggle to Do Their Job

NATO's ostensible reason for launching the war in Kosovo was to degrade the ability of the Yugoslav army and police to conduct military operations in Kosovo. But these military and paramilitary forces were not struck at all in the first week of the war. NATO planners, principally those in the United States, believed that a few symbolic attacks would soon bring Serbian leader Slobodan Milosevic to his senses and he would agree to the peace demanded by the Alliance at Rambouillet. On March 24, 1999, U.S. secretary of state Madeleine Albright stated, "I don't see this as a long-term operation."[1] This assessment turned out to be a grave mistake.

Firmly convinced that the war would be a short one, NATO initially deployed only 350 to 400 aircraft for the air operation. This contrasted with the 2,600 allied aircraft that had initially been on hand for operations against Iraq in 1991. Moreover, the allies did not deploy any ground forces capable of offensive operations against Yugoslavia. Although there were about 13,000 NATO troops stationed in Macedonia, for the most part these were lightly armed peacekeepers ready to go into Kosovo had

Milosevic agreed to the terms demanded at Rambouillet. They were in no way prepared to fight their way into the province.[2]

Canada's own ill-preparedness far exceeded that of other NATO allies. When the "balloon went up" and war began, Canada had only six CF-18s deployed at the Aviano air base in Italy. Since a full wartime squadron normally consisted of up to 24 aircraft — the number that Canada had deployed in the Gulf in 1991 — the government could hardly have been expecting a serious military contest. Yet the signs had all been there for all to see. How was it that they had been missed?

Serbia's attachment to Kosovo was historic and deep. Already in October, the Yugoslav parliament, not entirely the tool of Milosevic, had united behind the dictator and declared a "state of imminent war." It had approved emergency funding for the country's air defence system (a symbolic move, to be sure) and imposed an immediate war tax on all goods. On March 23 a debate in the Yugoslav parliament witnessed attacks against NATO and the Rambouillet agreement from representatives of all parties in the legislature.[3]

The signals of Serb determination to fight were there for all to see. Within the Department of National Defence, for instance, Tony Kellett of the Directorate of Strategic Analysis wrote a note at the end of March which stated:

> Since the latest round of threatened NATO air strikes began at the end of January, there seems to have been a widespread assumption that an air campaign would be sufficient to bring Milosevic to the bargaining table, honour satisfied and ready to accede to the demands put to the warring parties at Rambouillet … There is another viewpoint, however, that warrior myths are at the root of the Serbian national psyche and that losing in battle is acceptable as long as it is done defiantly and against great odds. Such an attitude is enshrined in the death of Prince Lazar, at the battle of Kosovo Polje … in 1389. He was supposed to have said that "it is better to die in battle than to live in shame" …
>
> It is no surprise that Milosevic has swung Serbian opinion behind him with his refusal to accede to the Rambouillet agreement.

Kellett concluded by warning that "it is hard to see Milosevic or the Serbs throwing in the towel under anything but the most severe attack."[4] The analysis contained in this note was impressive and sound. Yet its circulation within the department apparently only went as high as the assistant deputy minister for policy, Kenneth Calder.

It is doubtful that Defence Minister Art Eggleton ever saw Dr. Kellett's well-written assessment. He certainly seemed to have his own delusions that the conflict would be over quickly. Indeed, the day operations were initiated, Eggleton was asked in the House about the measures he had undertaken to protect the safety of Canadian troops in Bosnia in the midst of this "war." He responded by saying, "I prefer to think of this as a humanitarian mission, an effort to stop what is being done in Kosovo, as opposed to a war."[5]

Challenging perspectives that suggested the war could be longer and more difficult than anticipated were simply ignored in Canada. There could be no starker contrast than the discussions in the United States Congress and other NATO legislatures.

In October briefings provided to members of Congress caused the Senate majority leader, Trent Lott, to remark that he was "stunned" that the administration had no Plan B in place if a limited bombing campaign didn't work. By March much of the U.S. Congress was most alarmed over what the administration was planning.

The dispatch of 4,000 U.S. troops to Kosovo under terms of the Rambouillet Accord was only approved by the House by the narrowest of margins.[6] Once the war began, this position changed in many NATO countries. In the Italian Chamber of Deputies a resolution was passed on March 26 by a vote of 318 to 188, calling on the Italian government to work with NATO to "re-open negotiations immediately and suspend the bombing."[7]

In the U.S. President Clinton's impeachment problems had certainly increased the level of partisanship in Congress. However, concern over the American role in Kosovo crossed party lines. Indeed, worry about a possible ground campaign had become so strong that on April 28 the U.S. House of Representatives reversed its earlier support for ground troops in Kosovo and instead passed a resolution requiring the president to seek congressional approval before sending any troops into the province. The resolution was passed by a vote of 213 to 210.[8] The Senate, however, continued to support the position of the administration.[9]

There was a natural impetus in all NATO nations to rally around the troops once war began. The same impetus was naturally felt in Canada's Parliament. In his reports home, the commander of the Canadian CF-18 contingent in Aviano, Colonel Dwight Davies, repeatedly noted the importance of a supportive home environment for the morale of the pilots who were being asked to risk their lives. For example, on March 26 he remarked, "It is heartwarming to see the incredible outpouring of support from every member of the CF, and from the senior leadership in particular." Similarly on March 30: "Appreciate unbelievable support and dazzling response from all the team back home."[10]

Rallying round the troops overseas was thus a natural response as soon as war broke out. Unfortunately, however, unlike the U.S. Congress, the Canadian Parliament had left the Canadian Forces woefully unprepared for the war that they were now being asked to fight.

Canada and the Bombing Campaign

"What kind of convoluted logic is the prime minister using? What kind of cuckoo-land does he draw his ideas from? You do not become a peacekeeper when you have been shooting at the other side."

Lloyd Axworthy, House of Commons, January 15, 1991

It is not surprising that when the government looked at the contribution it should make to the allied effort, it decided to send the air force's CF-18s. The CF-18s were sent because they were the best weapons that Canada possessed. A few of these fighters had been equipped to deliver the precision-guided weapons (PGMs), or "smart bombs," that NATO wanted to use in large numbers in this bombing campaign. This capability had not been available to Canadian aircraft in the Gulf War of 1991.

At that time Canada's CF-18s did not have the smart bombs possessed by the Americans and other allies' air forces. When Canadian aircraft were finally committed to an offensive role late in the Gulf War (in fact just a few days before the war ended), they initially had to borrow bombs (though not of the PGM variety) from the U.S. air force.[11]

After the Gulf War this shortcoming in capability was partially addressed through a project initiated in 1994–95. The project involved the expenditure of $103 million ($85 million of that was spent up to March 31, 1999). But only 13 FLIR (Forward Looking Infra Red) systems, known as Nighthawk, were purchased for our aircraft. Some of these had to be used in Canada for training and to replace those that might be malfunctioning. In the end only six CF-18s deployed in Europe could be equipped with FLIR pods — about five percent of the total CF-18 force.[12]

The two types of smart bombs purchased were the GBU-12 laser guidance system for 500 lb bombs and the Maverick air-to-surface anti-armour missile. But the Canadian air force knew that its smart bomb supplies were essentially only sufficient for training and that, in the event of war, stocks would fast run out. While government ministers were also made aware of this fact early on in the campaign, Parliament was never informed, even on a confidential basis. Indeed, when questions about smart bomb stockpiles were raised in the House or in committee, the government refused to answer the questions.

The limited stock of PGMs and the fact that only six CF-18s were ready to deliver the weapons was indicative of a government that had never really expected to use the weapon systems it had purchased. The purpose of the purchase had been mostly political and symbolic: to equip a few of the CF-18s to enable them to train and occasionally exercise with American and allied units. Despite the experience of the Gulf War, no need was seen to plan for anything more. Yet when Canadian fighters were in the vanguard of the attack on the Serbs, there was no dissent in Parliament.

This was in sharp contrast to 1991, when a possible offensive role for Canada's fighters in the Gulf War was bitterly attacked by both the opposition Liberals and NDP. Lloyd Axworthy was among the most vehement critics of any Canadian role in that conflict, arguing that a country participating in war could not later participate in peacekeeping. Eight years later, however, on April 15, 1999, when he was asked before the House of Commons Foreign Affairs Committee whether Canada could continue with its peacekeeping role given its role in the bombing campaign in Kosovo, Axworthy responded with a simple "Yes."

The Air Force Struggles to Do Its Job

From the outset, the air force faced a serious problem in keeping pace with the evolving nature of the bombing campaign. The answers to some of its problems gradually became evident during the war. Other answers were only provided after the war was over. But Parliament was never told anything more than the rest of the country through the media. The government never permitted Parliament to have a serious role in examining military appropriations in the run up to the war, and so it certainly wasn't going to be frank now with Parliament about the condition that the Forces found themselves in as the war dragged on. These shortcomings were acute in some key areas.

It soon became apparent that the six CF-18s in Italy would have to be reinforced. From about April 4 another six fighters were dispatched. To equip these aircraft to deliver PGMs an emergency order had to be approved to borrow, not purchase, additional Nighthawk pods from Australia. When the decision was made later in April to deploy six more aircraft — bringing the total to 18 — additional FLIRs could not be found. That meant if all 18 CF-18s were committed to air operations at one time, these last six fighters were restricted to bombing with "dumb" munitions, to protecting coalition aircraft against the very limited Serb fighter threat or to supplying spare parts.

Canada was also the only NATO nation to deploy fighters that were not equipped with anti-jam radios. The requirement for anti-jam radios had already been identified in the Gulf War but no action had been taken to rectify the shortcoming. Fortunately the Serbs did not have sophisticated electronic warfare capability. CF-18 pilot Major Todd Balfe reports that Serb electronic warfare largely consisted of piping what he considered to be "really bad" ethnic music over the airwaves. Major Balfe noted that had the Serbs possessed more extensive capability, NATO would have politely asked the Canadians to stay on the ground.[13]

Prior to the war the air force made repeated requests to acquire smart guidance systems (GBU-10s) for larger 2,000 lb bombs. These requests were turned down. Once the war broke out the situation became urgent. The smaller 500 lb GBU-12s were not destroying all their targets. Again an emergency order had to be approved to acquire the GBU-10 system.[14] This delay meant that the first GBU-10s were not used until May 5–6, a full six weeks into the war.[15]

Most Canadians, including parliamentarians, were unaware that Canada's stocks of essential weapon systems were so limited. When the issue was raised the government's response was always evasive. For example, on March 26 Defence Minister Eggleton blandly stated that whether or not Canada had sufficient stocks of smart bombs depended on "how long the attacks go on." At the same press conference, he was questioned on the available budget for purchasing PGMs, to which he responded, "I don't think money is the issue. The issue is ending this humanitarian disaster. We're there with our allies to bring about the accomplishment of our aims and purposes, and we will be there with them and play the role that we are being asked by the supreme allied commander in Europe."[16]

The truth was that military officials were already sounding the alarm about the limited stock of smart weapons. A briefing note prepared for the deputy chief of the defence staff, General Henault, stated that there was a serious danger of running out of PGMs. Indeed, the entire inventory of smart weapons had already been shipped to Europe by March 30. The only means of replenishing stocks was to secure emergency supplies from the United States.[17]

An April 14 communication from one logistics officer, Major P. A. Desmarais, stated that "stock levels became a major concern as stocks were being depleted." Fortunately, he reported that another country (probably the U.S.) had responded on the previous day with a promise of munitions from its own stocks, thereby "solving the crisis."[18]

While the minister signed off on this purchase on April 20, a message just 10 days later from the commander of the Aviano task force described the process of procurement as "painfully slow."[19] At Aviano, Sergeant D. M. Neal of 1 Air Movements Squadron worked tirelessly to marry the newly arrived guidance systems to bombs. He thus "built" about two dozen smart bombs each day.[20] With the weather improving toward the end of April/early May, Colonel Davies noted that decisions were required as to when to reorder. This was a problem because the government was not providing additional funds to DND, and a handwritten question on the memo from Colonel Davies asked the question, "Who will pay in the future?"[21]

Parliament was told nothing of this, even privately, and there was never any indication that the government was looking for any additional money for DND. Both on April 16 and April 22, even as DND was scrambling to secure additional PGM supplies, Art Hanger asked questions in the House of Commons about those same supplies and about the increased funding that was now so urgent.

On April 16 Deputy Prime Minister Herb Grey made no commitments to increase the budget to pay for the war. On April 22 Minister

Eggleton also implied that no additional funds were required for DND. With regard to PGMs, he simply said that "we have the equipment that is necessary to do the job" and "they have the supplies that are necessary."[22]

As Colonel Davies had warned, smart bomb supplies remained a problem for the rest of the campaign. A May 19 briefing note for General Henault advised that the U.S. would not be able to deliver Task Force Aviano's required weapons due to heavy demands on its airlift. It was then necessary to task Canadian C-130s to pick up the additional PGMs and deliver them themselves.[23]

This was no easy task since Canadian transport resources were already stretched to the maximum. The air force had only 32 C-130 and five A-310 Airbus aircraft. On April 4 in a briefing for the press, General Henault stated that normally only about 75 percent of the C-130s (or about 24 aircraft) would be available for operations (the rest being in maintenance).[24] These aircraft were multitasked to support operations in Europe, North America and the deployment of Canadian ground troops and equipment to Europe which took place from April to June. Colonel Michael Ward, who commanded Task Force Kosovo — the ground forces — from March to December 1999, described the air deployment of the advance team as "a near catastrophe. From the first chaulk (air transport sortie) breakdowns interrupted the flow, and equipment was delivered out of sequence or not at all."[25]

Many Canadian C-130s were close to 35 years old and required extra maintenance simply to stay in the air. Likewise, none of the aircraft in the Canadian inventory could provide heavy lift; maximum lifting power was only about 17,300 kilograms per aircraft. This meant that the government had to lease Russian or Ukrainian Antonov heavy-lift aircraft at considerable cost. The irony that the Russians and Ukrainians "opposed" the war but were permitting a NATO country to rent its aircraft to supply its forces was not lost on anyone.

A memo from 1 Canadian Air Division headquarters on May 12 described both the C-130 and Airbus fleets as "severely taxed." Moreover, it warned that due to the heavy flying time, 40 percent of all of Canada's C-130s would have to undergo a major inspection within 90 days from about June 1. "This," it was warned, "will significantly impinge on aircraft availability."[26] The war ended before this became a problem, but this was simply very good fortune. The fact that nothing was done to correct this problem between 1999 and the next crisis in

2001–02 represents a glaring failure on the part of the government to acknowledge real defence problems and address them seriously.

Canadian CF-18s were not supported by their own air-refuelling aircraft during the campaign either. The decision to retire Canada's last 707 jet tankers in 1997 made it difficult for Canada to even deploy its CF-18s to Europe. Canada had been unable to deploy its CF-18s to participate in NATO air exercises over the Balkans in June 1998 because no supporting U.S. tankers were available to refuel the Canadian fighters.

Pilot shortage was a further problem. Although Canada had about 120 trained CF-18 pilots (as many as there were fighter aircraft) only about 80 were described by General Henault as "combat ready."[27] In actual fact, probably only around 40 were trained to the standard required.[28] By late April all of these 40 pilots were already in Italy, manning the 12 CF-18s that Canada had deployed there by that time. The high number of pilots reflected the needs of an operational squadron in time of war. As reported by CF-18 pilot Lt. Colonel David Bashow and other aviators, "In order to sustain operations, at least two pilots for each aircraft were needed for each daily mission ... Given the policy of holding a pilot in combat no longer than 60 days without a break, the Canadian air force was committed at the highest possible activity rate. In short, the operational commitment pushed the available pool of combat-ready pilots to the limit."[29]

On April 17 Art Eggleton admitted that "we are getting a little stretched on our resources in terms of pilots and could we do more? I don't know."[30] In fact, both the limited numbers of Nighthawk pods and smart bombs as well as the fact that all of the ready CF-18 pilots were already "in theatre" meant that Canada had reached its maximum capability level in deploying just 18 fighter planes.

Despite these impediments, the pilots and ground crew in Aviano gave it their all. A total of 224 missions were flown by CF-18s during the 78-day war. Each mission comprised between two and eight sorties (a sortie consists of a combat flight by one aircraft). After the increase in strength to a total of 18 operational CF-18s from April 27, Canadian aircraft flew a total of between 16 and 20 sorties per day when weather permitted. Aircraft service ability was reported at about 90 percent. Of 224 missions, 167 were air-to-ground attack missions and 57 were combat air patrols. In total, 678 individual sorties were flown during these missions (558 air-to-ground and 120 air-to-air). There were no air-to-air engagements between Canadian and Yugoslav aircraft, though on April 24–25 Canadian CF-18s closed to within eight miles of a Yugoslav fighter aircraft before the aircraft landed and no longer posed a threat.[31]

The government tried to spin the line that Canadian pilots had flown 10 percent of all NATO strike missions and led half of these. These figures sounded impressive but were misleading. In total, NATO flew 34,000 sorties during the war. Most of these missions were all-American operations. Canadian sorties numbered just 678 (or about two percent of the NATO total). In fact, Canadians really only flew in 10 percent of all multinational missions and served as the commanders or deputy commanders in half of these.[32] This is admirable, but it is far from being as impressive as claimed by the government.

The actual tangible results appear to have been somewhat mixed. Of 558 air-to-ground sorties flown, only 158 were successful in hitting their target (or 28 percent). On most of the occasions when a target was not hit, it wasn't even attacked due to an inability to positively identify the target. Canadian pilots appear to have been extremely conscientious and professional in this regard. The presence of military lawyers as part of the target assessment team also restricted the targets assigned to Canadian pilots. Thankfully Canada experienced no aircraft losses during the war.

Canada's Input in NATO Decision Making

"I don't know exactly who was at the meeting … I don't know what was discussed or what impact it had. I am still waiting to find out about it."

Art Eggleton
responding to reporters' questions on June 1, 1999,
about a NATO defence ministers' meeting

Canada was involved in the NATO bombing campaign from the first night. But with limited influence in the NATO council, the parameters of the operation were decided with very little Canadian input. Since before the war began Canada had effectively been along for the ride. As Professor Kim Richard Nossal, one of Canada's leading international relations experts, commented, "The Kosovo operation was led, moved entirely by the United States. What the Canadians did or said about it would have made very little difference to how the dynamic of that conflict was unfolding."[33]

On May 27 American and European defence ministers held a key meeting to discuss the progress of the war in Kosovo and possible military options. Even at this late stage the war did not appear to be going well.

Since it looked as though the air campaign might not succeed, the U.S. administration finally began to entertain notions of a ground war; president Clinton having initially ruled this option out. General Clark, NATO's supreme commander in Europe, produced plans for a ground war by mid-May. Key discussions were held in Bonn on May 27 between defence ministers from the "Contact Group" — the U.S., the U.K., France, Germany and Italy.

Despite the fact that we had 1,300 troops in Bosnia and 800 more en route to Macedonia, Canada was not invited. Initially, the Liberal government leader in the Senate, Al Graham, called the exclusion of Mr. Eggleton "totally and absolutely unacceptable."[34] However, Eggleton later claimed that the meeting had merely been an informal one of no importance. He said that the meeting was in fact similar to the bilateral discussions he had every day with various people. This comparison was, of course, invalid since even informal meetings between ministers of key NATO countries would set the parameters for later official meetings of the North Atlantic Council at which decisions would be made.

In theory, all allied governments had important input into the formulation of NATO strategy over Kosovo. Formally, decisions by the North Atlantic Council are taken collectively, based on the "consensus" of all the allies. In theory, therefore, Canada's voice is as important as that of any other ally on all issues. In reality, some NATO countries are more equal than others. On the issue of Yugoslavia, the member states on the inside were those forming the contact group. These countries took the lead in the formulation of allied policy on Yugoslavia.

Major-General Lewis MacKenzie recalls an interview he did with Prime Minister Chrétien for his own documentary, during which he asked the prime minister why Canada wasn't on the contact group: "The prime minister looked me in the eye and said, 'They didn't ask us.'" A few years later MacKenzie recalled how this answer had astonished him. "You don't wait to be asked. You insist … If you didn't get invited to the meeting, you should have been standing outside the bloody door when the meeting started."[35]

But the truth is that Canada had sought to get onto the contact group for years, especially after Italy was admitted in 1997. However, it was never successful. Despite the fact that we had had troops in Yugoslavia since 1992, our role in the alliance itself was insufficient to gain admission to this inner circle.

MacKenzie's discussion with the prime minister does illustrate the rather pathetic level to which the country's influence had been reduced by the time the Kosovo war erupted. Canada had unilaterally withdrawn its military forces from Germany and consistently cut its defence budget. We no longer had the ability to commit substantial forces to the security of NATO. Even token contributions, such as the 800 troops we were sending to the Balkans, took two months to deploy. In terms of political influence that meant in NATO circles we got exactly what we paid for. While like every other ally we had an ambassador at NATO as well as a three-star general on the alliance's military committee, in 1999 the highest Canadian on NATO's international staff was the director of information and press, and the highest-ranking Canadian officer serving at the allied military headquarters in Mons, Belgium, was only of colonel rank.

But on Kosovo all the allies followed the American lead. Throughout 1998–99 it was the United States that was driving a hard-line policy. Madeleine Albright dominated the negotiations at Rambouillet even if the British and French foreign ministers were the nominal chairs of the conference.

Faced with a united resolve on the part of NATO's larger powers, the lesser NATO states did not believe that they could step out of the allied consensus. Even Greece, whose population was largely pro-Serbian and anti-Albanian, did not oppose NATO military action (although its air force did not participate in the bombing). All seemed content to "go along to get along." In Canada the emphasis was to remain in the NATO consensus and avoid making waves. Many believed that Canada's declining influence in NATO allowed for nothing else. While in other NATO countries national legislators at least raised serious questions, in Canada for the most part they did not.

The Consequences of Soft Power

The Liberal government's approach to international relations deliberately downplays the importance of traditional instruments of power, such as military capability. Instead, the Liberals extol the virtues of so-called "soft power," described by Lloyd Axworthy as follows:

> Soft power is the art of disseminating information in such a way that desirable outcomes can be achieved through persuasion rather than coercion. Because it sets the terms of the debate, soft power influences the nature of the solution. It blurs, even counters, the perception of traditional power assets, such as military force, economic might, resources and population ...
>
> Canada is well placed to succeed as a leader in a world where soft power is increasingly important ... A country's image is key to the use of soft power. An attractive set of values and an image as a trustworthy partner encourage other countries to consider and weigh our views.[36]

The problem is that without the requisite capability, the use of persuasive rhetoric is of limited value. Neither adversaries nor allies are likely to "consider and weigh the views" of a country that can bring little in the way of hard power capability to the table. The soft power myth can only be sustained in an environment made safe by the hard power of allies.

Notwithstanding the impressive role played by the handful of CF-18s situated in Italy, the Canadian voice in allied decision making was low. To be sure, Canada's contribution was appreciated, as Colonel Davies recorded in his war diaries on several occasions, but it was hardly vital. And it had no impact in enhancing Canada's role in the formulation of NATO's grand strategy. General Wesley Clark, NATO's supreme commander during the war, makes no mention of Jean Chrétien, Lloyd Axworthy, Art Eggleton nor of any Canadian diplomatic or military contribution in *Waging Modern War*, his own 461-page account of the Kosovo campaign.

In Parliament, members, mostly on the government side, publicly continued to pretend that Canada's role and influence were significant. But in private almost nobody really believed this — not the media, not staffers and not parliamentarians. However, for the most part, no one on the Hill said that. There was no small child around to point out that the emperor had no clothes.

So the pretence went on throughout the war. The speeches and statements of Jean Chrétien and Lloyd Axworthy that referred to

Canada's major role went largely unchallenged. Alexa McDonough and others demanded that Canada launch new diplomatic initiatives. Axworthy scooted around Europe, even visiting Moscow at one point. But no Canadian diplomatic position or so-called initiative received attention outside Canada. Lloyd Axworthy's mission to Moscow at the end of April, which coincided with similar visits by the U.S. undersecretary of state, Strobe Talbot, was ignored by virtually everyone.[37] We claimed to be very active, but none of our allies seemed to notice.

Defence Minister Art Eggleton was even more of a non-factor in NATO councils. The same seemed to be true at home at the Cabinet table. Despite the fact that the war was stretching the resources of the Canadian Forces to the limit, he was unable to extract any more money for equipment or enhanced training. In the official Opposition we found this incredible, and we asked several questions on the issue, with Deborah Grey pointedly asking the minister on April 29, "If war is not a good enough reason to increase the defence budget then what is?" Extraordinarily, Eggleton responded that the troops had been given pay raises and that "we are doing a number of things that improve their quality of life." He also said that they had some of the latest and best equipment "which would help them do the job of peacekeeping."[38]

The prime minister also seemed to be out of the loop of the decision-making process in the alliance. His only face-to-face meeting with allied leaders occurred at the NATO 50th Anniversary Summit in Washington in April. When asked about the position that Canada was to adopt at the summit, he was at least a little more honest about Canada's real role. On April 20 he said with reference to a ground war that "if everyone agrees, I will not be the only one not to agree."[39] The next day in the House he reiterated that "if some day we are confronted with the necessity to send ground troops, we will do so with the others ... We will not be the ones to not be members of the team."[40]

Even as Canadian ground troops were on their way to the Balkans, decisions about the nature of their role in the war were being made not in Ottawa by their Parliament or their government, but for all intents and purposes outside the country.

Parliament and Possible Canadian Involvement in a Ground War
The make-up of the Canadian ground force contingent for Kosovo was already decided prior to the war, when NATO was looking for member

states to contribute to the planned peacekeeping force. It was perceived as politically necessary for Canada to "show the flag" within NATO. That meant sending a token force which would not unnecessarily stretch the army's very limited resources. Such a contingent would have very limited capability.

On February 19 Defence Minister Art Eggleton stated that Canada was considering deploying 500 to 800 troops to serve with a NATO force in Kosovo. "We could not do much more than this," he said.[41]

The force finally decided on would consist of reconnaissance, engineer, helicopter and command and support units; no infantry. These Canadian units would deploy alongside a British armoured brigade of approximately 5,000 troops. But there were serious questions about employing the Coyote reconnaissance vehicle and the Griffon helicopter in a medium- to high-intensity conflict.

The Coyote was a light armoured vehicle with highly sophisticated surveillance equipment and a 25-mm cannon. Art Eggleton had repeatedly lauded the vehicle, saying on February 17, for instance, "We are going to send our people in with the best equipment ... the Coyote, one of the best found anywhere in the world."[42] However, in April 1998 the auditor general had evaluated this vehicle based on internal DND studies which found that "a battle group equipped with Coyote-type vehicles was regarded as likely to be suitable for peacekeeping but not necessarily for peace-restoring operations." The auditor general's report noted that:

> [The Defence Department's] simulation study concluded that vehicles armoured to the same standard as the Coyote could not withstand the enemy fire they would encounter at the high end of mid-intensity combat without the support of heavy forces. It concluded that this type of vehicle could not be considered for a general purpose combat force; forces so equipped should be considered light units with limited capabilities and be given only limited tasks.[43]

The capabilities of the Griffons were even more questionable. In the same report the auditor general found that these helicopters had inadequate lift and range, inadequate defensive systems, limited reconnaissance capability and electrical shock problems for passengers.

An April 15 memo from the land staff assessed the threat to Canadian troops from Yugoslav forces as "high." It noted that:

> Enemy possesses anti-armour, anti-air and full range of manoeuvre and fire support capabilities, to include armoured, infantry, field artillery and close air support. It has been assessed that it is very probable that the VJ [Yugoslav army] and MUP [paramilitary police] may revert to guerrilla type ops and the destruction of lines of communication/infrastructure throughout the area.

The memo assumed that the Canadian units would be part of the NATO force operating as a "corps-level asset."[44] In reaction Colonel Leslie, the commander of the 1st Canadian Mechanized Brigade, from which the Canadian contingent would be drawn, warned on April 22 that "if there is a requirement to have Canadian Forces deploy outside of U.K. force protection due to ground/terrain, or if U.K. forces are unable to provide, this could result in an enormous risk and possibly delay the prudent deployment of our troops."

The next day he reiterated, "I am still concerned that the force protection issue has been dismissed away by the assumption that we will rely upon the U.K. forces for force protection. If our present force has to occupy itself with force protection, thus taking away from its primary task, then we will end up being more of a hindrance to any coalition."[45]

Another 1995 memorandum for ministers, which we obtained through an Access to Information request, noted:

> Alliance doctrine, which has always been supported by Canada, requires that forces provided to a NATO operation be self-sufficient. A contribution of forces without stand-alone capability would require them to be integrated with and supported by foreign units. Canada would not therefore receive the visibility or recognition that its level of involvement would otherwise deserve.[46]

That such an arrangement had been rejected in 1995 but adopted in 1999 was something that should have been discussed and critiqued in Parliament.

But it was as difficult as ever to get military-specific questions up for Question Period. Reform did ask a few such questions about the capabilities of the Coyote and the Griffon, but generally they were not seen to be "sexy" enough. Neither the Bloc nor the NDP ever asked military-readiness questions. What did make it to Question Period were the phrases that were likely to get sound bites.

For instance, on April 21 Bob Mills asked a question about a parliamentary vote on Canadian involvement in the war and used the phrase "Does the prime minister think he is some sort of king who can simply send his peasants off to war?"[47] It was the perfect sound bite and was broadcast on nearly every newscast that evening. Perhaps in a dysfunctional legislature this was the best that could be hoped for, but I believe that Canadians, and especially those military personnel whom we had put in harm's way, deserved better.

By early May members of the parliamentary press corps informed MPs that they were getting bored with the war and that they wanted to move on to other topics. Since the name of the game was press coverage, the parties generally obliged. Question sets (initial ask and supplementary questions) on Kosovo fell from five on May 2 to zero on May 12; thereafter only the official Opposition continued to ask one question per day related to the war.

Reprieve: The War Comes to a Conclusion

By May, with NATO moving toward a ground war, Canada was caught in a vortex. Despite the fact that the 800-person contingent being sent to Macedonia was ill-equipped and ill-prepared for independent ground combat operations, it was quite clear that Canada would be involved in any ground campaign. The government hadn't opted out of any other aspect of NATO policy up to that point or given any sign that it was pursuing any distinctively Canadian objectives. To use the prime minister's own words, we were "team players."

Since early in the year the army had been scrambling to produce options for the possible deployment of a viable Canadian contingent as part of the NATO force for Kosovo. The deployment of a viable and more significant contingent had been considered but rejected because of the negative impact on the army's other commitments. Despite this reality, on April 28 I witnessed the chief of defence staff, General Maurice Baril, tell the press in a media scrum that he could deploy

20,000 troops overseas if he had to. The next day Brigadier-General David Jurkowski, chief of staff and director-general of military plans and operations at National Defence Headquarters, acting on the cue of his boss, repeated the same claim at the daily DND press briefing.[48]

Even though the claim was outrageous and irresponsible, it went largely unchallenged. The media had little interest in the issue and hence it was difficult to convince people that the matter should be brought forward in Question Period. While Art Hanger and Jim Hart did confront General Baril on several occasions in committee about Canada's real capabilities, the limited time allotted to questions and answers in committee simply did not allow for the issue to be brought to the attention of the public in a serious manner.

Fortunately for Canada, and most particularly for our serving soldiers, the Milosevic government surrendered early in June. Always placing his personal survival first, Milosevic probably thought that he could get away with surrendering Kosovo now that he had put up a serious fight. He was mistaken and would be out of power, under arrest and on trial in The Hague within two years.

Even with the war at an end, ethnic cleansing began in reverse. Despite NATO's efforts, about half the Serb population of 200,000 in Kosovo was forced out of the province as a result of attacks by Albanians. Canada was compelled to increase its commitment in Kosovo and it agreed to deploy 500 more troops to the province to reinforce the small contingent already there. The new units deployed included two mechanized infantry companies, drawn from the battalions that had been identified as most suitable for deployment back in February, and for the first time main battle tanks — though only one troop of just four tanks.[49]

Overstretch prevented anything more, and within one year even this small contingent was withdrawn, thus avoiding the problem of troop rotations. Meanwhile, the air force returned to Australia six emergency PGM guidance systems it had borrowed during the war. The funds just were not there to keep them and, extraordinarily, the air force went back to the same low readiness level it had maintained prior to the war.

Both NATO and Canada were lucky. But the allies are now stuck in Bosnia and Kosovo for a very long time since withdrawal will inevitably lead to new fighting. This might seem to many to be a price worth paying, but there is no clear sense of what NATO's end strategy actually is or for how long this position will remain tenable. Indeed, to maintain the viability of its position, NATO was compelled in 2001 to become involved in yet another Balkan conflict — this time in Macedonia. Canada is simply "along for the ride" in all of this, while Parliament is sidelined and destined to remain so as long as the issue stays off the front pages.

After the end of the war the Reform Party did demand that the government allow Parliament to review the future of the country's foreign, defence and NATO policy, given the obvious challenges posed by the post–cold war environment. Informed observers know that the Canadian military has, by good fortune alone, won a series of reprieves in the crises in which Canada has become involved. It remains anyone's guess how long we will be so fortunate.

But true to form, as the memory of events began to fade, Parliament went back to sleep on foreign and defence policy issues until the next crisis of September 2001. In the Throne Speech that followed in the fall of 1999, the government took no action of its own to address the serious equipment crisis facing the Canadian Forces.

By way of contrast, after the war the British House of Commons conducted a major study on "lessons learned" in the war. A similar self-examination process occurred in the United States, debating readiness issues, American vital interests and NATO's future role. In Canada the Senate issued a report in 2000 on the future of peacekeeping but not specifically on "lessons learned" in Kosovo. But there wasn't so much as a murmur on Kosovo from the elected House of Commons.

Witnessing these events I began to realize that none of this was unique to my time in Parliament. The lack of effective oversight is chronic and goes back years, perhaps decades. And it is in this absence of real oversight that one can begin to understand how it is that Canada has gradually seen its international influence erode and how it is that the Canadian Forces have fallen into the sad state in which they find themselves today.

NOTES

1. Christopher Layne, "Miscalculations and Blunders Lead to War," in *NATO's Empty Victory*, Ted Galen Carpenter, ed. (Washington, D.C.: Cato Institute, 2000) p. 11.

2. News Digest for March 1999, Keesing's Record of World Events, Vol. 45 (March 1999), p. 42,847.

3. News Digest for March 1999, Keesing's Record of World Events, Vol. 45 (March 1999), p. 42847; Office of the Leader of the Opposition, Briefing Materials on Kosovo [internal brief], October 1998.

4. Tony Kellet, Serbia: How Obdurate Will It Be?[internal brief], March 29, 1999. Department of National Defence. Briefing note for ADM (Pol).

5. Canada, Parliament, House of Commons, *Debates*, Vol. 16 (March 25, 1999) p. 13510.

6. The Resolution was passed on March 11 by a vote of 218 to 201. United States. Congress, House of Representatives, *Peacekeeping Operations in Kosovo Resolution*, 106th Cong. (March 16, 1999), H. CON. Res. 42.

7. News Digest for March 1999, Keesing's Record of World Events, Vol. 45 (March 1999), p. 42,848.

8. House of Representatives, *Military Operations in the Federal Republic of Yugoslavia Limitation Act of 1999*, 106th Cong. (April 29, 1999), Bill H.R. 1569.

9. United States, Congress, Senate, *That the President of the United States is Authorized to Conduct Military Air Operations and Missile Strikes in Cooperation with Our NATO Allies Against the Federal Republic of Yugoslavia (Serbia and Montenegro)*, 106th Cong. (March 23, 1999) S. CON. Res.21.

10. Department of National Defence, War Diaries of the Commander of Canadian Air Forces (Task Force Aviano) [diaries], March 26 and March 30, 1999.

11. Major Jean Morin and Lt. Commander Richard Gimblett, *The Canadian Forces in the Persian Gulf: Operation Friction, 1990–1991* (Toronto: Dundurn Press, 1997), p. 173.

12. Lt. Colonel David Bashow, Colonel Dwight Davies, Colonel André Viens, Lt, Colonel John Rotteau, Major Norman Balfe, Major Ray Stouffer, Captain James Pickett and D. Steve Harris, "Mission Ready: Canada's Role in the Kosovo Air Campaign," *Canadian Military Journal* (Spring 2000) p. 60.

13. Bashow et al., p. 60; Major Balfe [interview]. Interviewed by Rob Roy of Stornoway Productions, May 2000.

14. Bashow et al., p. 60.

15. Department of National Defence, War Diaries of the Commander of Canadian Air Forces (Task Force Aviano) [diaries], March 26 and March 30, 1999.

16. Art Eggleton, [press conference], Department of National Defence, March 26, 1999.

17. Department of National Defence, Briefing Note for the Deputy Chief of Defence Staff [internal brief], April 1999.

18. Major Desmarais, [e-mail], April 14, 1999.

19. Task Force Aviano, Ammunition Reorder Levels [communication], May 1, 1999. Communication to National Defence Headquarters.

20. Bashow et al., p. 58.

21. Colonel Davies, Op Echo Operational Requirement Guided Bomb Unit Bombs [memo], April 20, 1999. Memo to the minister.; Commander, Task Force Aviano, Ammunition Reorder Levels [memo], May 1, 1999. Message to National Defence Headquarters.

22. House of Commons, *Debates*, Vol. 16 (April 16, 1999) pp. 13957–13958; House of Commons, *Debates*, Vol. 17 (April 22, 1999) p. 14221.

23. Briefing Note for the DCDS — Op Echo Weapon Sustainment Issue, May 19, 1999.

24. Department of National Defence, [press briefing], April 4, 1999.

25. Colonel Michael Ward et al., "Task Force Kosovo: Adapting Operations to a Changing Security Environment" *Canadian Military Journal* 1 (Spring 2000) p. 69.

26. 1 Canadian Air Division, [memo], May 12, 1999. Memo to National Defence Headquarters.

27. Department of National Defence, [press briefing], April 17, 1999.

28. Interview with air force officer.

29. Bashow et al., p. 60.

30. Department of National Defence, [press briefing], April 17, 1999.

31. Department of National Defence, War Diaries of the Commander of Canadian Air Forces (Task Force Aviano) [diaries], April 24–25, 1999.

32. Interview with air force officer.

33. Kim Richard Nossal [interview]. Interviewed by Robert Roy of Stornoway Productions, June 2001.

34. Jack Aubry, "Canada Left out of Council of War," *Ottawa Citizen*, June 2, 1999, p. A1.

35. General Lewis MacKenzie [interview]. Interviewed by Robert Roy of Stornoway Productions, June 2001.

36. Lloyd Axworthy, "Canada and Human Security: The Need for Leadership," *International Journal*, Vol. LII (Spring 1997) pp. 192–93.

37. Keesing's very detailed account of the war in April, May and June not only makes no mention of Axworthy's mission to Moscow, it does not mention any Canadian diplomatic initiative or role.

38. House of Commons, *Debates*, Vol. 17 (April 29, 1999) pp. 14480–14481.

39. Graham Fraser, "PM not opposed to Kosovo Ground Troops," *The Globe and Mail*, April 21, 1999, p. A4.

40. House of Commons, *Debates*, Vol. 17 (April 21, 1999) p. 14151.

41. Art Eggleton, comments made on *CTV News One*, 3:00 p.m. broadcast [television program], February 19, 1999.

42. House of Commons, *Debates*, Vol. 14 (February 17, 1999) p. 12043.

43. Canada, Auditor General of Canada, *Auditor General's Report* (Ottawa: Office of the Auditor General, April 1998) Chapter 4, paragraph 4.52.

44. Land Staff, [memo], April 15, 1999.

45. Commander 1 CMBG, [memos], April 22 and April 23, 1999.

46. Directorate of Cabinet Liaison, Memorandum for Ministers [memo], October 1995.

47. House of Commons, *Debates*, Vol. 17 (April 21, 1999) p. 14152.

48. Department of National Defence, Daily Press Briefing, April 29, 1999.

49. The light armoured vehicles of this force had to be hurriedly equipped with add-on armour through an emergency $12.5-million purchase that the minister approved on June 28. Synopsis Sheet (Effective Project Approval) Add-on Armour Kits for Light Armoured Vehicles — Op Kinetic +. Signed June 28, 1999.

CHAPTER FIVE

The Rise and Fall of Canada's International Influence

"The nineteenth century was the century of the United States. I think we can claim that it is Canada that shall fill the 20th century."
Sir Wilfrid Laurier, Canadian Club, Ottawa, January 18, 1904

In the first half of the 20th century, Canada earned the respect of the nations of the world by playing a growing role in international affairs. From World War I until after World War II, Canada's influence continued to expand steadily. Canada was a respected and influential player in the global community. It had a central role in the founding of both the United Nations and NATO.

Looking back on it now, it is difficult to imagine that in the mid-1950s Canada was a major actor on the international scene. Indeed, the 1950s came to be known as the "Golden Age" of Canadian diplomacy. For most of the 1950s Canada was a country that made serious commitments to international security. In March 1953 the Canadian Forces totalled about 104,000 regular troops (those numbers would rise to 126,000 by 1962).[1] More than 17,000 Canadian personnel were serving overseas in 1953. At the same time a strong economy enabled Canada to provide about $1 billion in focused aid for its allies in Europe. The entire Canadian population at the time was less than 15 million.

This earned the country political influence. In September 1954 Canada's foreign minister, Lester Pearson, was one of a group of only nine foreign ministers at the conference in London that established the terms for the restoration of German sovereignty, that country's admission to NATO and its rearmament. The settlement established the basis for the post-war political order in Europe for the next three decades. Canada's role at the conference was directly linked to the fact that it maintained military forces in Europe.[2]

Pearson, the architect of many of the Canadian successes, was certainly an idealist. He wanted to change the international order away from its dominance by sovereign states. He advocated a stronger non-military role for NATO, an idea that larger allies were never very keen on. In 1956 he was able to draft a report with the foreign ministers of Norway and Italy on improving political consultation and co-operation for smaller powers in the Western alliance. He also publicly criticized the American war in Vietnam in the 1960s. But at the same time he understood that real influence had to be based on a bedrock of real capability. Because Pearson understood this, Canada was able to help formulate allied policy in key areas. In a modest way, Canada helped to shape the cold war order in this period rather than simply be affected by it.

The High Water Mark of Canadian Influence

In the 1956 Suez crisis Canadian diplomacy was widely hailed as a major diplomatic achievement which served to extricate Britain and France from a difficult situation and to preserve peace in the Middle East. It was a role that Canada had earned by its past credibility and was able to play because it had the will and the resources to do so.

The combined forces of Israel, Britain and France invaded Egypt at the end of October 1956 in an attempt to seize control of the Suez Canal and depose Egypt's dictator, Gamal Abdal Nasser. The three countries acted because of the threat that Nasser represented to British and French interests in the Middle East and because of his support for military attacks by Arab guerrillas against Israel. Despite rapid success the goals of the mission met with intense political opposition from both the Soviet Union and the United States. The intensity of American opposition came as a shock to London and Paris, and a combination of diplomatic and economic pressure caused the attacking powers to agree to a cease-fire after only one week.

The government of Louis St. Laurent had opposed military intervention from the outset, fearing it would lead to heightened confrontation between Western countries and the Soviet Union as well as to a fracturing of the Commonwealth. Nevertheless, in public the government's opposition to the actions of its allies was restrained, with External Affairs Minister Lester Pearson merely regretting the use of military force. Formally, Canada tried to avoid taking an overt position for or against military action and, along with five other countries, it abstained from an American-sponsored United Nation's General Assembly resolution on November 2 which urged an immediate cease-fire.[3] However, Pearson was anxious to do what he could to mediate an acceptable political solution. As a result, on November 1 he left for New York to take personal charge of Canada's UN delegation.

Pearson's diplomacy was skillful and effective. By November 4 he had formulated a plan that would allow the British and French to save at least some measure of face by agreeing to turn over control of the canal to a United Nations emergency force. The plan was accepted and a temporary cease-fire agreed to by November 7. But implementation of this cease-fire still depended on the ability to have an international force in place and operational in Egypt quickly.

Diplomacy was not enough. Since Canada led the diplomatic effort, it also had to be able to ante up forces to form the core of the international force. It further had to be able to get the forces to the Middle East on a timely basis and to provide them with effective offshore support when they were in place. The latter factor was especially important, in the words of the chair of the Canadian Chiefs of Staff Committee, General Charles Foulkes, to provide "a firm base to which we could evacuate quickly" in the event of renewed hostilities.[4]

It was Canada's military capabilities in the mid-1950s that made the entire operation, and hence Pearson's diplomacy, possible. Indeed, the Canadian Forces were able to make military units available to the United Nations quickly. Canadian Lieutenant-General E. L. M. Burns had been appointed commander of the proposed force on November 4 and Canadian units were tasked by November 6. These forces centred on an infantry battalion from the Queen's Own Rifles of Canada. While the battalion was subsequently prevented from going to Egypt largely for political reasons, it was in Halifax and boarding its sea transport by November 14.[5] By November 15 lead elements of the Canadian contingent were ready to move to Egypt on transport provided by the Royal Canadian Air Force (RCAF) — though Egyptian government hesitation temporarily delayed this initial Canadian deployment.[6]

While other foreign contingents were transported to the region by a combination of national (usually sea) transport and by hitching a ride with the Americans, the RCAF airlifted a majority of the Canadian force on its own over the next several weeks. Early in January these troops were joined by the Canadian aircraft carrier HMCS *Magnificent*. *Magnificent* acted as the essential offshore base for the force, and she carried to Egypt 405 more soldiers, 100 tons of stores, 230 vehicles as well as four light aircraft and one helicopter. All told, just over 1,000 troops and their equipment were in place and, together with significant offshore support, operating as the core elements of the UN force within two months.

Canada's leading diplomatic and military role during the Suez crisis enhanced its already considerable influence at the United Nations and in world affairs. It also garnered Pearson a Nobel Peace Prize.

Diplomats at the United Nations, and their leaders at home, did not listen to Pearson simply because he had some "good ideas" or because he offered "leadership," as important as these factors may have been. Instead, they primarily listened because of what Canada could bring to the table. Since 1956 many in Canada, including parliamentarians, have lamented the loss of the influence that the country once enjoyed. But what they often fail to recognize is that it was real "hard power" capability that made such influence possible.

Policy Mismanagement and the Erosion of Canadian Influence

"[Being Canadian foreign minister] seldom involves the kinds of problems that are routinely faced by, for example, the minister of finance and health and welfare, with responsibilities for making decisions affecting the pocketbooks of Canadians."[7]

Mitchell Sharp, Canadian external affairs minister,
1968–1974

Changes that occurred in world politics after the 1950s are usually cited as the major reason for the decline in Canadian influence in the 1960s and 1970s. Most analysts argue that the decline of an immediate Soviet threat and a changing world order made Canada's sharp run-down in its military capability inevitable. All Western countries reduced their military expenditures in this period.

At the same time European countries (particularly West Germany) and Japan began to recover from the devastation that they had suffered during World War II. As their economies grew in strength, they began to play a more influential role in international affairs. This lessened in relative terms the weight of Canada in the international system.

However, despite the obvious importance of such factors, it is inadequate to argue that the sharp decline in Canada's influence was largely due to factors beyond its control. Canada made deliberate policy choices during this period and many of these choices were ill-considered and badly thought out. The way in which these choices were usually made fit a consistent pattern which left the key decisions to an "elite" few and limited any outside input. This political environment still prevails.

One of the more unfortunate aspects of the nature of the British parliamentary system is that it usually places policy leadership in the hands of amateurs who are usually lacking in background or professional knowledge of the portfolio for which they are responsible. Throughout Canada's history the country's foreign policy has been in the hands of individuals insufficiently accountable to the Canadian people, even though they have been making decisions that, in the most fundamental way, affect the lives of Canadians. In this context it is perhaps somewhat ironic that many Canadian historians express outrage that Prime Minister Sir Robert Borden was simply "informed" that Canada was at war in 1914 and that no political decision was made in Canada about going to war. The truth is that even today the elected representatives of Canadians have, at best, only had the most pro-forma input into decisions, great and small, related to the country's foreign policy.

Canada's lack of serious foreign policy discussion has deep roots. Prior to 1939 matters of high politics were largely left to the British government. British foreign policy became Canadian foreign policy. While Mackenzie King may have had the illusion that Canada could pursue an isolationist course, he was simply too ill-informed himself and lacked the skill to chart such a course effectively.

To be sure, the prime minister did attempt to play at foreign policy from time to time. Since he also served as his own minister of external affairs, there were simply no serious checks on his initiatives or ideas. In this sense, he had just enough unchecked power to be dangerous to the country's interests.

This is evident when one examines the impact that Mackenzie King's pre-war views of Hitler had on Canadian military preparedness prior to the war. In 1937 King visited Europe and met with several leaders, including Adolf Hitler. In a memorandum after the meeting he described the German leader as "a man of deep sincerity and a genuine patriot ... [a man whose] mind is absorbed in Germany and in what he wishes to do for the German people ... not equally concerned with matters outside Germany ... [and whose] interest in Spain arises unquestionably out of his feelings and fears concerning the spread of communism."[8]

The prime minister's benign views of Hitler meant that, in his mind, adequate military preparation for a possible conflict was mostly unnecessary. King was the first of many Canadian leaders who also believed in the unlimited virtues of international negotiation with foreign leaders who surely must share our own goodwill. In fact, in an appeal to Hitler only one week prior to the outbreak of World War II he naively wrote that "there is no international problem which cannot be settled by conference and negotiation."[9] There is no record that the German leader ever bothered to reply. As noted by the scholar Frank Underhill in 1944, "Mr. King never quite got it into his head during his economic studies at Toronto and Harvard that our civilization is dominated by carnivorous animals."[10]

It is certainly true that the leaders of countries other than Canada also underestimated the threat posed by the Third Reich. But in Canada the absence of any serious forum for discussing international problems and checking the government's proposed policies meant that the country was completely at the mercy of the prime minister's judgment. Although Parliament voted on whether to go to war with Germany in

1939, it had no role whatsoever in determining Canadian foreign and defence policy in the period leading up to the war. It was the emergency conditions of the First and Second World Wars that finally required the country to make serious contributions to stopping aggression.

The views of prime ministers continued to be definitive in shaping the nation's foreign policy after World War II. "Mackenzie King was still very much in charge of external affairs," wrote a noted historian of the period, "but long-term planning had never much interested him and post-war planning was not a subject to which a wartime prime minister could give steady attention."[11]

If it did not interest the prime minister, then it simply did not happen, and in the immediate post-war period Canada's role internationally and its military capability were simply allowed to run down.

Mr. King was able to take major foreign policy initiatives largely on his own. In 1946 he decided to pull Canada's occupation troops out of Germany over strong British objections. In 1948 Canada was the only major Western or Commonwealth country not to participate in the Berlin airlift — largely because the prime minister feared entangling obligations on the continent of Europe. These issues were not debated in a serious way in either the government or in Parliament.

Parliament was largely irrelevant in determining the nature of Canadian involvement in Korea in 1950. This was only the first instance where the national legislature was completely sidelined in determining the nature of Canadian military commitments overseas during the cold war. One might argue that limited accountability had its advantages. Lester Pearson, for instance, never had to get legislative approval for his foreign policy initiatives — that was always guaranteed. Canada was also fortunate in having Brooke Claxton as its minister of defence from 1946–1954. The formulation of Canadian foreign and defence policy in the early 1950s thus occurred within a relatively small circle of competent decision makers.

But regrettably, as competent policy leaders and managers, Claxton and Pearson were exceptions. Most Canadian leaders who followed them simply failed to manage Canadian foreign policy well. For instance, one consistent goal of Canadian policy in the cold war period was to develop and maintain a positive political relationship with Europe as a counterbalance to our relations with the United States. But among most of Canada's leaders there was never a particularly deep understanding of what it took to actually craft, implement and sustain such a policy. Consequently, policy with regard to Europe and NATO changed repeatedly, and often suddenly, in the years between 1955 and 1995. Sometimes policy shifts would occur with the entry into office of a new government. On other occasions the same government would radically alter a course which it had itself set. In such a policy environment, with almost no outside constraints, it was simply impossible to pursue any kind of coherent strategy.[12]

Therefore the concentration of power in the hands of a few and the exclusion of Parliament from any relevant role proved to be a negative thing. After 1957, for instance, during the Diefenbaker government, Canada was brought to the edge of international marginalization. Howard Green was a committed idealist and the minister of external affairs who became a "convinced and stubborn crusader against nuclear testing and proliferation and for disarmament."[13] In particular, he wanted to roll back the decisions taken to acquire nuclear-capable weapon systems for the Canadian Forces. These weapon systems were an essential element in allied strategy at the time — a strategy that Canada had already accepted along with all other NATO allies. Green's increasing influence over an equally inexperienced prime minister led the government to attempt to back away from the commitments it had already made. Canada's reputation as a reliable ally suffered serious damage, and this eventually led to the resignation of Defence Minister Douglas Harkness.

Although the Diefenbaker government's debacle on the nuclear issue is the most visible and well-known of its foreign policy blunders, there were others. For instance, Green tried to push the Germans and the Americans to pursue more flexible policies in Central Europe, particularly concerning the future status of Berlin, divided at that time between East and West. But Canada lacked the diplomatic weight to do this, and all that was accomplished by continuously beating a dead horse was the steady erosion of Canadian influence and credibility.

This was a great pity since in 1958 Canada's reputation in allied diplomatic circles had been quite high. For instance, a briefing note prepared in the German Foreign Office that year stated, "Within the North Atlantic Pact, Canada is one of the most important alliance partners for us, which provides its economic and financial capabilities in exemplary fashion for the common defence."[14] Likewise, British prime minister

Harold MacMillan was said to have, at least initially, "implicitly and greatly prized" his relationship with Prime Minister Diefenbaker.[15]

But one year later the German ambassador in Ottawa warned his government that in some respects Canadian policy had become "remarkably naive." He also made pointed comments about Green's general inexperience in foreign policy and that, despite his obvious enthusiasm for the UN, the minister seemed to have little idea which countries were members of the organization and which were not. In a face-to-face meeting, the ambassador reported that he had been forced to correct Green's mistaken view that West Germany was a member of the United Nations.[16]

In the same period British and American diplomats expressed similar misgivings. Early in 1959 a British High Commission cable to London warned that Diefenbaker was "temperamental and emotional" and that Britain would "have to watch taking him into confidence."[17] Likewise, American briefing materials prepared for President Kennedy's visit to Ottawa in 1961 described Green as having a "naive and parochial approach" to global politics.[18] Thus, even before the Diefenbaker government began to openly back away from its military commitments, Canada's reputation and credibility with its allies had begun to decline.

While such impressions may or may not have been correct in all of their particulars, they were nevertheless the product of a clear perception that the Canadian government did not know what it was doing in foreign policy. Pearson's return to office as prime minister in 1963 provided a temporary respite and allowed Canada's reputation a chance to recuperate. However, this proved to be very short lived.

Five years later, with the election of Pierre Trudeau, Canadian policy took another abrupt turn. Although the new prime minister had no experience in foreign or defence policy matters, he was nevertheless determined to reshape Canadian foreign policy to conform with his own ideological predispositions.

The prime minister treated discussions on foreign policy almost like a university seminar — with himself as a kind of novice instructor, teaching the course for the first time. Major policy decisions were taken without any real understanding as to the wider political, strategic and economic consequences. Not only was departmental advice from experienced officials completely ignored, but so was the Liberal-dominated

House of Commons Standing Committee on External Affairs and National Defence.

The committee recommended there be no changes to Canada's military commitments in Europe. Having received advice from numerous foreign policy and defence experts, and having also visited Europe to gauge the European perspective, the committee had come to see how politically damaging a unilateral troop reduction might be. But the reality of concentrated power proved to be decisive. In the face of the determined idealism of the prime minister, the views of the majority of Liberal members on the committee were of little consequence.

The policy review process was often chaotic. For instance, Mr. Trudeau's defence minister, Leo Cadieux, was shocked to arrive at a Cabinet meeting one day to find a paper prepared by the Prime Minister's Office proposing a 50 percent cut in the strength of the Canadian Forces. Cadieux threatened to resign and the paper was withdrawn, but the idea that such a revolutionary change could be proposed without any prior consultation of either the minister of defence or the external affairs minister is stunning to say the least.

The departments of External Affairs and Defence tried to fight desperate rear-guard actions to prevent the most radical of these ideas from coming to fruition. But given the prime minister's orientation, the die was cast and Canada's NATO policy underwent abrupt changes. The principal results were that defence spending was frozen, troops in Europe were arbitrarily cut by 50 percent and, equally arbitrarily, moved from their frontline position to a rear area location in the south of Germany. Simultaneously, Canada unilaterally announced that it would abandon most of the nuclear roles that had been taken on by the Pearson government in 1963.

The Canadian decision was taken less than one year after the Soviet invasion of Czechoslovakia and many feared that this would set a terrible example, encouraging isolationists in the U.S. Congress to follow suit. Thus, when Defence Minister Cadieux, made the announcement at NATO headquarters in Brussels, the allies exploded. According to Cadieux, the Belgian ambassador actually burst into tears when informed of the scope of the cuts.[19] The British defence secretary, Denis Healey, accused Canada in the NATO council of "passing the buck to the rest of us."[20]

The depth of the negative European reaction stunned Cadieux, who again considered resigning from Cabinet but was persuaded by friends to stay in order to head off even deeper potential defence cuts.[21] Earlier, on a visit to Ottawa, German foreign minister Willy Brandt, hardly known as an arch cold warrior, warned that Canada's desire for closer economic relations with Europe could not remain isolated from its defence policy decision.[22]

Mr. Trudeau's new defence policy decisions had been formulated without much thought to the broader political and economic implications for Canada's relations with Europe. Indeed, only three short years later Trudeau actually tried to launch a trade initiative to strengthen Canada's economic ties to Europe. Not surprisingly he found European leaders unreceptive. He soon discovered that the only way to move the trade initiative ahead was to revisit the defence decisions taken in 1969 and again accord NATO and Europe a higher priority.

Although Mr. Trudeau's initial decisions were eventually modified, their diplomatic impact was long-lasting. Moreover, they were accompanied by other periodic decisions that were ill-considered and further complicated Canada's relations with its allies. In 1971, for instance, during his visit to the Soviet Union and without consulting the Cabinet or the minister of external affairs, Trudeau agreed to a Soviet proposal for a diplomatic protocol between the two countries on political consultation. Earlier, the prime minister and External Affairs Minister Mitchell Sharp had also publicly mused about the possibility of recognizing the East German regime prior to the conclusion of the negotiations being conducted by West Germany. Both these moves encouraged the Soviet Union, surprised and concerned the allies and again made Canadian diplomacy appear jumpy.[23]

The ill-considered defence initiative of 1969 set the tone for Canadian relations with Europe for the next decade. Relations with Europe did not really recover until the mid-1970s, and then only partially. Mitchell Sharp records in his memoirs:

The mishandling of the NATO decision had unfortunate repercussions for years on relations between Canada and our allies in Europe and the United States. The prime minister himself discovered this when he sought to establish a contractual link with the European Economic Community ... From what I heard from contacts in Europe and the United States, the mishandling of the NATO decision in the early 1970s [sic] was one of the things that affected adversely the reception in the Western world of Trudeau's peace initiative in the early 1980s, 10 years later.[24]

The Trudeau "peace initiative" of 1983 is yet another example of naivety in foreign policy. To be sure, the initiative was well-intentioned. In his twilight years in office, the prime minister became very concerned about the growing tensions between the East and West, particularly in the aftermath of the downing of a Korean Airways passenger jet by Soviet fighters in September 1983, in which 71 Americans and Canadians were killed.

However, Mr. Trudeau's response — to launch a peace initiative to "inject a bolt of political energy" into superpower relations in order to "reverse the dangerously downward trend line in East–West relations"[25] — was naive in the extreme. Canada simply did not have the clout to play such a role. The German defence attaché in Ottawa at the time later recalled that "Canada liked to see itself as a big peacemaker," but that "the notion that one could solve the East–West divide by simply sitting around the table and talking was naive."[26]

The American reaction was scathing. One official in the Pentagon remembered his reaction to the news of the initiative: "Oh, God, Trudeau's at it again! But why worry if Trudeau has no influence on other people?" Lawrence Eagleburger, then the third-ranking official in the State Department, was scathing and contemptuous in his response, calling the initiative "resembling nothing so much as [the actions] of a leftist high on pot."[27] Robert Ford, Canada's ambassador to the Soviet Union, recalled that "the Russians just laughed at it ... Trudeau had no clout in Moscow."[28]

Mr. Trudeau totally ignored the advice of the Department of External Affairs, whose officials knew the mission was doomed to fail. "Trudeau," officials recalled, "couldn't be stopped despite the best efforts of External Affairs and others."[29]

Most defence analysts generally refer to the Trudeau era as the one in which defence policy was erratic. But if anything, defence policy became even more schizophrenic during the Mulroney government. During the 1984 election campaign Mulroney promised to increase the defence budget by four percent annually in real terms. But as soon as he was elected his government actually reduced previous Liberal appropriations for defence.

The Mulroney government's series of defence policy flip-flops, which were so damaging to Canada's reputation, also went largely uncriticized and unnoticed in Parliament. With regard to Canada's European commitments, the Mulroney government first announced its intention, in March 1985, to enhance the Forces' strength in Europe by 20 percent; then six months later it floated a plan to withdraw all Canadian Forces from Germany and instead enhance its commitment to Norway. One year after that this plan was shelved and it was announced that Canada would actually strengthen its commitment in Germany further. This policy was, in turn, ditched less than two years later, when the budget of April 1989 was gutted in the face of general cuts to government spending.

After the end of the cold war the Mulroney government first publicly promised Canada's allies, on two occasions in June and November 1991, that it would retain a European-based military commitment to NATO's rapid-reaction forces. But only four months later, in February 1992, that promise was broken — again for budgetary reasons. By the end of the Mulroney government in 1993 it was probably understandable if the allies had ceased to take anything Canada said with regard to its NATO commitments too seriously.

Parliamentarians were so far out of the loop that most of them likely had no clue that the country's reputation had been seriously damaged. Indeed, through all the series of defence flip-flops between 1985 and 1992, many were probably largely unaware that the defence policy had even changed.

But allies certainly noticed. As Commander (Ret) Peter Haydon, senior fellow with the Centre for Policy Studies at Dalhousie University, commented, the country's reputation with its allies had been given a coup de grace:

> The refusal, the constant refusal in the Canadian government to honour its commitments was nothing short of ... an embarrassment to those of us that were trying to work in the NATO staff, to carry our fair share of the ... collective defence burden. A constant embarrassment. There was nothing you

could do about it ... The politicians could be given good military advice but they would ignore it. The decisions were made for political purposes.[30]

The "Axworthy Doctrine" and the Collapse of Canadian Influence

"We promised to develop an independent foreign policy for Canada. What does that mean? It means first and foremost to have the political courage to say what we think. To dare say what we think, sometimes in spite of others, to say it often before others, but also to always say it better than others."

Foreign Minister André Ouellet, House of Commons,
March 15, 1994

Canadian foreign policy under the Chrétien Liberals has been termed by one analyst as "speak loudly and carry a bent twig."[31] Lacking the hard-power resources possessed by most major and even medium-sized powers (credible military capability, focused aid policy promoting national strategic objectives, national intelligence capability and so on), the Canadian government has embraced the notions of "co-operative security," "human security" and "soft power." Not only has the government adopted these concepts, it has in fact become the leading proponent of the perspective internationally. This was particularly the case during Lloyd Axworthy's time as foreign minister, from 1996 to 2000, although it continues today.

In Chapter 4 we saw how quickly such idealistic notions melt in the heat of forthcoming conflict. Real influence in the international arena depends on what you can bring to the table. Our closest allies aren't impressed by ideas and rhetoric alone when they are looking for tangible contributions. Statements like the claim made by Mr. Axworthy in 1997 that Canada was able to contribute to the resolution of global ethnic conflicts because it was "putting together a roster of qualified Canadian human rights experts available for rapid deployment"[32] does little more than provoke laughter.

The central tangible hard-power instrument in the hands of the Canadian government — the Canadian Forces — has not been provided with either good policy guidance or effective funding to adjust to the post–cold war security environment. Serious capability shortcomings have been allowed progressively to grow. Some of the most serious gaps in capability which now exist include:

1. **Poor power projection capability:** Power projection capability encompasses the ability to deploy and sustain military forces away from bases both within and outside the national territory. Despite the fact that Canada's forces must protect a huge national territory, the Canadian Forces have a very limited ability to "project power." Both air and sea transport is very limited. Two-thirds of existing transport planes are more than 35 years old and there is no heavy-lift air transport capability. This makes it difficult to even meet domestic security requirements. During the 1997 Manitoba flood and the 1998 ice storm American heavy-lift aircraft had to be called upon to lift Canadian troops and equipment to respond to the crises. The army also has poor tactical mobility once deployed, since it has no heavy-lift or attack helicopters.

   The navy has no dedicated offshore support/amphibious capability, meaning that it is difficult to sustain and support troops once they are deployed overseas. The two operational support ships are 30 years of age and are devoted primarily to refuelling and re-supplying ships at sea. In most circumstances they cannot adequately support troops operating ashore.

   While the army is pledged to deploy up to a brigade plus a battalion group (a total of at least 6,000 ground troops) overseas within 90 days, testimony before the House of Commons Standing Committee on National Defence in 2001 revealed that it is unlikely that this could ever be done. Instead, it is probable that no more than one or two battle groups (with perhaps a combined maximum strength of 2,500 ground troops) can be deployed and sustained overseas in the long term in low-intensity operations. The deployment of troops in a medium- to high-intensity combat environment is another matter entirely. The inability to sustain forces deployed overseas arises from the fact that the army's total strength has dwindled to just 18,600 troops, of which perhaps half can be considered frontline personnel. Many troops are now forced to serve back-to-back rotations overseas.

2. **Disappearing air power:** The air force has not had any strategic (jet) refuelling tanker aircraft since 1997, meaning that Canada cannot deploy its CF-18s overseas without allied support. This situation will not be rectified until at least 2004.

    Meanwhile, the force of fighter aircraft is rapidly declining. CF-18 numbers are being reduced by one-third (from 120 to 80 aircraft) just to pay for the modernization of the remaining planes. Even fewer aircraft will be available for regular frontline service. This will mean increasing reliance on U.S. aircraft to police and defend Canadian airspace.

    Flying hours have also been seriously pared back. For instance, the air force's main sovereignty protection aircraft, the Aurora, has had its flying hours cut to just 8,000 hours per year for the entire fleet (or no more than about 37 hours per aircraft per month).

3. **Low naval-readiness levels:** About half of the navy's 16 major warships are maintained at reduced readiness to save money and because of personnel shortages. This makes it very difficult to sustain deployments (such as in the Indian Ocean/Persian Gulf region).

    The navy's four air defence and command destroyers are now about 30 years old, and failure to replace them will end the ability to deploy integrated task groups overseas. In the meantime, the navy's air arm has rusted out and the Sea King helicopters are now nearly 40 years of age, requiring about 40 hours of maintenance for every hour in the air. The project office to replace the Sea King was opened in 1981, and in 20 years hundreds of millions of dollars have been spent, but no helicopter has been successfully ordered.

    The navy's ability to protect Canadian waters has significantly eroded, and while the navy continues to operate in the Atlantic and the Pacific, it has no capability at all in Canada's third ocean — the Arctic.

This erosion of capability will soon make the Canadian Forces ineffective as a means of national policy. This has profound implications for Canadian sovereignty, for Canada's ability to respond to internal emergencies and for Canada's reputation (whatever is left of it) internationally. While increasing numbers of informed parliamentarians from all parties recognize the seriousness of the crisis, the government, which for a long time has pursued defence policy with ideological blinders on, has been free to ignore it.

If one compares Canada's defence effort to that of other countries with similar or smaller economies, it is readily apparent that not only is the amount of money devoted by Canada to defence relatively small, it is also quite badly managed and spent. The end result is that Canada gets little bang for the bucks it spends on defence.

This is illustrated in the table on the following pages, which compares Canada's defence spending and capabilities in 2000–2001 to that of four countries: Italy, the G7 nation closest to Canada in terms of national wealth, Spain, Australia and the Netherlands. These latter three countries have smaller national economies than does Canada; they spend about the same amount on defence annually; but they spend it better and generally produce more effective military forces with better power projection capabilities.

One common denominator for all these countries is that they have better systems of parliamentary oversight, where the national legislatures are more seriously engaged in foreign and defence policy issues. Three of the countries (Italy, Spain and the Netherlands) have at least partial systems of proportional representation which allow for the nomination of policy experts to Parliament, thereby improving the quality of parliamentary debates. Australia has an elected Senate, whose committee on defence plays an important role in scrutinizing the country's defence budget. Constitutional provisions in Italy, the Netherlands and Spain also require the national parliaments to ratify international agreements — thus more directly involving the legislatures in foreign policy and security issues.

Canadian Defence Spending and Capability
Compared to Selected Small- and Medium-Sized Countries

	Canada	Italy	Spain	Australia	Netherlands
Population	31.8 million	57.2 million	39.7 million	19 million	15.9 million
GDP ($U.S.)	705 billion	1.1 trillion	570 billion	380 billion	347 billion
Defence Spending ($U.S.)	7.3 billion (1% of GDP)	21 billion (1.9% of GDP)	7.2 billion (1.3% of GDP)	7.1 billion (1.9% of GDP)	6.2 billion (1.8% of GDP)
Total Regular Military Personnel	58,000 (volunteer forces)	230,000 (reducing; conscription being eliminated)	143,000 (reducing; conscription being eliminated)	51,000 (volunteer forces; increasing to 54,000)	50,500 (volunteer forces)
Power Projection Ground Forces	1 battalion and/or 1 "battle group" (1,000 to 2,500 troops)	1 division with 3 brigades (about 15,000 troops)	1 division with 3 brigades (about 15,000 troops)	1 brigade (5,000+ troops; 30 days notice or less	1 airmobile brigade and 1 "light brigade" (about 7,000 troops)
Special Operations Forces	JTF2 (about 250 troops)	Special navy commandos and 1,200 marines	4 army SF battalions (1 Spanish Legion) and 5,600 marines	500 SAS troops and 1 commando battalion	3,100 marines
Main Battle Tanks	114 Leopard Is	1,349 (various types)	688 (various types)	71 Leopard Is	320 Leopard IIs (reducing)
Attack Helicopters	0	45 A-129s	28 with anti-tank missiles	(22 Tigers ordered)	19 Apaches (increasing)

	Canada	Italy	Spain	Australia	Netherlands
Heavy-Lift Helicopters	0	36 Chinooks	17 Chinooks	6 Chinooks	13 Chinooks
Aircraft Carriers	0	1 (second being built)	1 (second planned)	0	0
Amphibious Ships	0	3	4	3	1 (second ordered)
Major Surface Warships	16 (half at reduced readiness)	21	15	10 (increasing to 14 by 2006)	12
Submarines	2 (and 2 being delivered)	6	8	6	4
Jet Combat Aircraft	87 operational CF-18s (reducing)	337 (including 75 Tornados and 18 navy Harriers)	221 (including 90 F-18s and 17 navy Harriers)	71 F-18s and 35 F-111 strike aircraft	138 F-16s
Tactical Transport Aircraft	32 C-130s (19 date from 1960s)	14 C-130s and 23 G-222s (12 C-27J ordered)	12 C-130s and 34 C-212s	24 C-130s and 14 Caribous	2 C-130s and 6 F-50s/F-60s
Specialized Combat Support Aircraft	0 (2 Airbus to be converted to tanker role by 2004)	2 707 jet tankers (UAVs — unmanned air vehicles — ordered)	4 707 jet tankers	4 707 jet tankers (radar aircraft and UAVs ordered)	2 DC-10 jet tankers

Budget figures for 2000; other information for 2001. Main source: International Institute for Strategic Studies, *Military Balance, 2001-02* (London: International Institute for Strategic Studies, 2001) pp. 49–50; 62–66; 71–73; 185–186.

Opening the Canadian foreign and defence policy decision-making process to legislative input will not, in and of itself, solve Canada's defence problems. But it will force real debate on real issues in the Canadian Parliament. In particular, it would force government to justify both its policy decisions and the way in which it spends the resources given it by Parliament for national defence.

Effective oversight would likely require better management of the country's national security on the part of the executive. Recommendations from legislators related to national security would have to be taken more seriously. For instance, in recent years both the Reform Party caucus (in 1999) and Liberal caucus committee members (in 2002) suggested that Canada acquire its own national intelligence capability. Canada is in fact the only G8 country not to possess such a capability. However, on these occasions, as in so many others, the government felt entirely free to ignore the views of opposition and back-bench MPs.

A further consequence of the absence of serious debate in Parliament is that the Canadian government has been able to base much of the country's foreign and defence policy on rather tenuous assumptions. It has been able to do this without having to fear the reaction in Parliament. Canadian governments have asserted in particular that traditional measurements of power are no longer relevant in the post–cold war world. They have argued that Canada's international influence in forums like the United Nations remains high. Canada, we are told, is after all one of only seven countries that are part of the G7 group of leading industrialized nations. Canada is also commonly said to fill niche roles, such as providing foreign aid.

But as even rudimentary discussion in a first-year university seminar would soon reveal, multilateral diplomacy at the UN and simply sitting at the G7 table do not protect national sovereignty. Remember once again John Manley's words that "you can't just sit at the G8 table and then when the bill comes go to the washroom".[33] Neither has our foreign aid been sufficiently focused or co-ordinated to buy Canada a great deal of valuable international influence. Unlike the assistance provided by some countries such as Australia or New Zealand, which is focused on particular regions of immediate political, strategic and economic importance, Canadian aid is widely dispersed over many recipients. Moreover, very little of it is used to support specific national interest objectives. Instead, most of it goes to underwrite development projects — some of which are worthy and others of which are not. Indeed, according to the auditor general, much of Canada's assistance is poorly monitored and cannot ensure consistent or effective results.[34]

If one actually looks critically at many of the so-called successes of Canadian foreign policy over the past several years, they prove on closer examination to be little more than Pyrrhic victories. The most prominent international agreement pushed by Mr. Axworthy in his time as foreign minister was the treaty to ban antipersonnel land mines. But the Canadian army never contributed to the global land mine problem because it has never used land mines irresponsibly. Instead, they were used, in the Korean conflict for instance, to defend usually outnumbered Canadian troops.

The antipersonnel land mines ban is essentially a "coalition of the willing" or a "coalition of the virtuous." The world's main mine users and producers (such as Russia, China, India, Pakistan, South Korea and others) have refused to sign. Reports also suggest that many states that have signed may have done so cynically; that loopholes can easily be used to circumvent the treaty, such as employing anti-tank mines (allowed by the treaty) in an antipersonnel role (which although banned by the treaty is practically impossible to enforce). It is highly questionable whether the main indiscriminate users of such weapons — guerrilla groups and ill-disciplined Third World armies — will actually be constrained by the treaty's terms. Even Canada made a rather hypocritical decision to shelter behind possible U.S. antipersonnel mines when it deployed troops to Afghanistan in 2002. (The United States has not signed the land mines treaty.)

By the time I arrived on Parliament Hill in September 1998, this "human security agenda" was in full swing and had expanded to include a UN ban on the employment of child soldiers, the restriction of the global small arms trade, the establishment of an international criminal court and the elimination of nuclear weapons. Most of these initiatives betray a high degree of naivety as to what is realistically achievable on the international stage. Some initiatives, such as the campaign to eliminate nuclear weapons, are doomed to remain either irrelevant or generally ignored by the world's major powers. Often it seemed that greater resources and people hours were devoted to promote these campaigns than to protect Canada's hard interests.

Indeed, in 2001 I learned that in the four years that Mr. Axworthy was minister of foreign affairs, the human security and land mines sections of the department grew from six professional staff to 30. At the same time the Canada–U.S. relations division had a staff of only one dozen people. Likewise, even though tens of thousands of Canadian jobs were at stake during Mr. Axworthy's tenure in the softwood lumber dispute with the United States, the staff of the softwood lumber division in his department oscillated between just 12 and 25 people.[35]

None of the initiatives so proudly launched by Mr. Axworthy has served to enhance Canada's influence with its major allies — the countries whose policies affect Canada in the most direct way. At present about 95 percent of Canadian trade occurs with the United States, Europe and the Asia–Pacific region (80 percent with the U.S. alone). As Canada's profile and credibility with our major allies is reduced, so too is the country's ability to influence events that impact on Canadians. This development should certainly concern all Canadians.

The Consequences of Unrestrained Idealism in Canadian Foreign Policy

"Canada has never exhibited the balanced political and military culture of a genuine nation-state."
Gerard Vano in *Canada: The Strategic and Military Pawn*

A strong idealistic streak has always permeated Canada's political culture. As early as 1920 Canada's delegate to the League of Nation's Assembly lectured that body, saying in the aftermath of the First World War that "it was European policy, European statesmanship, European ambition that drenched this world in blood." He was thanked by then Prime Minister Arthur Meighen "for stating to the conference, as frankly as you did, the price the world has paid for the European diplomacy of the last hundred years."[36]

U.S. secretary of state Dean Acheson once referred to Canada's tendency to claim the moral high ground in foreign policy as akin to being lectured by the stern voice of the daughter of God. And although Canada may not quite be the fireproof house far from inflammable materials once claimed by Canadian senator Raoul Dandurand, Canadian leaders have often acted as though this were the case. Since 1945 they have done so because Canada has had the luxury of resting comfortably under the protection of the United States, even while it has often been grandstanding on the international stage.

Gerard Vano, a scholar who has examined Canadian strategic issues in a historical context, has argued that the roots of this are to be found in Canada's colonial history. In strategic/military terms, he argues, Canada has always defaulted control over military matters to its imperial patron state — be it France, Britain or, now, the United States. Therefore, "Canada has never exhibited the balanced political and military culture of a genuine nation-state."[37] The analyst R. J. Sutherland also noted in the early 1960s that "Canada has no particular tradition of strategic calculation."[38] Another analyst, R. B. Byers, writing in the 1980s, asserted that Canada never developed its own security policy (combining the military, diplomatic and economic dimensions of policy in a single cohesive framework).[39]

Naivety in foreign policy and the absence of serious debate go hand in hand. Unwittingly, and even though many Canadians have continued to regard Canada as a kind of "fireproof house," the country has steadily become ever more subservient and dependent on the United States.

If we are to have any chance of reversing this trend, then we require a national political institution where real discussion and debate takes place and in which the country's political leaders discuss international challenges in a serious manner. Foreign policy in Canada can no longer be monopolized by a small elite representing a relatively narrow segment of Canadian opinion, nor can this elite remain largely unchallenged in its policy decisions and spending choices. There is simply too much at stake for all Canadians not to have a voice.

NOTES

1. D. Stairs, "The Military as an Instrument of Canadian Foreign Policy" in H. J. Massey, *The Canadian Military: A Profile* (Toronto: Copp Clark: 1972) p. 99.
2. Roy Rempel, The Anglo-Saxon Powers and German Rearmament [unpublished paper], 1994. Presented at the Society for the Historians of American History in Boston.

3. The Resolution was passed by a vote of 64 to five (Britain, France, Israel, Australia and New Zealand).

4. J. L. Granatstein and David Bercuson, *War and Peacekeeping: From South Africa to the Gulf — Canada's Limited Wars* (Toronto: Key Porter Books, 1991) p. 195.

5. Terence Robertson, *Crisis: The Inside Story of the Suez Conspiracy* (Toronto: McClelland and Stewart, 1964) pp. 285–291. The Egyptians had raised objections to Canada's leading role in the UN force due to its membership in NATO and its close ties to the United Kingdom. Under the circumstances, Lester Pearson thought that the deployment of a unit such as the "Queen's Own Rifles" might further intensify Egyptian opposition to Canada's leading role. With other nations providing sufficient infantry units, it was decided to forego the deployment of an infantry battalion from Canada and deploy light armoured reconnaissance and support units instead.

6. Lt. General E. L. M. Burns, *Between Arab and Israeli* (Toronto: Clarke Irwin, 1962) pp. 206–218.

7. Kim Richard Nossal, "The PM and the SSEA in Canada's Foreign Policy: Dividing the Territory, 1968–1994," *International Journal* (Winter 1994–95) p. 207.

8. "Memorandum by MacKenzie King on His Interview with Adolf Hitler, Berlin, 29 June, 1937," from the King Papers reprinted in James Eayrs, *In Defence of Canada: Appeasement and Rearmament* (Toronto: University of Toronto Press, 1965) pp. 226–231.

9. Eayrs, p. 79.

10. Eayrs, p. 47.

11. John Holmes, *The Shaping of Peace* (Toronto: University of Toronto Press, 1979) p. 26.

12. See discussion in Roy Rempel, *Counterweights: The Failure of Canada's German and European Policy, 1955–1995* (Montreal: McGill-Queen's Press, 1996).

13. H. Basil Robinson, *Diefenbaker's World: A Populist in Foreign Affairs* (Toronto: University of Toronto Press, 1989) p. 97.

14. Author's translation: "Kanada's Stellung in der Welt und die deutsch-kanadishe Beziehungen" [Canada's place in the world and German-Canadian relations] in "Informations-und Besprechungsmappe,

Staatsbesuch des kanadischen Premierministers John G. Diefenbaker" [Briefing notes for Prime Minister Diefenbaker's visit to West Germany in 1958] German Foreign Office Files: 305 82.21.

15. Robinson, p. 61.

16. German Ambassador, Ottawa to Foreign Office, Bonn, 29 September 1959, Foreign Office Files: Vol. 123 301-81-04-91.20.

17. High Commission Ottawa to Commonwealth Office, January 23 and 26, 1959, Public Record Office, London PREM 2712.

18. Cited by Jocelyn Ghent-Mallet, "Deploying Nuclear Weapons, 1962–63" in John Kirton, ed., *Canadian Foreign Policy* (Toronto: Prentice Hall, 1992) p. 103.

19. Leo Cadieux [interview]. Interviewed by Roy Rempel, October, 1986.

20. Marilyn Eustace, *Canada's European Force, 1964–1971* (Kingston: Centre for International Relations, Queen's University, 1982) p. 108.

21. Discussion in Jack Granatstein and Robert Bothwell, *Pirouette: Pierre Trudeau and Canadian Foreign Policy* (Toronto: University of Toronto Press, 1990) pp. 27–28.

22. Rempel, *Counterweights*, p. 53.

23. Rempel, *Counterweights*, pp. 70–71.

24. Mitchell Sharp, *Which Reminds Me — A Memoir* (Toronto: University of Toronto Press, 1994) p. 175–176.

25. Cited in Beth Fischer, "The Trudeau Peace Initiative and the End of the Cold War: Catalyst or Coincidence?" *International Journal*, 49 (Summer 1994) p. 614.

26. Colonel Roland Foerster [interview]. Interviewed by Roy Rempel, November, 1991.

27. Granatstein and Bothwell, *Pirouette*, pp. 371–372.

28. Granatstein and Bothwell, *Pirouette*, p. 374.

29. Granatstein and Bothwell, *Pirouette*, p. 366.

30. Commander Peter Hayden [interview]. Interview with Kitson Vincent and Robert Roy of Stornoway Productions, 1994.

31. Denis Stairs, "Canada in the 1990s: Speak Loudly and Carry a Bent Twig," *Policy Options*, 22 (January–February, 2001) pp. 43–49.

32. Lloyd Axworthy, "Canada and Human Security: The Need for Leadership," *International Journal*, Vol. 52 (Spring 1997) p. 186.

33. Paul Wells, "We Don't Pull Our Weight," *National Post*, October 5, 2001, p. A1.

34. Canada, Auditor General of Canada, *Auditor General's Report*, (Ottawa: Office of the Auditor General, October 2000) Chapter 14.

35. Information provided by the Department of Foreign Affairs through an Access to Information request.

36. James Eayrs, *In Defence of Canada: From the Great War to the Great Depression* (Toronto: University of Toronto Press, 1964) p. 4.

37. Gerard Vano, *Canada: The Strategic and Military Pawn* (New York: Praeger Publishers, 1988) pp. 71–110.

38. R. J. Sutherland, "Canada's Long Term Strategic Situation," *International Journal*, 17 (Summer 1962) pp. 199-223.

39. R. B. Byers, *Canadian Security and Defence: The Legacy and the Challenges* (London: International Institute for Strategic Studies, Winter 1985).

CHAPTER SIX

War in a Time of "Peace"

The Canadian Forces have been steadily cut since 1968, largely because Canadian prime ministers have believed wars involving Canada are a remote possibility. Throughout this period of continuous cuts, Parliament has not been relevant on defence issues. Many reports have been drafted in Parliament in these years arguing that military readiness is inadequate. Four very good Senate studies on defence were published between 1982 and 1989 after lengthy hearings. But these were quick to gather dust on shelves after perhaps one day of spotty press coverage. There has been simply no obligation on the part of any prime minister to be concerned with anything that parliamentarians, especially unelected senators, say.

While some might say that the ambitious defence white paper drafted by the Mulroney government in June 1987 was an exception to this neglect of defence, it was an isolated event. Indeed, when that white paper was released there was virtually no discussion in Parliament on the strategic rationales behind the government's proposals. Instead, most of the discussion focused on the relative merits of particular equipment projects proposed in the white paper, especially the plan to purchase nuclear-powered submarines for the navy. Ignoring the larger strategic issues to focus on particular weapons systems was like having a debate on medicare that focused exclusively on the construction of hospitals.

In any case the government was never committed to its new defence policy, and less than two years later it abandoned the white paper when budgetary priorities changed. While the white paper's plans to significantly increase Canadian military capabilities in Central Europe had clearly been overtaken by events, other aspects, namely the objective of maintaining viable forces to protect Canada's offshore seas and territorial sovereignty, were still valid. Yet not a single question about the demise of the white paper was asked in Question Period after the April 1989 budget — except in so far as envisaged defence cuts might result in the closure of bases in members' ridings.[1]

This meant that when the world turned more violent after 1989, Canada was left largely unprepared. During the cold war the engagement of the two superpowers around the globe actually served to control regional conflicts. The United States, the Soviet Union and their allies usually endeavoured to ensure that regional conflicts were carefully managed or contained so as to avoid direct superpower confrontations.

After 1989 this was no longer the case and it contributed to new international instability. In an effort to help manage the international instability that resulted from rapid change, Canadian military operations around the world increased. For the first time since Korea Canadian Forces were deployed on active operations and Canadian troops were killed and wounded in action. Between 1992 and 1995 nearly a dozen Canadian soldiers were killed in Bosnia and more than 100 were wounded.

The Canadian government has lurched from crisis to crisis, trying to be a "player" everywhere but without any clear sense of the national interest to help set priorities. Varied commitments have been made in places like Croatia, the Gulf, Bosnia, Somalia, Haiti, Zaire, Kosovo and East Timor. But decades of neglect of the Armed Forces have left the troops on the ground ill-equipped for many of the operations they have been asked to undertake.

The Gulf War

> "Wars have to come to an end. Cease-fires have to be negotiated, truces have to be honoured, peacekeeping has to take place, bridges have to be built, reconstruction has to occur and that is the peculiar Canadian talent."
>
> Lloyd Axworthy, House of Commons, January 15, 1991

Iraq's invasion of Kuwait on August 2, 1990, was the first indication that the post–cold war world would be anything but peaceful. For most Canadians this was probably a bolt out of the blue. Why had Iraq invaded Kuwait? Was it of any importance to Canada? What were Canadian interests in the region? Where, in fact, was Kuwait?

It wasn't just ordinary Canadians who were asking these questions on August 3. Undoubtedly Prime Minister Brian Mulroney, Cabinet ministers and many members of Parliament were asking them as well. Despite the long and bloody Iran–Iraq war of the 1980s, events in the Persian Gulf had been of no interest in Parliament prior to 1990 — even though a Canadian peacekeeping force had been deployed to police the cease-fire finally agreed to by Iran and Iraq in 1988.

Following the U.S. decision to confront Iraq over its aggression against Kuwait and to defend Saudi Arabia (announced on August 5), Canada stated (on August 10) that it would send two Destroyers (HMCS *Athabaskan* and HMCS *Terra Nova*) and a support tanker to the Gulf. *Athabaskan* was already nearly 20 years old in 1990 and oriented to anti-submarine warfare. But Iraq had no submarines and the main threat would be from aircraft or fast patrol boats armed with anti-ship missiles. During the Iran–Iraq war an Iraqi Mirage aircraft mistakenly attacked and seriously damaged a U.S. frigate operating in the Persian Gulf with an Exocet anti-ship missile. *Athabaskan's* air defence armament was weak, consisting of relatively short-range Sea Sparrow anti-aircraft missiles which had only a very limited anti-missile capability. She also had no surface-to-surface missiles. *Terra Nova* was even more antiquated, dating from the early 1960s. She neither carried her own helicopter nor did she have missile armament of any kind.

The Canadian navy had been allowed to rust out. No ships had been built since the early 1970s and although the first of the new Halifax-class frigates were by then under construction, they could not be made ready in time to sail to the Gulf. A Senate report in 1983 had recommended a comprehensive rebuilding of the Canadian navy — but it was ignored by both the Trudeau and Mulroney governments.

Nevertheless, the government now ordered that the navy send ships to the Gulf. The only solution was to improvise. Harpoon surface-to-surface missiles, which had been acquired for the Halifax-class ships that were still being built, were fitted to the older Canadian ships, as were Phalanx radar-guided gattling guns, to provide some measure of anti-missile defence. In addition, army personnel were put aboard the ships with light, hand-held surface-to-air missiles. These were hurriedly purchased from Great Britain as an emergency measure when it was revealed that existing older Canadian air defence weapons had a 33 per-cent misfire rate.[2]

Even though these systems modernized the two ships, given their age and relative obsolescence both vessels could only be deployed in the mid to southern waters of the Gulf in the event of conflict. Both *Athabaskan* and *Terra Nova* were forbidden by National Defence Headquarters in Ottawa to operate north of 28 degrees latitude. *Athabaskan* moved north of that line on only one occasion (on February 19), when the cruiser USS *Princeton* struck a mine and was in need of towing. *Athabaskan* was the closest ship in the vicinity and requested emergency permission to move north of 28 degrees. In anticipation that such permission would be granted now that the Iraqi air threat was sharply diminished, *Athabaskan* went to the aid of the *Princeton*.[3]

The Canadian navy endeavoured to make the best of a bad situa-tion. The role assigned to the navy — commanding the logistic force — was a testament to the skill of Canadian personnel. But the role was not essential to the allied effort. Indeed, as our naval attachés in London and Washington found, both the British and Americans questioned the value of committing Canadian warships, given their lack of modern weapons systems — though they were interested in seeing a Canadian tanker committed to re-supply their own vessels.[4]

Partly because of the weakness of the naval contingent deployed to the Gulf, the government sought to provide a more substantial contri-bution. The most potent weapon system that Canada could provide was its CF-18 fighter aircraft. These were ordered dispatched to the Gulf on September 14.

These virtually brand new fighter aircraft were assigned to provide air cover to the Canadian warships once they reached the Gulf. But when they were deployed they were restricted to air defence operations exclusively and were not even permitted to bring any air-to-ground weapons with them. Nor did they have any specialized anti-ship weapons of any kind to deal with possible surface threats. In 1983 the Senate committee examining Canada's maritime forces had recommended, based on naval advice, that "it would be advisable to equip some of the CF-18s ... [to] fire Harpoon [anti-ship] missiles."[5] But no action was taken.

In this sense the Canadian government made a completely unrealistic distinction between "defensive" and "offensive" operations and thought it could draw an artificial line between them. This, as we shall see, seriously hampered Canada's CF-18 pilots once war broke out.

Canada's two opposition parties of the day, the Liberals and the NDP, ignored defence preparedness. Instead, they objected to the nature of the military role that Canada was assuming and argued that there was no specific UN sanction for offensive military operations. Liberal leader Jean Chrétien alleged that Canada was playing Rambo in the Middle East: "At the moment, we in Canada are looking more belligerent than the Americans ... The international reputation of our country has never been so low."[6]

For most of September and October almost no questions were posed in Question Period related to the crisis in the Gulf. Only as the crisis intensified and became a major news story did the issue begin to draw opposition attention. The November 8 announcement by the United States that it would deploy offensive military forces to the Gulf for the purpose of throwing the Iraqis out of Kuwait drew strong media interest. Opposition politicians then began to focus more intensely on Canadian policy as a way of enhancing their own political fortunes at the expense of the government.[7]

However, of all questions that were asked, only one focused directly on the operational readiness of the forces that Canada had deployed to the Gulf. That question, posed by NDP MP Jack Whittaker on October 30, noted the auditor general's own critique of the readiness of the Canadian Forces and especially the military's ability to handle major casualties. But Defence Minister Bill McKnight simply dismissed the auditor general and his experts as "not qualified military strategists."[8]

The Mulroney government (like the Chrétien government eight years later) was most anxious to use Parliament to legitimize the political and military actions that it had already undertaken and to ignore much of the rest. On October 23 parliamentarians voted 170 to 33 (with the NDP opposed) to support Canada's actions in the Security Council as well as the dispatch of Canadian military units. That was followed by a similar debate and vote on November 29, in which Parliament again voted, entirely predictably given the government majority, to support the UN's actions to ensure Iraqi compliance with UN resolutions. This time the Liberals joined the NDP in opposing the government motion.

These debates ignored the matter of Canada's real interests in the Gulf, as they did the actual capabilities of the Canadian Forces. The debates were thus largely irrelevant to the serving men and women Canada had deployed to the Gulf. Given the operational problems confronted by Canada's air and, particularly, the naval contingent this seems astonishing, but considering the complicity of every official party then represented in Parliament with the unfettered rundown of the Canadian Forces, it was probably understandable.

On December 19 Parliament adjourned for a long Christmas break while events in the Gulf moved steadily toward war. The imminence of hostilities led to the recall of parliamentarians on January 15 for an emergency debate and vote. Unlike the Chrétien government eight years later, the Mulroney government was at least willing to allow a debate and vote. But the discussion largely occurred in a void, and MPs who had given almost no attention to foreign and defence policy issues in the previous decade were ill-equipped to discuss the matter seriously.

Svend Robinson asked questions about Canadian policy vis-à-vis a possible American nuclear strike against Iraq — a scenario that lacked even the remotest plausibility.[9] Lloyd Axworthy, in turn, claimed that Canada's role as a peacekeeping nation was being destroyed: "Wars have to come to an end. Cease-fires have to be negotiated, truces have to be honoured, peacekeeping has to take place, bridges have to be built, reconstruction has to occur and that is the peculiar Canadian talent." He related a discussion with one Canadian who had supposedly stated that Canada would lose its "innocence" in this war and that it would "no longer be possible for Canadians to see themselves in a world where, by wearing a little maple leaf on our lapel, that we would be seen as Boy Scouts and that we would have open access. All of a sudden, we would have the scales drop from our eyes and we would now see ourselves in a world where there can be ruthless dictators detaining internationals."[10]

The fact that these MPs were the principal foreign affairs spokespeople for their parties set a rather poor and ill-informed tone for the general debate. Jean Chrétien even went so far as to argue that if war actually broke out, "our troops should be called back."[11]

Several prominent Liberals, including former prime minister John Turner, rejected the decision of the Liberal caucus to oppose the war and publicly broke with their colleagues. Mr. Turner was then kicked out of his Centre Block office by the Liberal whip.[12]

After war broke out on January 17, and in the middle of the parliamentary debate, the Liberal leadership, sensing that the wind of public opinion might no longer be blowing its way (especially given the likelihood of Iraqi attacks against Israel), abruptly flip-flopped and instead decided to support the motion proposed by the government. That motion, which passed in the House by a vote of 217–47 on January 22, was largely academic. By that time Canadian personnel had already been at war for five full days. Thereafter, Parliament adjourned for most of the rest of the war, though parliamentary committees did meet in the interim.

In the meantime most Canadian personnel were being kept well out of harm's way. The Canadian task group had been instructed to move south of 28 degrees latitude as soon as the code word "Barber Pole" was transmitted to them. On receiving this warning, Canadian ships immediately were deployed out of range of Iraqi aircraft, and the CF-18s were restricted to patrol duties over the Gulf. They did not undertake their first "sweep and escort" missions to protect allied strike aircraft over Iraq until January 24 — a full week into the war.

The Canadian aircraft still had no bombs with which to actually attack enemy ground targets. They had not been allowed to bring any to the Gulf. The air force had no smart munitions of any kind. And the failure to acquire anti-ship weapons in the 1980s also came back to haunt the air force when, on January 30, Canadian CF-18 pilots David Kendall and Steve Hill were asked by the Americans to attack an Iraqi patrol boat in their sector. Lacking any air-to-surface weapons, they made several strafing runs, racking the ship with 20-mm cannon fire. Then, in desperation, they launched an air-to-air missile which not surprisingly missed the ship. Later, as opposition MPs decried this "escalation" in Canada's war role, the pilots were actually reprimanded for making too many strafing runs on the ship — though thankfully they were later mentioned in dispatches for their actions.

Although Canadian fighters provided nominal air protection for allied bombers, there were no air-to-air engagements between Canadian and Iraqi aircraft because the air threat had been quickly eliminated by the allies. By February the air force was pressing for a more relevant role, but the government delayed taking such a decision until February 20, making Canada the last country to commit its air contingent to an air-to-ground role. This caused a hysterical reaction from opposition foreign affairs and defence spokespeople. Mr. John Brewin of the NDP called the government decision "despicable" and said that Canada would now be "complicitous with Saddam Hussein in the killing of tens of thousands of people," while Lloyd Axworthy claimed that the Canadian announcement would undermine what he termed a "crucial" Soviet peace proposal then being put forward.[13] How the commitment of 24 CF-18s to bombing operations that already comprised some 2,000 allied aircraft would compromise a non-existent peace process was not immediately clear.

Nevertheless, the main impediment to Canadian bombing operations didn't come from parliamentarians but rather from the fact that there were no Canadian bombs "in theatre." When the decision to engage in bombing missions was finally taken, the Canadian air commander had to go shopping to the Americans for emergency bomb supplies. The provision of American bombs allowed the Canadians to begin bombing operations on February 24 — the day the ground offensive began. In all, CF-18s flew 56 ground attack sorties from February 24 until the end of the war four days later, using a combination of American and Canadian bombs, which had finally begun to arrive on February 25.[14]

One attack on an Iraqi patrol boat and 56 bombing sorties were the only Canadian combat actions during the Gulf War. While the air force was seriously constrained in its role by the fact that it initially had no bombs in theatre, no precision-guided munitions and no anti-ship weapons, neither the navy nor the army was in any shape at all to be seriously involved in the fighting.

The only ground forces that Canada deployed to the Gulf were a small infantry unit to protect the Canadian air base in Qatar and a field hospital. The field hospital was a welcome contribution and was heavily involved in treating wounded Iraqi soldiers after the war was over. Canadian interests in the Gulf probably did not warrant a larger ground force contribution and Canada's military effort was in line, for instance, with that of Australia, which only deployed two (albeit capable) warships to the Gulf but did not commit any of its own F-18s. The only Western countries to dispatch large ground, air and naval contingents to the Gulf were the major powers — the United States, Britain and France. But in Canada's case it was also evident to most observers that the dispatch of a viable ground contingent would simply be beyond what was feasible.

To be viable and an asset rather than a burden to its allies, it was judged that a Canadian ground force would have to be at least brigade size, reinforced to a strength of about 12,000 personnel with three mechanized infantry battalions, an armoured regiment, an armoured artillery regiment as well as air defence units and a host of support elements. On November 23 a plan code-named *Broadsword* was presented to the chief of defence staff for the dispatch of a Canadian brigade to the Gulf. This plan was rejected on the same day it was presented.

Broadsword revealed that it would take 135 days to dispatch the Canadian brigade in Germany to the Persian Gulf together with supporting elements from Canada, and then ready that formation for combat in the desert.[15] Thus, had Canada taken a decision in late November to deploy a brigade to the Gulf, it would likely not have been ready for operations at least until sometime in April.

There were additional problems as well. Leaving aside the basic reality that the Canadian army had never trained for desert operations and had no such specialized equipment, much Canadian ground equipment was at least a generation behind that of the British and American allies. Canada's Leopard I tanks were based on 1960s designs, as were its M-113 armoured personnel carriers. Unlike the British and American armies, the Canadian army had neither attack helicopters nor multiple-launch rocket artillery systems. Moreover, Canada had no heavy air or sea transport to actually move such a force to the Gulf and would have had to hitch a ride with its allies. Thus, while there was periodic speculation, even encouraged by the government, that Canada might dispatch ground forces to the Gulf, this was never a serious possibility.

Three days prior to the end of the war Parliament resumed sitting. But by then the frenzy of interest that had characterized parliamentary discussions in January had all but disappeared. After very limited questioning of the government by NDP leader Audrey McLaughlin and Lloyd Axworthy on February 25 and 26, the issue was swept off the parliamentary agenda by the federal budget — which also ignored the need to rebuild the Canadian Forces. With the war over and won, the issue was no longer topical. No more questions were asked on the Gulf War thereafter and, as would be the case eight years later, the opportunity for Parliament to discuss "lessons learned" for the Canadian Forces, for the Canadian government and for Parliament itself disappeared.

The Gulf War should have signalled that military preparedness remained important despite the end of the cold war. It should have given an impetus to a comprehensive review of Canadian defence policy to determine Canada's interests in the post–cold war era and the type of military capability that Canada required to support its diplomacy. The Gulf War had certainly revealed how inadequate Canada's military capability was.

This failure to seriously review policy contributed to the resignation of the vice-chief of the defence staff, Admiral Chuck Thomas, in April. In his resignation statement Admiral Thomas criticized the government for failing to encourage and facilitate public participation on the future of the Canadian military.[16] But Admiral Thomas would later comment, "When I resigned as the vice-chief of the defence staff because I didn't think that the advice that was being put forward was valid or affordable … I was never called before the parliamentary committee on defence to explain myself. Never. That wouldn't have happened in the United States."[17]

While parliamentary committees looked at some of the challenges of post–cold war peacekeeping,[18] there was simply no interest by government in a comprehensive policy review, especially one that seriously involved Parliament and testimony from disgruntled military officers. Parliament itself had no ability to force any meaningful policy review on its own. So while government dithered and Parliament stood on the sidelines, Canadian soldiers gradually became ever more embroiled in operational missions for which they were ill-equipped and ill-prepared.

Battles in Croatia

Our wheeled vehicles had no blast blankets … so if your vehicle hit a mine, which is highly likely if you go off the road, it's gonna

151

take that shrapnel out instead of hitting you in the leg or the buttocks and none of that stuff is there. We got APCs that are older than [the defence minister] is. I mean, guys have been shot in Cougars. The Cougar was never meant for combat ... It was bought for a training vehicle so guys could pretend to be driving tanks ... What do we do? We're Canadians. We'll put those Cougars in the theatre of war and maybe the guys will make believe it's a tank. I mean that's stuff we deal with all the time.

> Matt Stopford, Princess Patricia's Canadian Light Infantry,
> Croatia and Bosnia, December 1999 [19]

Less than one year after the end of the Gulf War Canada became involved in another operational mission, this time in Europe. From 1992 to 1995 Canadian soldiers were situated in the middle of an ongoing war in Bosnia — ostensibly to protect civilians of all ethnic groups. Simultaneously, they were assigned to keep an often-faltering peace in Croatia.

Neither mission worked out as planned. Croatia was supposed to be a traditional peacekeeping mission of the type so often engaged in during the cold war. A UN force was situated between the two belligerents (the Croats and ethnic Serbs) following fierce fighting in 1991. But for the Croats the cease-fire period was simply used as an opportunity to rearm and prepare for an all-out offensive that would push the Serbs out once and for all.

Jim Davis, a soldier who served in Bosnia and Croatia, reports that when the Canadians deployed to Croatia only a traditional peacekeeping mission was anticipated:

[From the first day] everybody sort of got in that Cyprus frame of mind and they went out to their various little camps — we had three main camps at that point. And they set up. They lined their vehicles up like they're on a parade square back in Canada. They lined up their little pup tents that the troops were sleeping in, the kitchen set up and there was a little mess tent where the guys could have some pop and chips ... No machine guns sighted, there were no trenches dug, there was no defensive work whatsoever. The vehicles were locked up, the weapons were put away. Nobody had any ammunition.

152

It was soon apparent just how tenuous the cease-fire was. Davis reports how the Croatians wasted no time in testing the Canadians by shelling their positions. They began by slowly "walking" mortar rounds toward the Canadian headquarters encampment, first at one kilometre ... then 800 metres ... then 500 metres ... then 100 metres ... and then right on top of the Canadian position. Davis adds:

> It [was] just pandemonium ... There's no place to hide, there's no trenches to dive into ... the guys were all running around. Of course the only hard shelter there was, which was the vehicles, the big armoured personnel carriers but they were locked up so all the guys ran to them and then they couldn't get the doors open because our normal Canadian standing operating procedure says you lock them up ... And a couple of guys, you know, climbed up on the vehicles because you had to get on top to unlock the driver's hatch to get down to drop the ramp so the guys could get in. And the bombs are going off and the guys are getting blown off the carriers, a couple of minor wounds there ... it was absolute chaos ....[20]

Other Canadian infantry companies in the area were being hit simultaneously with mortar and heavy artillery fire. It was a co-ordinated attack for the purpose of intimidating the Canadians right from the outset.

Canadian troops had been dropped into an active theatre of war with little in the way of adequate preparation or effective support. Since Canada had no aircraft carrier–based air power or amphibious capability, when Canadian troops came under serious attack they could not be reinforced, withdrawn or supported by national means.

The "cease-fire" between Croats and Serbs was tenuous and broke down on several occasions. In September 1993 Canadian troops fought pitched battles against the Croatian army at the "Medak Pocket." On that occasion the Croats pushed across the cease-fire line in what was known as Sector South. The Canadians were ordered into the area to supervise the restoration of the cease-fire line to where it had been prior to the Croat offensive. But the Croats weren't anxious to give up what they had won, not least because they were also in the process of committing horrific atrocities against the Serb civilian population. The result was steady fighting between Canadian and Croatian troops over a four-day period.

Fortunately Canadian casualties at Medak were light — only four wounded. Croat casualties were significantly higher. The Croats finally withdrew after they completed the grizzly process of removing the bodies of murdered civilians from the area. According to the report submitted by the Canadian commander, Colonel Jim Calvin, to the UN:

> A total of 164 homes and 148 barns and outbuildings were destroyed. This comprised every single building in the Medak Pocket. Nothing was spared ... As of the submission of this report, 16 bodies had been found in the area ... Particularly alarming is the large number of surgical gloves that were found scattered throughout the Pocket. These numbered in the hundreds. Speculation is that they were used to manhandle bodies in a large evacuation process ....[21]

The atrocities committed were horrific, and these would have a serious effect on the Canadians who witnessed the aftermath.[22] One might have expected the commander of Croatian forces at Medak to be indicted and tried as a war criminal. Instead, Canadians would meet him again, this time as an ally. By 1999 General Agim Ceku was commanding KLA forces in Kosovo in their battles against the Serbs.

Despite the successful action by Canadian troops, National Defence Headquarters was anxious to keep events quiet, both to avoid embarrassing questions in the middle of the federal election campaign and so as not to draw attention to the fact that Canadian troops in the Balkans were engaged in operations that went far beyond traditional peacekeeping.[23]

For such operations, the equipment and support available to Canadian Forces were inadequate. The army's M-113 armoured personnel carriers were reported to be regularly breaking down. Likewise, no tanks were deployed with Canadian troops. There was little in the way of offshore support available to back up or evacuate Canadian troops in the event of serious combat. The last Canadian CF-18s had been evacuated from Europe when Canada closed its air bases in Germany in 1992–93. In the event of a serious attack on Canadian Forces in Croatia, the plan was simply for troops in the northern part of the country to abandon their supplies and equipment, get in their APCs and try to drive to Hungary, several hundred kilometres away. It is anyone's guess how the troops in southern Croatia, who fought at Medak, would have coped in the event that combat with the Croatians continued beyond a few days.

Parliamentarians were for the most part totally unaware of many of the specific threats that Canadians faced on a day-to-day basis. But they should certainly have been aware of the serious equipment and support problems confronted by Canadian soldiers. However, even for those MPs who were aware, there was next to nothing they could do in the face of a government determined to chop the defence budget. Indeed, between 1993 and 1999 Canadian defence spending was cut by 30 percent in real terms. Equipment problems multiplied and Canadian troops simply had to soldier on as best they could.

Canada's role in Croatia ended ignominiously in August 1995 when the Croats assaulted the ethnic Serb enclave in an all-out attack. Canadian and other UN troops were simply pushed aside by the Croatian army as it advanced into the Krajina, putting hundreds of thousands of Serb civilians to flight. Canadian military posts were either bypassed or captured, with large numbers of Canadian troops being led into custody with guns to their heads. Canadians could provide little protection to those Serb civilians who remained behind, and many were liquidated by Croatian death squads.[24]

Bosnia: Breaking Faith with the Armed Forces

"Where we do know that an attack has come from one side or another [on our forces], [we] make a protest through the United Nations."

Defence Minister David Collenette, House of Commons, October 21, 1994

Canada's involvement in Bosnia was an extension of its mission in Croatia. Under pressure to "do something" when the war broke out in that country in March/April 1992, the UN received the agreement of the Serbs and Muslims to take control of the airport at Sarajevo in order to provide humanitarian assistance to local civilians.

The mission in Bosnia was announced by External Affairs Minister Barbara McDougall on June 10, 1992, in the House of Commons. This doubled the number of Canadian troops in the former Yugoslavia from about 1,200 to more than 2,000 — half in Croatia and half in Bosnia. There was no debate in the House of Commons on a deployment that was later described by Major-General MacKenzie as our most dangerous operation since Korea. The condition of the Canadian army notwithstanding, it was a mission that no party in the House of Commons opposed — indeed, both the opposition Liberals and New Democrats actually pressed for Canada to put troops on the ground. "When is Canada going to stand up against the outright aggression of Serbia in that region?" Lloyd Axworthy asked the minister on May 12.[25] The minister herself had claimed, on June 10, that this mission would ensure that Canada remained at the forefront of the "movement toward global peace."[26]

The Canadian decision to become militarily involved in Bosnia was directly linked to Major-General MacKenzie's role as the prospective UN commander in Sarajevo. General MacKenzie, who was then deputy commander of UN forces in the Balkans, lobbied for a Canadian battalion to be sent to Sarajevo to take on the airport security role. On June 6 MacKenzie told his superior, Indian general Satish Nambiar, that the UN should set up a command in Sarajevo with himself as the commander. He argued that a Canadian battalion would be the only unit suitable for deployment to the city since "no nation I know would allow one of their units to go to Sarajevo unless one of their officers was in charge of the operation."

When General Nambiar balked at this, MacKenzie told him in that case the Canadian battalion would be unavailable. Nambiar responded that he didn't believe him, so MacKenzie said that he would confirm it. He left and went to his own office, lit a cigarette and called no one. When he returned five minutes later, he told Nambiar, "Sorry sir, I was right. The CDS said that there is very little chance that the Canadian government will authorize the involvement of the Canadian battalion in Sarajevo unless I'm placed in charge." Nambiar then agreed and General MacKenzie reports:

> I cranked off two quick messages to New York and my own National Defence Headquarters in Ottawa with our proposal. Then I sent a warning order to [Lt. Col] Michel Jones of the Van Doos to report to our headquarters the following day with his

reconnaissance group, ready to proceed directly to Sarajevo on short notice. The main body of the battalion would follow only after the Security Council was satisfied that the whole operation was viable.[27]

Given that MacKenzie's warning order to the Canadian battalion was issued prior to any consideration of the matter in Ottawa, and since MacKenzie states that "the main body of the battalion would follow only after the *Security Council* was satisfied that the whole operation was viable," [emphasis added] there was apparently no expectation that the Canadian government would offer any objections.

There is certainly no indication that any serious debate or discussion took place in Ottawa at the political level about this deployment. Indeed, Minister McDougall's announcement in the House of Commons on June 10 came just four days after MacKenzie's discussions with General Nambiar, indicating that Ottawa was only too anxious to facilitate the mission going ahead.

Canada was seen by the government to be in the "peacekeeping business" and this was the highest profile peacekeeping mission going. While General MacKenzie was wearing his "UN hat" and was anxious to carry out his mission using the troops with which he was the most familiar and in which he had the most confidence (his own), the Canadian government seemed to be largely thinking about the public relations value of the mission (of being at the forefront of the "movement toward global peace," for instance). The potential dangers of the mission and the tangible interests that Canada had in Sarajevo, or in Bosnia for that matter, seemed to have been largely outside the realm of discussion.

Canadian troops deployed in Bosnia were extremely vulnerable. The first Canadian contingent, made up of troops from the Royal 22nd Regiment (the Van Doos) and the Royal Canadian Regiment (RCR), deployed into Bosnia on June 29. It was exclusively an infantry force, with no heavy armour and no artillery. The heaviest pieces of equipment deployed were the M-113 APCs, some of which were at least equipped with TOW anti-tank missiles.

Parliament failed to consider any of these factors prior to the entry of Canadian troops into Bosnia. Only four questions had been asked of the government by the opposition from the outbreak of fighting in Bosnia in March/April to the entry of Canadian troops, and none of these focused on the problems likely to be encountered.[28] It was only on September 15, 1992, 10 weeks after the deployment, that the House of Commons Foreign Affairs Committee even considered the issue of Bosnia — and then for only 90 minutes.

On that day, Lloyd Axworthy finally questioned External Affairs Minister Barbara McDougall on the matter of air support for Canadian troops. He suggested to McDougall:

> We should have a more open parliamentary system for review-ing troop commitments like this because I think Canadians would like to know under what risk we're putting our troops. Are they going to be properly equipped to undertake not just small-arms retaliation if they're fired upon but the heavy armoured equipment to break through blockades on roads? Why do they not have air cover? Why are we sending our troops in to cover convoys and move into dangerous areas without proper air cover to go along with them?[29]

The government could not provide military capability that it did not possess, and Minister McDougall gave the type of response that Mr. Axworthy would himself give a few years later when he was in government:

> The people we've sent will be well equipped and well trained. The Canadians are the best trained, and this is coming out more and more as we see other countries, particularly other big powers, entering into this peacekeeping exercise. Canadians are the best trained, particularly at the decision-making level. They get the best response, and are well equipped to do what they do as peacekeepers ...
>
> There is another action we could take aside from air cover. For example, if diplomatic persuasion does not work, then we could establish a no-fly zone. Once again, that is something else that has not been ruled out. However, we want to be careful about escalating or providing opportunities for confrontation if we think the discussions are getting somewhere.[30]

For most of the rest of the conflict, the availability of air power and other support to troops on the ground was an ongoing problem. Even after January 1994, when NATO became more involved in the conflict, the UN chain of command had great trouble assuring its peacekeepers credible air cover on a timely basis. With such intermittent support, bombing could do more harm than good and often provoked Serb (for the Serbs were the only targets for NATO air strikes) retaliation against peacekeepers on the ground.

There were a multitude of everyday "low-level" threats associated with being present in a war zone — mines, getting caught in crossfires and being deliberately targeted by one side or the other. Corporal Jordie Yeo was a Canadian who experienced the latter threat when he was wounded around one of the UN "safe areas," Srebrenica, in September 1993.[31] Canadians had been given the impossible task of protecting that area with just 170 peacekeepers. Yeo, a reservist from Montreal, had volunteered to serve in Bosnia. He was on foot patrol around Srebrenica when he was hit in a grenade attack. He was lucky in that he survived. Others did not.[32]

Corporal Daniel Gunther was one of the less fortunate. He was sliced in half by a Serb anti-tank rocket near Sarajevo in June 1993. Although the attack had been described in the "Significant Incident" report as "a deliberate attack," the press release in Ottawa announcing Corporal Gunther's death implied that it was accidental — the result of a mortar shell landing 20 metres away. The press release sanitized the story, probably in an effort to avoid embarrassing Defence Minister Kim Campbell, then in the middle of the Tory leadership race. Campbell was never told of the real circumstances surrounding Gunther's death.[33]

As terrible as these instances were, they could have been much worse. In December 1993, for instance, 11 Canadian soldiers serving with the 12th Armoured Regiment were captured by Serb forces, punched, kicked, hit with rifle butts and threatened with death. In the style of a mock execution, shots were fired at them. This incident is scarily similar to the murder of 10 Belgian soldiers captured in Rwanda in the following year. That event caused the Belgian government to withdraw its troops from that UN mission, with the surviving Belgian soldiers symbolically cutting up their blue UN berets as they left the country.

The mock execution incident occurred only two weeks after the Liberals took office in 1993. When the facts came to light (after a story in the *New York Times* rather than in the Canadian media) the new prime minister, Jean Chrétien, hinted that Canada might withdraw from Bosnia. Within two days, however, after a meeting with British prime minister John Major, Chrétien stated that Canada would not cut and run. While he tried to claim that the government would not make a final decision until after a parliamentary debate on January 25, in actual fact the decision had already been made.

The prime minister had found out how restricted his options were and how limited Canada's influence was at NATO. From January 1994, as NATO became more involved in the conflict against Serb forces, the hostility of the Serbs against peacekeepers from NATO countries increased. NATO involvement had been precipitated by a mortar attack on a Sarajevo market on February 5, 1994, in which many civilians were killed. But several foreign experts, including Canadian officers, were convinced that the Muslim government dropped both the February 5 and the subsequent August 28, 1995, bombs on its own citizens in order to gain international support. The latter attack opened the way to full-scale NATO intervention in the fall of 1995.[34]

Canada tried, but did not have the influence, to arrest NATO's growing air role. The countries most strongly in favour of intervention in Bosnia were those that did not have troops on the ground — the United States and Germany. Parliament, in the meanwhile, remained largely ignorant and uninvolved. It was clear in 1995 that Canada had been out of the loop in the decision-making process leading to these strikes. Pursuant to a question from Reform member Monte Solberg, Defence Minister Collenette admitted on May 30 that "if such air attacks as were deployed last week were to be used again, we would prefer some modification to the approval process so that Canada would certainly be part of that decision in a more formal sense."[35]

In May 1995, 370 UN soldiers, including 55 Canadians, fell into Serb hands after NATO launched air strikes. One of these men was Captain Patrick Rechner of Vancouver, who was chained to a lamp post near a Serb ammunition dump. The world media was then invited to photograph him to illustrate the point that further NATO air strikes would mean the death of the UN hostages. Fortunately Canadians were able to dodge another bullet as the crisis was successfully resolved. Canadian and UN troops were finally pulled out of their vulnerable outposts.

Canadian efforts to downplay the seriousness of this situation were in marked contrast to U.S. actions when an American fighter was shot down over Bosnia on June 2 and the pilot was reported missing.

President Clinton immediately held a news conference on the issue. Congress, the administration and the media began to devote their full attention to the situation. In spinning the Canadian government's ability to shut out Parliament and the public, one former Ottawa bureaucrat claimed that "it helps ... to have a relatively sophisticated news media that understands our people are not in imminent danger and that negotiations can and will work, and that isn't breaking into TV programs with hourly updates on the 'Hostage Crisis Day Six' or whatever."[36]

Of course Canadian soldiers *were* in imminent danger. In fact, they were in imminent danger throughout the Bosnian war. Eleven Canadians were killed in the Balkans between 1992 and 1995, and over 100 were wounded. These casualties could easily have been much higher.[37] In most of these "Significant Incidents," the reaction of DND public affairs officers was the same — keep the story out of the press and make sure parliamentarians don't find out. They apparently feared that if Canadians knew the full story of the dangers facing their troops in Bosnia and the deplorable condition of their equipment, they might be recalled. And they might have been right. But their efforts to use the Canadian engagement in the Balkans as a way to get more money for the Canadian Forces were never successful. Indeed, throughout the entire period from 1992–95 the defence budget continued to fall. Equipment remained unreplaced and soldiers in the field struggled to do their jobs as best they could.

And where was Parliament during all this? Certainly parliamentarians were quite visible at some of the moments of highest drama, such as when Canadian soldiers were being held hostage in front of the world television cameras in the spring of 1995 or when there were major escalations in the fighting. But MPs remained irrelevant to the actual making of Canadian policy. Despite the best efforts of some, they were unable to play any role in addressing the funding crisis that afflicted the Canadian Forces.

The first parliamentary debate on Yugoslavia took place in November 1991, before Canadian troops were committed to the Croatian mission. It wasn't much of a debate, however, since only one question was asked of External Affairs Minister Barbara McDougall throughout the entire discussion. The possible deployment of Canadian troops was also not discussed in any detail since the parameters of a possible UN mission were not yet known. But the "debate" did at least provide the parties with the opportunity to put their "perspectives" on the record. These universally lamented the situation in Yugoslavia, while the opposition called on the government to "show leadership."

Questioning of the government in the House during the three years of the Bosnian war followed the usual pattern. There were long periods in which no questions were posed, followed by a frenzy of questioning whenever the news was especially bad. After 1993 only the Reform Party consistently asked about Canadian military preparedness. By November 1994 Reform spokespeople were calling for a withdrawal of Canadian troops because their safety could not be adequately guaranteed.

From time to time parliamentarians heard from Canadians who had served, or were serving, in the Balkans. Major-General Lewis MacKenzie, Canada's UN commander, had pointed out on numerous occasions that all sides were guilty of atrocities. MacKenzie consistently reported that the Serbs were responsible for the majority of atrocities, but the Bosnian government and Croats also shared responsibility.[38] In 1994 the commander of the Lord Strathcona's Horse, Colonel Ray Wlasichuk, went over the heads of his superiors and wrote directly to his own MP, Stephen Harper, to correct the view that it was only the Serbs who were the aggressors in the war. In this case it was Bosnian forces, rather than Croatian or Serb soldiers, who had repeatedly attacked Canadian troops.

A warrant officer under Wlasichuk's command, Tom Martineau, had been wounded, and the colonel was outraged when he heard about the $50 million in aid Canada was giving to the Bosnian government exactly at the time when his men were being shot at by Bosnian troops. He complained that this was only the latest of 13 attacks on his battle group by Bosnian government forces. Mr. Harper raised the issue in the House while protecting Colonel Wlasichuk's identity, only to have Defence Minister David Collenette respond that "where we do know that an attack has come from one side or another, [we] make a protest through the United Nations." That was cold comfort indeed, but there was little more that a single MP could do.[39]

The best place for detailed consideration of the complex situation in Bosnia was in either the Foreign Affairs or the Defence committee. But there were no special hearings on the situation in Bosnia in either 1994 or 1995, and on those rare occasions when either the minister of foreign affairs or national defence would appear before committee to discuss the Estimates or other general matters, only a few questions would be asked about the Balkans. In April 1995, for instance, as the crisis in the Balkans was escalating, Defence Minister Collenette appeared before the Defence Committee. Only one MP, Jim Hart of Reform, asked any question at all on Yugoslavia. The Bloc's defence critic asked a number of questions on bilingualism in the Forces, but showed no interest at all in the situation confronting Canadian troops in Yugoslavia. He also asked the minister why he thought military morale was so low.[40]

Malaise in the Canadian military skyrocketed during the 1990s. Soldiers' needs were consistently ignored or were often swept under the carpet. Because of growing personnel shortages, soldiers who had never trained together were regularly cobbled together in ad hoc units hurriedly formed to meet commitment obligations. This patchwork approach to meeting commitments continued throughout the decade.

In the meantime the Forces were stigmatized by the Somalia scandal. Colonel Jim Calvin, who commanded Canadian troops at Medak in 1993, gives a sense of the atmosphere to which Canadian soldiers returned:

> When we came home in October of 1993 Somalia was just breaking ... the focus was all on what had happened with that particular tour, and not even the entire Somalia tour, just the bad part of that tour ... for the next two years that consumed most of the focus of the public's attention on the military. And all the other things that had happened, including our tour, were cast into the background.[41]

By not addressing the serious problems that had come to light during three years of operations in the Balkans, Canada's political leaders utterly failed in their responsibilities to the country's soldiers.

Zaire, 1996: "The Bungle in the Jungle"

> "Sometimes it is useful to raise our heads, clear our minds and see us as the world sees us."
>
> Prime Minister Jean Chrétien, House of Commons,
> November 18, 1996

In 1996 the Chrétien government decided to launch a military operation deep in the heart of Africa. Officially the military intervention in Zaire was launched unilaterally by the prime minister in response to news reports he had seen on television and based on reports filed by his nephew, Raymond Chrétien, who had been appointed as the UN special envoy to the Great Lakes region of central Africa.

Actually, the primary impetus for Canada to lead the force seems to have come from the Americans. In response to a growing refugee crisis in Zaire, the Clinton administration was facing pressure to take action. Given the quagmire that U.S. forces had fallen into in Somalia in 1993, where 18 U.S. soldiers were killed and a hundred wounded in the now famous Black Hawk Down operation, the Americans were unwilling to take the lead role in Zaire. Instead, on November 8 officials in the State Department telephoned their Canadian counterparts in the Department of Foreign Affairs to suggest that Canada take nominal leadership of the operation, which would still be heavily supported by the United States.[42]

With Canada front and centre the Americans could still pull the strings behind the scenes and reduce or increase their involvement as required. In a political sense it would also be easier to walk away from the mission if necessary. It is interesting that the Americans turned to Canada rather than to countries that were more capable militarily, such as the United Kingdom or France. In Canada the Americans found a political leadership only too willing to oblige. Within a day, with virtually no time devoted to weighing the pros and cons, the prime minister was all too ready to agree.

But the situation in central Africa was anything but straightforward. There were four foreign armies and about 10 militia groups from five different countries operating in Zaire in a conflict which emerged, in part, out of Rwanda's bloody civil war of 1994. That war had witnessed the slaughter of some one million people from the Tutsi ethnic group.

After that war the Tutsi-dominated Rwandan Patriotic Front assumed power. With the Tutsi now in control of the government, some 1.5 million to 2 million refugees (mostly Hutu) took refuge in neighbouring countries (mostly in Zaire). Among these refugees were the Hutu militias (the "Interahamwe") that perpetrated the massacres against the Tutsi in Rwanda in 1994.

In the two years that followed, the Rwandan government supported groups in Zaire (such as the Alliance for the Liberation of Zaire-Congo, or ADFL) that opposed that country's dictator, Mobuto Sese Seko. Zaire, in turn, repeatedly put pressure on the Rwandan Hutu refugees in Zaire to return to Rwanda. In October 1996 the ADFL began a military campaign (with Rwandan support) in northeastern Zaire against both the Hutu population in the refugee camps and the Zairian government.

On November 2 ADFL rebels and Rwandan forces captured the Zairian city of Goma. About one million Hutu refugees assembled in the Mugunga refugee camp (west of Goma) or fled into the hills. Food shortages and disease reached crisis proportions. The images of a people in peril were broadcast on television. On the weekend of November 9 Jean Chrétien watched these events with great concern. After a flurry of calls to various leaders, he decided to call ministers back to Ottawa and respond positively to American overtures: Canada would lead a military intervention in central Africa. As John Hay, a scholar who has studied Canadian policy in this crisis, records, this decision forced senior officials to assemble "all of [the Foreign Affairs Department's] rather scarce expertise on central Africa and military operations in the same enterprise."[43] For all but a few specialists in the government, the bloody conflicts of central Africa were remote and little understood.

The decision to lead the mission was taken and relayed to senior officials on November 9. They were ordered to prepare briefings and policy options for Sunday and Monday. On Sunday senior officials from Foreign Affairs and National Defence met with the prime minister and Lloyd Axworthy and were told Canada would lead the mission. The prime minister, according to Deputy Foreign Minister Gordon Smith, "had made his mind up when he walked in ... There was no holding him back." The deputy minister of national defence, Louise Frechette, and the acting chief of the defence staff, Admiral Larry Murray, were said to have left the meeting "shaking their heads and wearing expressions that others read as terror."[44]

They had good reason to be worried. Zaire was more than 12,000 kilometres from Canada as the crow might fly. The distance was even greater when one considered that aircraft would have to route, and be supported, through a series of airports along the way.

The Canadian air force had no heavy-lift transport aircraft. Its airlift capability was very modest — less than 40 medium-lift C-130, 707 and Airbus A-310 transport aircraft. Normal maintenance on about 25 percent of these aircraft would reduce available numbers even further.

Canada had no overseas bases to provide support to an intervention operation. It had no national intelligence capability and, as noted above, little expertise of any kind on central Africa, especially as it concerned the particulars of the military conflict in northern Zaire. It had no strategic or tactical reconnaissance capability to adequately assess the situation on the ground. The conflict region was well over 1,000 kilometres from the closest ocean. So even if the Canadian navy had possessed a credible offshore support capability, which it did not, it would have been impossible to support Canadian troops from the sea.

Even had the logistics situation been different, the Canadian army itself had no rapid deployment force suited for jungle/tropical operations. The Airborne Regiment had been disbanded the previous year. Operations in that region of Africa would have required good tactical mobility, but the army had neither heavy-lift transport helicopters nor attack helicopters.

In reality the very idea of Canadian command and control of such a mission was ludicrous. But, apparently, nobody decided to end his or her career by telling the prime minister this. The prime minister explained his motivation to the House of Commons on November 18:

> We acted because deeply ingrained in our very being as Canadians is a clear and basic understanding that we are citizens of the world, that we take that citizenship very seriously and that when it is time to stand up and be counted, Canada is there.
>
> Sometimes it is useful to raise our heads, clear our minds and see us as the world sees us ... a new world nation, without the burdens of history that weigh so many nations down ... a diverse bilingual country that knows the importance of accommodation and understanding ...
>
> We are not entering into combat with an enemy. Our only enemy is human suffering. Our only foe is hunger and disease. Our only adversary is pain and misery.
>
> We have already won an early battle against moral blindness and self-interest by galvanizing the world community into action.[45]

All these words notwithstanding, the military capability to do what the prime minister demanded did not exist. The only way to make the mission work was if American support could be sustained. On November 12 senior Canadian officials travelled to Washington to discuss the mission with their U.S. counterparts. David Meren, who has studied prime ministerial diplomacy, reports that details of the mission were "being worked out literally on the back of an envelope on the plane down to Washington."[46]

A lengthy series of meetings was held at the White House, chaired by U.S. national security advisor Tony Lake. Canadian officials recall that the meeting involved several hours of uncomfortable grilling on the details of the Canadian proposals. The Americans wanted firm answers on how exactly this mission was to be accomplished and what exactly the objectives would be on the ground. Divisions in the U.S. national security leadership were clearly evident. Within a few days U.S. defense secretary William Perry told the press that the U.S. army "is not the Salvation Army."[47]

On November 13, following a telephone conversation between Chrétien and President Clinton, it was announced in Washington, albeit in very guarded language, that "the United States is willing, in principle, to participate in a limited fashion in this mission under certain conditions."[48] Six conditions to be exact, including a dominant role for U.S. forces. Although this public support was tenuous, it allowed the UN Security Council to pass Resolution 1080 on November 15, calling for the creation of a multinational force for Zaire.

To some the situation for refugees on the ground seemed to be changing for the better. Already, on November 20, the U.S. scaled back its involvement on the ground to less than 1,000 troops. Thereafter, negotiations were held with potential participating countries at the U.S. air base in Stuttgart, Germany, to iron out the nature of each country's involvement. It turned out that no country except Canada was willing to commit to anything.

According to one participant, "Clearly the instructions that were given by the various countries to their militaries were, 'Be involved in the discussions, find out what's going on, but don't commit yourself to anything.'" This angered many of the Canadians involved: "Bullshit," one senior Canadian official retorted, "we're the only ones there. If this is so goddamn important, where are you all?"[49] He may have answered his own question.

Indeed, Canadians were already on the ground. Virtually all of Canada's airlift resources that weren't in repair had already been committed, including 20 C-130s, two 707s and four Airbus aircraft. In addition, one Antonov heavy-lift aircraft had been rented from Russia. These aircraft were operating over an "air bridge," first to Britain, then to Crete, Djibouti, Nairobi, Kenya, and finally into the conflict zone. Due to a shortage of technical support personnel, staff from Canadian Airlines had to be hired on contract.

However, the first 34 Canadians sent to Africa ran straight into trouble. Having landed in Rwanda, they were immediately taken into custody by the local authorities. The next contingent of 117 Canadians had to divert to Entebbe, Uganda, to avoid similar trouble. At Entebbe the deployment was chaotic, with "an inappropriate mix of personnel on the ground ... without adequate communications to execute command, control and communications functions."[50] According to Major Phil Lancaster, who served on General Roméo Dallaire's staff in Rwanda and in central Africa during the Zaire mission, "It was clear that the people going in really didn't understand Africa. They understood Kosovo, they understood Europe ... but they didn't understand Africa ... We stumbled around like naive fools, it looked that way I'm sure in the eyes of the Rwandans. Our good intentions were wasted, absolutely wasted."[51]

Meanwhile, the situation on the ground was unclear. The numbers of refugees appeared to be declining, although reported numbers were fluctuating widely. Canada's deputy foreign minister reported around 600,000 refugees on November 20, while the Canadian special emissary to the region, Raymond Chrétien, estimated between 300,000 and 500,000 at about the same time. The U.S. commander on the ground, Major-General Edwin Smith, who had the most accurate intelligence, estimated only 175,000 — a figure that Lloyd Axworthy himself supported on November 17, when he said there were probably between 150,000 and 200,000 refugees.[52]

On the other hand, fighting was increasing — on November 21 the ADFL had ended its cease-fire. By the end of the month Zairian forces were also in combat with Ugandan troops. This seriously complicated the situation for any intervention force, especially the lightly armed Canadians who, more than ever, would be dependent on robust American support.

The Pentagon had always been dubious on this count and by November 25, after a meeting with Canada's new defence minister,

Doug Young, Defense Secretary Perry remarked that "at this stage there's been no definitive decision on whether or not there should be [a military deployment]." Axworthy was said to be "apoplectic" on learning of these remarks and Doug Young's general concurrence with them.[53]

In public, however, Axworthy's reaction was to spin the Zaire mission as a terrific success. On November 27, in response to a Bloc question in the House of Commons inquiring why the international community was totally incapable of acting, Axworthy responded (if in a somewhat annoyed tone):

> In case the honourable member did not notice, about 10 days ago over half a million refugees returned to Rwanda, which was the original purpose of the mission ... It may stretch the imagination of the honourable member but frankly if that was the objective of the mission and most of it has now been achieved, the question is what to do to ensure that it is completed ... There is no lack of political will. I will be glad to table my telephone bill in the House of Commons to show how much will we have been exercising in the last several days.[54]

In fact, there may still have been hundreds of thousands of refugees left in the jungle.[55] But politically Canada had lost international and especially American support for the operation. While Canada was able to get the international community to make sympathetic noises for a time, once the situation on the ground changed (even slightly and superficially) and international media attention shifted, support from other countries, especially from the United States, evaporated. While the mission in Zaire was terminated in December, the war in that country continued and expanded. It continues to this day.

The results of the Zaire mission were later reviewed in a "lessons learned" exercise in the Department of National Defence. The officer responsible for logistics commented that "while it may seem heresy, my professional opinion is that Canada should not accept a lead nation role in an operation of approximate or greater magnitude unless significant improvements are made to CF operational support." The officer responsible for planning concurred, saying, "The CF is simply not equipped to act as the lead member of a multinational force of such size and scope."[56]

In 1998 two foreign affairs and national defence bureaucrats published their own study of the Zaire mission in which they concluded:

> Canada did not have the influence to direct the MNF — Multi-National Force — in ways its "larger" partners did not want to go, nor could Canada effectively influence the parties on the ground ... Canada had few levers beyond moral suasion to pressure larger nations ... Almost all troop-contributing nations, including Canada, made the presence of U.S. ground forces a condition of their participation ... By taking the lead without contributing combat troops, Canada was in a weak military and political position.[57]

Although the government repeatedly heralded the Zaire mission as a major triumph, the facts are not supportive of this conclusion. In a way the government's public line is not surprising since Canada had for some time been pressing for the creation of a UN rapid reaction capability and had even produced a lengthy policy paper toward that end in September 1995.[58] But nothing had actually been done to establish any Canadian rapid reaction capability. To admit failure in Zaire would have made Canadian rhetoric at the UN even more hollow.

In launching the Zaire operation Lloyd Axworthy noted, "The lessons we acquired in our diplomatic, political and military textbooks on the cold war do not apply to the new situations ... We cannot use narrow national interests as an excuse for inaction or delay."[59] Throughout the exercise the lack of real capability and the risks posed to Canadian troops were simply not allowed to be an excuse for not acting.

In Parliament all parties were also anxious to show that they supported humanitarian intervention overseas. Given the fact that everything on the Hill is explained and justified in sound bites, it was probably seen to be too difficult to inject reality into a discussion in which the media and others were clambering for the government to take action. Indeed, the official Opposition Bloc Québécois was in the forefront even prior to the announcement of a Canadian mission, calling on the government to "do something" and "show leadership."[60]

The Reform Party appeared to be torn in its approach. But Jim Hart, the party's defence critic, argued that while the intentions of the government were noble, the mission goals were unclear and the mission proposal carelessly formulated. "This mission is falling apart," he said. "The government should just admit it and keep our people out of harm's way until we can clearly define a mission for them to accomplish." He reminded the House of the words of the former chief of defence staff, General Jean Boyle, when he said just a few months before, "If the government asked me to go into a high-intensity theatre with the equipment I have today, I would have to say I can't do it."[61] Mr. Hart might also have noted that the Zaire mission clearly violated all the criteria that the government had itself established for overseas missions in its own 1994 defence white paper.[62]

As out of step as the government may have been with its own criteria, none of the issues raised in Parliament mattered one way or the other to the actions of the government. With the media for the most part playing the role of uncritical cheerleaders, the government could push ahead with virtual impunity.

To his great credit, the Reform Party's foreign affairs critic, Bob Mills, introduced a private members' motion a few months later designed to at least open a discussion about enhancing the role of Parliament in the process of committing Canadian troops to overseas missions. But the principle behind the motion was rejected by the government, as was the very idea that decision making by the executive on such matters required any sort of oversight. Indeed, Canada's future foreign minister, Bill Graham, commented:

> The suggestions that unilateral decisions are being made behind closed doors have ignored the facts. Such assertions have no basis whatsoever in reality. The process, as it now exists, is one of the most open in the world. How many other countries have established Internet sites and conducted surveys to determine public support for involvement in peacekeeping missions?[63]

Certainly the initial decision to lead an intervention in Africa was not discussed in Cabinet or in Parliament. Instead, it was agreed to and pushed by the prime minister and discussed in very limited consultation with Lloyd Axworthy, Raymond Chrétien, Minister for International Co-operation Don Boudria and Doug Young. Raymond Chrétien later reported that he never recommended Canadian leadership of a multinational force and would "never have imagined such a thing."[64] No real thought appears to have been given to the logistical and practical difficulties involved in deploying a military force to central Africa.

The prime minister and Lloyd Axworthy seemed totally oblivious to hard political and military realities on the ground in central Africa — namely to the growing and complex civil war in Zaire. Some of the key players in the region (notably Zaire and its main backer, France) supported a multinational force primarily to stabilize the political situation to their advantage, while their opponents (the Rwandan government and the Zairian opposition movement) saw the possible deployment of a multinational force as thwarting their own objectives. The Americans, in turn, seemed to be looking for a naive party to take the heat off the issue of intervention. They found one. For the prime minister and the minister of foreign affairs, events in Zaire were reduced to the simplest interpretation.

The "Bungle in the Jungle" stands in sharp contrast to the successful mission that Canada launched at Suez 40 years earlier. Although parliamentary oversight was probably not much better in 1956 than it was in 1996, in 1956 Canada had a foreign minister who knew the limitations of Canadian power and who understood how to craft and build diplomatic support for his initiative. More importantly, Lester Pearson understood that diplomatic success had to be based on hard-power capability — and Canada had real military capability in 1956.

Parliament has the duty to ask the hard questions, but without any relevant role most of its members have not felt pressed to seriously inform themselves about the issues at hand. If Parliament had possessed real oversight responsibility and had the simultaneous ability to ask questions about the Zaire mission with some authority, then the mission might not have been entered into as lightly as it was.

This surely had been one of the key lessons of the Somalia debacle in 1992–93. In that case Canada had hurriedly deployed forces to that country, even though Canadian interests there were limited, Canadian military units were ill-prepared and Canadian knowledge of the Somali environment was limited.

The Somalia Commission of Inquiry (which was looking into events in Somalia as the abortive Zaire mission took place) concluded:

> The quintessential condition of control of military and all aspects of national defence is a vigilant Parliament …

Parliament must exercise greater diligence in critically monitoring the terms agreed to or set by the government for the employment of Canadian Forces overseas and safeguarding members of the Armed Forces from unreasonable risks; it must also monitor the operations of commanders and troops in the field.[65]

What the Somalia Commission may have missed is the fact that Parliament is simply incapable of acting in this way without significant reform. The Somalia report, which attacked the entire process of command and control of Canada's overseas missions, was also largely ignored by a government that felt it could afford to do so.

Dubious missions continue today. I recall visiting the Department of Foreign Affairs in the summer of 2001 and being told by one official that the recent mission in Ethiopia–Eritrea, which had involved deploying a token force of 550 soldiers to East Africa without any immediate national support available, had been undertaken primarily due to the political need perceived in the Department of Foreign Affairs to "do a mission in Africa."

Feelings of unease also prevailed in the Standing Committee on National Defence in January 2002, when that body was briefed on the mission that was to be undertaken by 750 Canadian Forces personnel in Afghanistan — a mission that made those troops entirely dependent on American forces in virtually every respect.

Lack of oversight means that the government can do what it likes in foreign and defence policy, even when it puts Canadian lives on the line without any serious constraint. The absence of any oversight is a consistent theme over the past 40 years. It is an approach that we can no longer afford.

NOTES

---

1. Canada, Parliament, House of Commons, *Debates*, Vol. 1 (April 25–May 5, 1989).
2. Major Jean Morin and Lt. Commander Richard Gimblett, *The Canadian Forces in the Persian Gulf: Operation Friction, 1990–1991* (Toronto: Dundurn Press, 1997) pp. 41–42.

3. Morin and Gimblett, pp. 204–05.

4. Morin and Gimblett, pp. 24–25.

5. Canada, Standing Senate Committee on Foreign Affairs, *Canada's Maritime Forces* (Ottawa: May 1983) p. 49. Report of the Sub-Committee on National Defence.

6. Edison Stewart, "Chrétien Stirs Metro Liberals with Plea for 'Give and Take,'" *The Toronto Star*, November 22, 1990, p. A4.

7. From September 24, when the House resumed sitting, until October 19, only three questions plus supplementaries were asked on the Gulf crisis. From October 22 to November 7 questions were asked on seven of 12 sitting days. From November 8 to December 3 questions were asked on all but one sitting day. Thereafter, until the House adjourned on December 19 only three question sets were asked. House of Commons, *Debates*,. Vols. 10–13 (September 24–December 19, 1990).

8. House of Commons, *Debates*, Vol. 11 (October 30, 1990) p. 14881.

9. House of Commons, *Debates*, Vol. 13 (January 17, 1991) p. 17198.

10. House of Commons, *Debates*, Vol. 13 (January 15, 1991) pp. 17026–17027.

11. House of Commons, *Debates*, Vol. 13 (January 15, 1991) p. 16993.

12. Geoffrey York, "Crisis in the Gulf: MPs Opposed to War Feel Uneasy," *The Globe and Mail*, January 19, 1991, p. A9.

13. Geoffrey York, "Canada Switches CF-18s to Offensive Role in Gulf," *The Globe and Mail*, February 21, 1991, p. A1.

14. Morin and Gimblett, pp. 173–175.

15. Morin and Gimblett, pp. 132–133. Sean Maloney asserts that analysis on the option of deploying a Canadian brigade began as early as September 14, when the British informally floated the idea of deploying a Canadian brigade to serve with the British division in the Gulf. Sean Maloney, *War without Battles: Canada's NATO Brigade in Germany, 1951–1993* (Toronto: McGraw-Hill Ryerson, 1997) p. 450.

16. David Leyton Brown, ed., *Canadian Annual Review of Politics and Public Affairs, 1991* (Toronto: University of Toronto Press, 1991) p. 122.

17. Admiral Thomas [interview]. Interview by Kitson Vincent and Rob Roy of Stornoway Productions, October 1994.

18. See, for instance, Canada, Senate Standing Committee on Foreign Affairs, *Meeting New Challenges: Canada's Response To A New Generation of Peacekeeping* (Ottawa: February, 1993).

19. Matt Stopford [interview]. Interview by Rob Roy of Stornoway Productions, December 30, 1999.

20. Jim Davis [interview]. Interviewed by Rob Roy of Stornoway Productions, December 30, 1999.

21. Colonel Jim Calvin, *Report on Medak Pocket Operations, 15–21 September 1993* (October 31, 1993). Report from Colonel Jim Calvin, CANBAT 1.

22. Warrant Officer Matt Stopford describes finding women in the area who had been raped with hot pokers or tied to chairs and burned to death by Croatian forces. Matt Stopford [interview]. Interviewed by Rob Roy of Stornoway Productions, December 1999 and January 9, 2000.

23. See discussion in Scott Taylor and Brian Nolan, *Tested Mettle: Canada's Peacekeepers at War* (Ottawa: Esprit de Corps Books, 1998) pp. 123–143.

24. Taylor and Nolan, pp. 218–223.

25. House of Commons, *Debates*, Vol. 8 (May 12, 1992) p. 10589.

26. House of Commons, *Debates*, Vol. 9 (June 10, 1992) p. 11715.

27. MacKenzie notes that he had a later conversation with CDS General de Chastelain who "confirmed" that it would in fact be difficult for the Canadian government to agree to deploy a battalion to Sarajevo without a Canadian commander there. However, this is debatable given both the high profile of the Sarajevo mission internationally (especially after a surprise visit to Sarajevo by President Mitterrand of France on June 28) and the commitment of small Canadian contingents to international missions with foreign commanders before (Croatia) and since (Kosovo). Lewis MacKenzie, *Peacekeeper: The Road to Sarajevo* (Vancouver: Douglas & McIntyre, 1993) pp. 306–307.

28. The four occasions were May 12, May 13, May 21 and June 2, 1992.

29. Canada, Parliament, House of Commons, Standing Committee on External Affairs and International Trade, *Minutes of Proceedings and Evidence* (September 15, 1992). Section 41:15.

30. House of Commons. Standing Committee on External Affairs and International Trade, *Minutes of Proceedings and Evidence* (September 15, 1992). Section 41:16.

31. Two years later Serb forces finally overran Srebrenica, which was then being "guarded" by Dutch peacekeepers. Several thousand Muslim men are believed to have been subsequently shot by the Serbs.

32. Yeo's treatment at the hands of the DND bureaucracy when he came home was shameful. Despite being wounded in action, Yeo, a part-time militiaman, had his pay revoked because he was no longer on active duty. Jordie Yeo [interview]. Interviewed by Rob Roy of Stornoway Productions, December 1999. See also Taylor and Nolan, p. 238.

33. Taylor and Nolan, pp. 118–121.

34. Colonel John Stray, *Selling the Bosnian Myth to America: Buyer Beware* (Leavenworth, Kansas: Foreign Military Studies Office, October 1995); David Binder, "Bosnia's Bombers," *The Nation*, October 2, 1995.

35. House of Commons, *Debates*, Vol. 11 (May 30, 1995) p. 13008.

36. Jeff Sallot, "Why Ottawa's Keeping Its Cool; What Crisis?" *The Globe and Mail*, June 6, 1995, p. A12.

37. All told, 213 UN soldiers were killed from 1992–95 and more than 1,700 were wounded. Cited by Alex Moens and Lenard Cohen, "Learning the Lessons of UNPROFOR: Canadian Peacekeeping in the Former Yugoslavia," *Canadian Foreign Policy*, 6 (Winter 1999) pp. 85–102.

38. Canada, Parliament, House of Commons, Standing Committee on National Defence and Veterans Affairs, M*inutes of Proceedings and Evidence* (February 18, 1993), p. 8.

39. Colonel Ray Wlasichuk [interview]. Interviewed by Rob Roy of Stornoway Productions, December 28, 1999; House of Commons, *Debates*, Vol. 6 (October 21, 1994) p. 7037.

40. House of Commons, Standing Committee on National Defence and Veterans Affairs, *Minutes of Proceedings and Evidence*, Meeting 21 (April 25, 1995) p. 20.

41. Colonel Jim Calvin [interview]. Interviewed by Rob Roy of Stornoway Productions, December, 1999.

42. CBC Television 's *Fifth Estate* (November 18, 1997); Gordon Smith, former deputy minister of foreign affairs [interview]. Interviewed by Rob Roy of Stornoway Productions, October 2001.

43. John B. Hay, *Conditions of Influence: A Canadian Case Study in the Diplomacy of Intervention*, Occasional Paper No. 19 (Ottawa: Norman Patterson School of International Affairs, 1999) p. 9.

44. Hay, p. 9.

45. House of Commons, *Debates*, Vol. 5 (November 18, 1996) pp. 6380–6381.

46. David Meren [interview]. Interviewed by Rob Roy of Stornoway Productions, June 2001. Mr. Meren completed his master's thesis on prime ministerial interventions in foreign policy at Carleton University.

47. Hay, p. 20.

48. Hay, pp. 15–16.

49. Hay, p. 23.

50. Canada, Department of National Defence, *Lessons Learned Questionnaire: Operation Assurance* [internal study], November 1997.

51. Major (Ret.) Phil Lancaster [interview]. Interviewed by Rob Roy of Stornoway Productions.

52. Hugh Winsor, "Military Mission to Zaire on Hold," *The Globe and Mail*, November 18, 1996, p. A1; Paul Knox, Graham Fraser, Anne McIlroy, Jeff Sallot and Hugh Winsor, "Commitment Fades for Aid Mission," *The Globe and Mail*, November 20, 1996, p. A1; Brian Milner, "Mandate in Africa Muddied," *The Globe and Mail*, November 21, 1996, p. A1.

53. Hay, p. 24.

54. House of Commons, *Debates*, Vol. 6 (November 27, 1996) p. 6791.

55. CBC Television's *Fifth Estate* [television program], November 18, 1997.

56. Department of National Defence, *Lessons Learned Questionnaire: Operation Assurance* [internal study], November 1997.

57. James Appathurai and Ralph Lysyshyn, "Lessons Learned from the Zaire Mission," *Canadian Foreign Policy*, 5, No. 2 (Winter 1998), pp. 93–105.

58. Canada, Department of Foreign Affairs and Department of National Defence, *Towards a Rapid Reaction Capability for the United Nations* (Ottawa: September 1995).

59. House of Commons, *Debates*, Vol. 5 (November 18, 1996) p. 6346.

60. See, for instance, questions asked by the Bloc in the House of Commons. House of Commons *Debates*, Vol. 5 (November 5, 6 and 8, 1996) pp. 6130, 6184, 6311.

61. House of Commons, *Debates*, Vol. 5 (November 18, 1996) p. 6382.

62. Department of National Defence, *Defence White Paper 1994* (Ottawa: Department of National Defence, 1994) p. 29.

63. House of Commons, *Debates*, Vol. 8 (March 12, 1997) p. 8981.

64. Hay, p. 7.

65. Canada, The Somalia Commission of Inquiry, *Dishonoured Legacy, The Lessons of the Somalia Affair,* Executive Summary (Ottawa: Minister of Public Works and Government Services Canada, 1997) p. ES–46. Report of the Commission of Inquiry into the deployment of Canadian Forces to Somalia.

CHAPTER SEVEN

Myth and Reality in Canadian Government

"The proper office of representative assembly is to watch and control the government."

John Stuart Mill,
Considerations on Representative Government, 1861

The theory of responsible government holds that the executive — the prime minister and Cabinet — is responsible to the legislature. The theory is that executive action and policy making must have the confidence of the legislature; that the executive governs at the pleasure of the legislature; and that it is incumbent upon government to ensure that its policies and budget proposals have the support of a majority of members of the legislature.

This is certainly the impression that most members of Parliament seek to convey. In 2001 the Library of Parliament produced a householder for MPs to use and distribute to their constituents. It included the claim that "the Commons makes decisions on spending public money and imposing taxes … When you fly in an airplane, visit a national park or buy a product in a store, you are doing something that has been touched by a law made in Parliament."[1]

In another parliamentary publication, the following statement is made about the supposed role of Parliament in the making of Canadian foreign policy:

> Parliament still plays a vital role. Key officials, such as the prime minister, the minister of foreign affairs and international trade and other members of the executive, are directly accountable to Parliament ... Any changes to Canadian law that may be necessary to implement Canada's treaty commitments must be approved by Parliament in legislation. Finally, Parliament can ultimately grant or withhold funds and confidence from the government.[2]

Many academics make similar assertions. Commenting on the issue of defence oversight in a report commissioned by the minister of national defence in 1997, Laval University professor Albert Legault claimed,

> "The House and the Senate ... have a role to play in formulating defence policy. The House controls one of the most vital defence functions because it disposes of the government budget and approves on an annual basis the National Defence Estimates ... In the area of defence, it has never happened — to our knowledge — that a House or Senate report has been neglected by the executive."[3]

All of this is virtually complete myth. In nearly four years on the Hill, I have never seen the House or the Senate come close to playing any such role in influencing the activities of the government — particularly in foreign and defence policy. It may be that individual government MPs, working with particular interests groups, may exercise influence from time to time, but neither the House as a whole nor its component committees do. Every aspect of parliamentary activity is so tightly controlled by a majority government that Parliament has no independent role of its own.

Many point to Question Period as the most important tool available to the opposition in exercising oversight over the activities of government.

The traditional view is that Question Period is an important symbol of government's responsibility to Parliament. For instance, in *The Canadian Polity*, Ronald Landes argues:

> Although the government is rarely defeated in the legislature, it is, nonetheless, kept from doing everything its little heart desires. Probably the best check against government pigheadedness, incompetence or downright malfeasance is the oral Question Period in the Commons. When the House is in session, the opposition members, or once in a while a brave government backbencher, can challenge the government over its past, present or projected behaviour. Since the government ministers do not know what the questions will be, the opposition attempts to embarrass them over policy, patronage or corruption.[4]

First of all, in my time on the Hill I have never seen any government backbencher seriously challenge the government during Question Period. Questions from government members are usually planted and don't even serve the purpose of allowing the government to highlight its policies — for no one is listening to those questions and answers. Instead, they exist exclusively to allow Liberal backbenchers the opportunity to demonstrate to constituents back home that they have spoken in the House and, more importantly, to take time away from opposition questions.

Second, the process of Question Period is so politicized that it has very little value as real oversight. No independent observer takes the process terribly seriously. As discussed in Chapter 1, questions and answers are strictly limited to 35 seconds each. The purpose of the questions is as much to embarrass the government as it is to hold it to account. This distinction is important. The tendency on every issue is to try to make the government look bad. It is rarely designed to get at the facts of an issue. And it is NEVER supposed to allow the government to point to any successes it might have had.

Similarly, government responses are not designed to answer the question posed. The purposes of the answers, like the questions, are to capture the 10-second sound bites on television. Thus, both questions and answers in Question Period are entirely spin oriented. While an opposition party like Reform came to Ottawa to do things differently, MPs soon found the pull of the system too great to resist. Most of the parliamentary press corps is uninterested in reporting questions that don't seem to have immediate appeal for their listeners, readers or viewers. MPs who have no power other than to attract press attention soon try to dance to the media's tune.

In my time on the Hill I have worked on what is called Question Period preparation. An MP from caucus, supported by a Question Period co-ordinator, leads the process. Every day at 8:00 a.m., when Parliament is sitting, the "QP group" meets to discuss the morning's headlines. Someone reads the key headlines from a "Quick Scan" document which has been prepared very early that morning. The MP and the QP co-ordinator usually take the lead in determining which issues should be brought forward in Question Period.

Discussion on the selection of questions is short and is focused on the political mileage to be gained in asking the question. Favoured questions are those that are most likely to catch media attention. Humour is highly valued. The morning meetings are relatively short — about 30 minutes. After question topics are selected at the morning meeting, the process of writing begins, in time for the practice session taking place at 1:00 p.m. — about one hour prior to Question Period itself. MPs assigned to ask questions meet to rehearse and refine their questions. An effort is made to ensure that the news angle is clear and that each question has a media hook.

A similar process is followed in every opposition party. The process consumes at least half of the parliamentary day. This lengthy and laborious process occurs solely for the purpose of producing 35-second questions that aren't designed to get any serious answers. The daily ritual creates an atmosphere in which serious oversight is forgotten.

The process of generating answers to the questions asked is somewhat different. The government does not know which specific questions will be asked on a given day. But like opposition staffers, Liberal researchers, as well as staff in the ministers' offices or departmental officials, need only read the day's headlines. Talking points are prepared on key issues. Instant responses are written with "main messages" for the minister to use.

Many MPs know that Question Period is largely nonsensical. Some MPs use the time to answer letters or possibly to work on other material on their laptops. Clifford Lincoln, a back-bench Liberal MP, admitted to the press that he uses the time to sign letters and do crossword puzzles.[5]

Liberal MPs are required to show up to demonstrate their solidarity with the government. Those government MPs anxious for promotion will cheer and scream loudly as opposition members ask their questions. If a Liberal MP is "lucky," he or she will get a seat behind a government minister or even the prime minister and be seen on television by constituents. Opposition MPs, in turn, get chances to ask questions of key ministers, and possibly even the occasional question to the prime minister. Even if they can't question the prime minister, they can at least sit across the aisle and yell at him.

Since every question is asked in a confrontational and outraged tone, I believe that the public has numbed to the whole process. It is left with no ability to judge when an issue is serious and when it is not. This has destroyed the value of Question Period as an oversight mechanism. Paul Wells of the *National Post* expressed the frustration of many when he called Question Period "the biggest eyesore in the parliamentary day … Opposition MPs fire aimlessly, read like drones from prepared scripts or embark on endless fishing trips without even knowing what their own point is. Government ministers duck, pass tough questions to hapless subordinates or rag the puck until the paltry 35 seconds allotted for each answer has elapsed."[6]

In my experience the antics of Question Period actually bring Parliament itself into disrepute. The daily melodrama has ceased to have any purpose in an environment in which the answers given have no relation to the questions asked. Former British prime minister Harold Wilson is once reported to have said that "if Britain ever had a prime minister who did not fear questions, our parliamentary democracy would be in danger."[7] I would submit that Canada has long since passed that point.

Government vs. Opposition

The resources available to the government in any departmental area are immense. The partisan nature of Canadian politics means that the civil service is largely at the disposal of the party in power. In the defence sphere, this effectively arrays the minister of national defence and nearly 8,000 military and civilian personnel at National Defence Headquarters against an official Opposition defence critic and two staff members — the defence critic's own executive assistant and a researcher like me. If one were to add one or two deputy defence critics to the Opposition side and Library of Parliament staff members (who serve all parties), the total number of persons acting on the Opposition side is still less than 10.

In what might be termed an understatement, a leading authority on Canadian government, Donald Savoie, writes, "It is important to recognize that, when sitting in opposition, politicians have limited access to substantial policy advice." Savoie is also largely correct when he says:

> Opposition parties, and in particular the leader of the Opposition, have resources to hire staff. However, the staff, much like assistants in ministerial offices, are partisan, young and only in exceptional cases do they have experience in government. Their grasp of policy issues is superficial, and their purpose is less one of understanding the details of policy than to promote the partisan interests and electoral chances of their party or the member of Parliament they work for.[8]

Paradoxically, the 10 professional staff in the Opposition leader's office are both overtasked and underused. At one time I was the Opposition researcher for defence and Aboriginal affairs. Thus, I was responsible for analyzing the combined budgets of two departments totalling about $18 billion per year. When I dropped the Aboriginal portfolio in 2001 and took over foreign affairs and trade in addition to defence, I was covering about $14 billion in departmental spending in addition to theoretically monitoring trade issues with a value of about $600 billion. Needless to say, there was simply no way for one researcher to provide any serious oversight on the goings on in these areas.

On the other hand, the ad hoc and reactive culture of Parliament means that researchers are often not consulted on policy initiatives or on questions being asked in Parliament. There is great pressure to get instant reactions out and into the press in response to events. A failure to respond immediately and decisively likely means being left out of the day's story. Too often press releases from members' offices in all parties are written on the fly, with little or no consultation.

By way of contrast, ministers have almost infinite resources at their immediate disposal. Even though the concentration of political power in the PMO means that most ministers undertake few substantive policy initiatives during their term in office, their large staffs greatly assist them in the political spin game — Parliament's very raison d'être. In this regard each minister's personal office has a normal complement of about 12 staff members. The pay rates for ministerial staff are also considerably higher than for Parliament Hill staff, making it possible to attract people with greater experience.

The staff of the communications divisions of government departments are also heavily involved in the spin game. Effectively, they serve the governing party. Moreover, staff from all divisions and directorates may be called upon to write speeches for government members of Parliament. For example, within the Department of National Defence, the Directorate of Public Affairs is composed of about 100 staff. By way of contrast, the Directorate of Strategic Analysis, which is charged with providing the government with strategic assessments of challenges facing Canadian national security, has fewer than 10 professional staff.

One of the biggest problems with today's Department of National Defence is the extent to which the entire department, including the senior leadership of the Canadian Forces, has become politicized. Senior officers — particularly the chief of defence staff — who appear before committees are severely restricted in what they are able to say about the state of the Armed Forces and still keep their jobs. As the former vice-chief of defence staff Admiral Chuck Thomas commented, "There is a structure in the United States where military officers are called before … committees, they are expected to testify to their own experience … In Canada you are expected to speak within the policy that is stated by the minister … It needn't be like that."[9]

In addition to the skewed resources that favour the government, opposition parties face immense challenges in organizing themselves into a cohesive team to counter the government. Not only are staff resources for the opposition on the Hill limited, it is also often the case that politics, rather than expertise, is the decisive factor in selecting policy critics. "We need to give that guy something to do" is an oft-heard phrase when it comes to appointing MPs to critic roles. Generally the talent pool for both Cabinet ministers and opposition critics is sorely limited.

In every opposition party nearly every MP is given some policy area to critique, even though the particular individual concerned may have very limited expertise in that area. There are certainly those who have an impressive ability to master their designated policy file. But even for these MPs, the superficial nature of politics on the Hill limits the impact that they can expect to have. The strongly partisan nature of Canadian politics makes nuanced discussions — which probably more accurately reflect the complexity of most issues — rare. The partisan nature of politics and the fact that parties never have something good to say about one another probably make the public suspicious of much of what politicians have to say.

An MP who has been a policy critic in opposition is expected to also be a potential Cabinet minister when in government. A few have the ability to make the transition effectively, but many may have only known the artificial and superficial politics of Parliament Hill. Therefore, they end up being ill-equipped to effectively lead and manage their departments. In the present government this means that only a few of the 20 percent of Liberal MPs who are Cabinet ministers are policy leaders in the true sense of the word.

Donald Savoie has noted that the limited talent of many Cabinet ministers has reinforced the trend toward the centralization of power in Canada. He matter of factly points out that "advisors to Prime Ministers Trudeau, Mulroney and Chrétien all made the point that some ministers have to operate under a kind of receivership in that they can hardly be trusted to lead an important policy review or even an internal review of departmental programs". This means that the prime minister inevitably turns "to his most trusted ministers to assist in developing and implementing initiatives, leaving other ministers to protest if they dare."[10]

The PM vs. the Backbenchers
You may ask how it is that 135 Liberal backbenchers can be held in check by 37 Cabinet ministers, and how 36 members of Cabinet can be held in check by one prime minister. On the surface the answer appears relatively straightforward — the 135 backbenchers want to become Cabinet ministers and the 36 Cabinet members want to remain in their jobs.

But that really only tells part of the story. The larger question is how 135 backbenchers have for the most part tolerated a situation in which they are marginalized, ignored or bullied by the party leadership. Many protest quietly, but, at least until very recently, few have dared to do so publicly. Preston Manning was often fond of asking the Liberal backbenchers rhetorically, "There are more of you than there are of them. Why don't you do something?"

From the very outset of their political careers, MPs in the traditional parties have been brought to heel in a party system that does not tolerate dissent and that rewards unswerving loyalty. They learn that the way to advance is to toe the party line. Many have become engaged in politics because they love the political game and, thus, to step outside the norm, buck the trend and suffer the consequences becomes unthinkable.

This is one of the reasons why new parties that promised to change the system, like the New Democrats and the Reformers, were so loathed by the mainstream political parties when they arrived in Ottawa. They were committed to reforming the system. But the pull of the system is strong, and even for parties that have rejected the status quo, the pull toward compromise is a continuous one.

Nearly all observers of the Canadian parliamentary scene today recognize that Parliament has become completely dysfunctional. Journalists and academic analysts increasingly make comments illustrating that they see through the façade of Canada's supposedly democratic system. Thus, the legitimacy of the present system is slowly being destroyed. That would have been unthinkable even 20 years ago.

For instance, one political analyst, James Allan Evans, has commented that "Canadian politics is coming to resemble Mexico's before the election of Vincente Fox. The prime minister can decide when elections take place. He can dispense patronage at will. He appoints senators and Supreme Court justices and the governor general. He can reward supporters with great collops of taxpayers' money."[11]

Veteran journalist Jeffrey Simpson has stated that Canada's political system gives us an "elected dictatorship with few checks and balances." He has also noted that Parliament is "a talking shop. Its deliberative functions long ago atrophied; its legislative function is highly scripted ... a form of organized intellectual mendacity."[12]

The former editor of *Saturday Night*, John Fraser, wrote in 1993:

The yokels who loiter at their parliamentary desks behind the leader are powerless. Pierre Trudeau once labelled Canadian MPs "nobodies" the moment they were 50 yards from Parliament Hill. This was charitable. Our backbenchers are nobodies on or off the Hill ... Backbenchers in this country are so stripped of significance that the traditional necessity of appointing party whips to enforce parliamentary voting discipline seems ludicrously funny; circus seals honking their horns show more independence of thought and action.[13]

Eight years later things had changed little. If anything, they had become worse. In May 2001 former prime minister John Turner used the opportunity afforded by the unveiling of his portrait on Parliament Hill to urge Prime Minister Chrétien to "give these members a voice, let them speak their minds, let them speak their consciences and let them represent the interests of their constituents." Chrétien showed how completely he had missed the point when he later responded that Mr. Turner had been saying the same thing since 1964.[14]

Early in 2001 MPs had a rare opportunity to express their views on the issue of parliamentary reform. Only about 40 MPs (or 13 percent of the House membership) did so. The Canadian Alliance spoke strongly for parliamentary reform through its spokesperson, Scott Reid. Reid, who had only been elected to Parliament in 2000, is a former freelance journalist who has published several books on constitutional issues. He is also a long-time advocate of democratic reform. Thus, he approached the issue with a thorough knowledge of the subject matter.

The Canadian Alliance (and Reform before it) has championed the issue of democratic reform, and thus its position calling for the reform of Parliament was predictable. What was striking, however, was the willingness of some MPs from every other party to join in this call — at least as far as it extended to reforming the House of Commons itself. Most who spoke in favour of democratic reform did so from personal conviction. It is safe to say that most who opposed it did so on orders to defend the status quo.

What individual MPs had to offer was interesting. Bloc Québécois spokespeople suggested that Parliament could learn much from the Quebec National Assembly, where the opposition chairs half the committees of the legislature. Lorne Nystrom of the NDP, who had sat in the House in the late 1960s and early 1970s, stated, "We are the most handcuffed parliamentary system in the world. We model ourselves after the British Parliament. [But] it is common to have a bill defeated in the British House of Commons."[15] Joe Clark commented that it was civil servants rather than elected members of Parliament who ran the country. He also admitted that when he had been in office in the 1980s and early 1990s, his government too had "feared free votes too much."[16]

As I sat and watched the debate that evening, several Liberal MPs, in what were certainly career-limiting moves, also publicly expressed their own frustration. I was very impressed with the comments made by former Quebec Cabinet minister Clifford Lincoln:

> In the British House of Commons dissenting votes have been a significant fact of life for a long time. In the 1970s dissenting votes accounted for 25 percent of all voting divisions in the British Parliament. In the first session of 1983–87, when the Tories were in power, 62 divisions took place in which 137 Tory backbenchers cast a total of 416 votes against the government. Here that would be viewed as heresy because any type of expression that is contrary to the wish of the government is seen as disloyalty ...
>
> We should look at what the Finns do, what the Swedes do and what the Brits do. Then we could say that surely there must be a way to improve this place.[17]

Liberal MP Dennis Mills was even more blunt:

> To be brutally frank, and I say this to all members of the House, I am totally fed up with the current system. I am not fed up because it will make any difference to me personally. What bothers me is the contempt that the entire machinery of government has toward each and every member of the House of Commons. I do not care what party it is, it is contempt. Those are strong words but I stand by them.[18]

These comments, coming from such a diverse array of political perspectives, have to be taken seriously. They represent a consensus. The House of Commons is dysfunctional in its primary role of holding the government to account.

How then does the prime minister keep control? He does it because Parliament is dominated by a culture of subservience, patronage and punishment. It is a culture that has evolved over time, but it has also been consistently strengthened and reinforced by every government that has dominated the Commons in the last 30 years. Beginning with the Trudeau government in 1968, through the Mulroney years and now the Chrétien Liberals, party discipline has been tightened and parliamentary reform resisted. When the Chrétien government came to power in 1993, the same process of consolidating power and crushing any dissent continued. This despite the fact that a Liberal committee report, which had been prepared prior to the election by Don Boudria and Peter Milliken among others, had recommended liberalizing parliamentary rules and procedures.

But after the election things changed. In 2001 now government House leader Don Boudria was no longer advocating major reforms. Instead, he proposed such "meaningful" measures as making Friday Question Period a theme day for special questions; increasing parliamentary exchanges with other countries ("If this means being criticized occasionally by the media for flying off to some other country, that is too bad," he said); eliminating the consensus rule for committee travel so that the opposition could not oppose travel plans; and so on.[19]

Under Jean Chrétien, prime ministerial powers are more extensive than they have ever been. Donald Savoie points out that "power in the federal government has shifted away from line ministers and their departments toward the centre, and also, within the centre itself, power has shifted to the prime minister and his senior advisors at both the political and public service levels and away from Cabinet and Cabinet committee."

Increasingly, the business of the country is conducted through enabling legislation in which Acts of Parliament "devolve" authority to the governor general in council — i.e., the prime minister and those appointed by him. And his powers of appointment are sweeping. In the Canadian system the prime minister appoints (without oversight):

- the governor general;
- all senators;
- all federal judges, including the entire Supreme Court;
- all members of Cabinet;
- all ambassadors;
- senior civil servants; and
- the chief of the defence staff.

There are a host of other appointments as well — to boards, commissions and other bodies — all told, 2,240 appointments, all at the discretion of the prime minister.

The *Ottawa Citizen* investigated 80 federal appointments made in July 2000 and found that half of them went to Liberal cronies, financial backers, former MPs and unsuccessful candidates. A similar investigation of the Mulroney Tories in 1990 revealed that one-third of the appointments went to former PC MPs and party supporters.[20]

Prime ministerial powers of sanction are also considerable. Independent-minded MPs can easily find themselves stripped of committee posts and chairmanships. Long-standing Liberal MP Warren Allmand, who voted against the budget in April 1995, was removed as chair of the Justice Committee; Liberals who opposed long-gun registration in 1996 were removed from various Commons committees; and George Baker was removed from his position as chair of the Fisheries Committee in 1998 when he dared to criticize federal bureaucrats from the Department of Fisheries and Oceans.[21]

In 1999 Liberal MP Albina Guarnieri found herself stripped of her committee chairmanship merely for circulating a petition calling on the government to use all necessary means to protect children from a court ruling that declared the possession of child pornography legal in B.C. Although 63 Liberal backbenchers signed that petition, when it actually came time to vote on a similar opposition motion in the House of Commons in February 1999, only four Liberals dared to support it.

The prime minister's ultimate sanction is to expel an errant member from the party. John Nunziata was the last unfortunate MP to suffer that fate. His crime was to vote against the government's budget after it failed to keep its election promise to abolish the GST. While Nunziata managed to win re-election in 1997 as an independent member, he was finally defeated by the Liberal machine in the 2000 election.

Finally, in November 2002, more than fifty Liberal backbenchers broke ranks with the prime minister to support a Canadian Alliance motion giving them the right to elect, by secret ballot, their own committee chairs. This change in procedure may appear to be a small one. It may also have had more to do with the politics of infighting between Jean Chrétien and Paul Martin. But it illustrates how many government MPs have become fed up with the current state of affairs.

Parliamentary Committees

In *Politics in Canada*, noted political scientists Robert and Doreen Jackson argue:

> Some recent reforms and innovations have enhanced the ability of individual MPs to perform their parliamentary tasks more

effectively. The new standing committees enable individual members to have more input into policy formulation. Reduction of the maximum length of speeches in the House allows more members to take part in debates, and the possibility of a 10-minute rebuttal/debate after each speech has provided more interest and flexibility.[22]

In theory parliamentary committees in Canada can be used to test the waters for government policy initiatives. Two noted experts on Canadian government, Richard Van Loon and Michael Whittington, argue, for instance, that "it is becoming more common in Canada for House committees to be used as investigatory bodies to examine policy proposals before the legislative stage. In this way, the committees may be able to have some influence at both the priority-setting and the formulation stages of the policy process."[23]

But in my experience the "consultations" carried out by parliamentary committees are in reality almost always part of the spin process. For instance, the "Quality of Life Study" carried out by the House of Commons Defence Committee in 1998 has often been hailed as a major inquiry by Parliament that forced the government to take action on conditions affecting soldiers and their families. In reality this study simply mirrored work that was already being done within the Department of National Defence. The committee was largely conscripted to play a public relations role and prepare the ground for increased appropriations that government had already decided to give to DND to fund its quality-of-life programs.

For the most part parliamentary committees are yet another tool of government. Occasionally committees may issue recommendations that government dislikes, but when that occurs they are almost always ignored. Committee appointments are made by party leaders. If an MP wants to be on his or her preferred committee, perhaps a committee that often travels to exotic locations, then he or she has to toe the line. In this sense, according to former Liberal MP Ted McWhinney, the Standing Committee on Foreign Affairs and International Trade is a preferred assignment: "Foreign Affairs is prized because it has a lot of money for travel ... and you will end up in interesting and not unpleasant places in the spring before the snow has melted in Ottawa, so there's intense lobbying to get there."[24]

The ability of members to retain these perks depends on the will of party leaders. When MPs, either the government or opposition, step too far out of line they are removed from committee. This makes parliamentary committees highly partisan and, generally, they largely mirror the ineffectiveness of the House. Rarely is any government bill changed by a committee and certainly never without the government's acquiescence.

Out of frustration, some committees do on rare occasions produce reports that conflict with government policy. But such reports almost never actually change that policy. The Trudeau government ignored the Defence Committee in 1969 on the matter of scaling down Canada's military presence in Europe, just as the Chrétien government ignored the Defence Committee in 2001 on the matter of funding for the Armed Forces in the war on terrorism.

My experience with the House of Commons Defence Committee suggests that when MPs of all parties are exposed, even in a limited fashion, to defence challenges and problems, they respond in a reasonable and considered way. In 2001 eight months of testimony from witness after witness pointing to a readiness crisis in the Canadian Forces produced a fairly hard-hitting report calling on the government to review the country's defence policy and invest significantly more dollars in national defence. That policy objective was endorsed by MPs from every political party represented on the committee, including the Liberals, the NDP and the Bloc Québécois. But it was just as quickly ignored by the government.

Ministers themselves appear before committees relatively rarely — usually once or maybe two or three times a year at most. Presently, when committees meet either to hear from ministers or officials or to consider other business, sessions usually only last for about 90 to 120 minutes at a time. If a minister is appearing before a committee, he or she will usually use about 20 minutes of that time to make a prepared statement. On occasion, two or even three ministers may appear before the same committee. On those occasions about half the committee's time may be taken up with the ministerial statements.

Once ministerial statements are completed, each opposition party has between five and 10 minutes to question a minister or an official in the first round. Answers take up part of those five to 10 minutes. There is little opportunity for detailed questioning of any kind. After each party, including the Liberals, has asked questions, a second round of questioning begins that is limited to no more than five minutes per party. If time permits, a third round will follow the second round.

When I first arrived on the Hill, I expected that the committee process would really allow ministers to be held to account. Perhaps my vision of events was based on the questioning and sometimes days of hearings that accompany U.S. congressional committee sessions. This turned out to be extremely naive.

During questioning ministers or officials often make points that should be debated and challenged. However, the rigid time limits coupled with MPs' lack of background knowledge to take the ministers or officials to task means that all too often witnesses are not questioned effectively. The flow of questioning is also interrupted when time expires and another party takes over with its own agenda.

Questioning of ministers by government MPs usually occurs with a great deal of deference. An extreme example is found in the "questioning" of Lloyd Axworthy by Sheila Finestone on February 17, 1999, during the Kosovo crisis. Ms. Finestone had no questions at all to ask about the brewing crisis in Kosovo, but she did use her time to laud the minister with rhetoric that might even have made Joseph Stalin blush:

> We are such a privileged country to have Mr. Axworthy as the minister of foreign affairs, and I mean this from the bottom of my heart ... I want to observe ... that members around this table and in the House of Commons can share a degree of pride because the minister truly believes in transparency and openness and consultation with the NGOs ... The minister has helped us put Canada forward with the values that we represent ... I thank you for allowing us to play the role of being a transparent and open, co-operative people, which we reflect when we go ... It speaks for the vision of this minister who believes that each and every one of us should be involved, irrespective of political affiliations.[25]

It's no wonder that within 18 months she was appointed to the Senate.

Because committees have only a limited tangible purpose, some MPs try to avoid them altogether. When the MPs are forced to show up, they often arrive with inadequate preparation. It may seem strange that many government and opposition MPs walk into committee cold and do little or no preparation work. But with the press usually elsewhere, many feel there is simply no political mileage to be gained in expending a lot of effort on committee preparation. As a result, questioning is often too simplistic and time, of which there is precious little in committee, is wasted.

Former Canadian ambassador to Yugoslavia, Joe Bissett, commented when he was testifying before the Foreign Affairs Committee on the Balkans:

> It wasn't a committee that was interested in hearing a former ambassador's views. It wasn't a committee that seemed really intent on getting at the facts and coping with some of these issues. It was obviously a committee that was nervous about my appearance because I might say something that would embarrass Lloyd Axworthy or [Defence Minister] Eggleton and the government.[26]

The amateur character of some discussions can at times be embarrassing. Although the media may pay little attention to many of the events that happen in Parliament, other countries' diplomats, who occasionally attend committee sessions, know exactly what Parliament is all about.

To prevent MPs from accumulating too much expertise, the government tries to keep its members moving from committee to committee. This further contributes to superficial debates and to a mindset among many MPs that they are simply seat warmers. Presently, the turnover in membership in House of Commons committees is between 65 and 70 percent over the life of Parliament. This contrasts with an average turnover of 16 percent in Britain and 10 to 20 percent in the Australian House of Representatives. In Germany and the Scandinavian countries, membership on committees normally prevails for the life of that legislature.[27]

A tight reign is also kept on all aspects of committee activities. Committees must receive authorization from House (that means unanimous consent from party leaders) to travel. Since the reports they are working on are purely advisory and likely to have no impact, some members end up seeing travel purely as a perk or, less charitably, a junket. This makes the issue of committee travel highly political.

Chairs of committees in nearly every European country and in Britain are split between opposition and government parties. In Canada every committee, except the Public Accounts Committee, has been chaired by a government member. Until November 2002, that chair was was effectively chosen by the prime minister. The House vote to change the method of selection to a secret ballot may dilute the prime minister's power somewhat, but it may still result in the chairs being chosen largely from the governing party through backroom deals between the prime minister and senior members of his own caucus. Indeed, partisanship remained as strong as ever immediately after the House vote as several Alliance MPs were booted out of their roles as committee vice-chairs by the governing Liberals in retaliation for embarrassing the government.

In 2001 the activities of the House Industry Committee became incredibly politicized when the Liberal chair, Susan Whelan, ruled "out of order" probing questions that opposition leaders were asking the prime minister's ethics counsellor, Howard Wilson, about the "Shawinigan Affair." A few months prior to that, and just before the federal election, the Liberals effectively silenced the testimony of the auditor general by "forgetting" — en masse — to show up for his presentation before committee on the HRD scandal. This denied the committee the quorum it required in order to meet. The same stunt was pulled on September 20, 2001, after the World Trade Center bombing. The Liberal whip called MPs out of the Finance Committee one by one to ensure that the Committee was denied quorum to discuss an Alliance proposal to call customs officials for a discussion on border security arrangements.

These tactics are more characteristic of banana republics than of a supposedly serious parliamentary democracy. Again, committees in other Western legislatures are much more independent than those in Canada. In Germany committee membership is determined by consensus decisions of a special council of MPs in the Lower House. Committees in Germany conduct their work outside the public eye and therefore grandstanding for the press is less prevalent. Members of committees are often experts in particular subject areas and, as such, exercise considerable influence in amending government bills.[28] This is partly due to the fact that half the members of the Lower House are elected on the basis of proportional representation, thus permitting the party to place specially qualified candidates on their party lists at election time.

In Norway parliamentary committees play a similar expert role, and measures decided on by a particular committee are usually also adopted by the parliament as a whole. The defence committee of the Norwegian parliament plays an important role in determining the defence plans of the nation, including funding levels.[29] In 2001, for instance, the Norwegian parliament totally dismantled the government's defence plans, rejecting many of the cuts that had been proposed to pay for the modernization of the armed forces. Debates over funding levels actually occurred on the floor of the parliament, rather than exclusively in the backrooms of the bureaucracy.[30]

The powers of the Italian parliament are probably the most extensive of any of the major European legislatures. Agendas for the Chamber of Deputies are usually fixed through the unanimous consent of parliamentary leaders. Where no agreement is possible, the Speaker determines the agenda — but only after attempting mediation between the parties. Committees in Italy are extremely powerful and in certain circumstances can even legislate directly without requiring the approval of the whole House.[31]

In Australia Senate committee members are chosen at the beginning of every Parliament and they remain members until the next election. The committees review the government's spending proposals in detail on an annual basis. Departments having their spending estimates considered by the committees are expected to table detailed explanatory notes with the estimates which break down expenditures by programs, sub-programs and individual components. Because the government is not directly responsible to the Senate, the Upper House has the opportunity to go through the estimates in a more non-partisan fashion than would the Australian House of Representatives.

In Canada Parliament does not fulfill its supposed function, which is to investigate the details and nuances of government policy and expenditure proposals. As far as foreign and defence policy is concerned, it is impossible for MPs to play a meaningful role in preparing Canada to respond effectively to the post–cold war environment. This means that the making of Canadian national security policy remains the preserve of a relatively small elite that has consistently downplayed and neglected the importance of military capability.

Many, in fact probably most, MPs are clearly frustrated with the existing system and, as a result, many have simply given up. Since they have no real power, many simply don't see any point in devoting a great deal of energy to the process.

There Must Be a Better Way

No other Western country emasculates its legislators in the way that Canada does. The United States is obviously at the top end of the scale in terms of having serious legislative oversight and guaranteeing the independence of members of Congress. Members of Congress and senators routinely cross party lines when voting, and since the chairing of committees is usually determined on the basis of seniority, they cannot easily be disciplined by their party leaderships.

As an example of the real powers of Congress, appropriation requests coming from the White House never emerge unchanged by the legislative process. Most laws originate on the floor of either the House or the Senate and do not come from the administration. Debates cannot be easily terminated by majority party leaders over the objection of the minority since this requires a 60 percent majority vote.

The president must also get support from a majority of senators for all senior executive and judicial appointments, and must secure a two-thirds majority to ratify any treaty. Congress has about 2,000 staff members and can appropriate vast resources to research the work of committees. John Hamre, former deputy secretary in the U.S. Department of Defense and chief of staff of the Senate Armed Services Committee, notes that the House Armed Services Committee alone has about 25 professional staff, with a potential staff of about 700 to 800 from various other congressional offices such as the budget office and the Congressional Research Service.[32]

Each member of Congress and senator also has a sizeable staff of his or her own. Former congressman Lee Hamilton, who served as the chairman of both the House Foreign Relations committee and the House Intelligence committee, points out that "it is the constitutional responsibility of Congress to look into all the activities of the executive branch … People know that somebody is looking over their shoulder, and when they know that somebody is looking over their shoulder they behave themselves. If they know somebody is not looking over their shoulder, that's when things go amiss."[33]

Paul Hellyer notes that when he was opposition critic for defence in the late 1950s and early 1960s, he was actually able to tap into the resources of Congress to fulfill his oversight duties in Canada: "I used to get all kinds of people, including Gerald Ford, to send [me information] … It was astonishing the information they had, including about Canada."[34]

Most European countries accord their legislatures significant responsibilities, including over foreign affairs and defence. This is unthinkable in
Canada, where shallow take-note debates are the substitute for substantive discussion. At times even MPs who have argued for greater back-
bench autonomy are reluctant to request it in the area of foreign policy.
For instance, during the take-note debate on deploying Canadian troops
to Afghanistan in 2002, Clifford Lincoln, who in the past pronounced
himself fed-up with the way parliamentarians are ignored in the
Canadian political system, nevertheless largely abdicated his responsibilities when he said: "I do not know of any parliament where we vote on
these issues to decide whether or not to send troops. There are debates but
I am quite satisfied to leave the issue to the executive …."[35]

But the truth is that in many parliamentary systems, legislatures
play a key role in determining the parameters of military commitments
and, more importantly, the nature of the defence and foreign policy that
leads to military commitments. Italy and Germany are among the most
notable examples of strong legislative involvement. Indeed, in Germany
the Lower House of parliament (the *Bundestag*) is constitutionally obligated to vote on every operational deployment of troops overseas.

Most of the weaker legislatures also possess at least some practical
ability to control the actions of the executive. The British Parliament is,
for instance, very weak when compared to the German or Italian parliaments. Nevertheless, in 1990, government MPs brought down Prime
Minister Margaret Thatcher. Irish prime minister John Burton suffered
the same fate a few years later (as did Australian prime minister Bob
Hawke in 1994 and New Zealand PM Jim Bolger in 1997).[36] This is
much more difficult in Canada.

Ordinary members in these parliaments also have a somewhat
greater ability to initiate legislation. A survey carried out by one scholar
found that between 1978 and 1982, about 10 percent of private members' bills passed the British Parliament, and in Australia about nine percent did. In Canada the figure was less than two percent.[37] Little has
changed in the past 20 years, and nearly all the private members' bills
that do pass to become law deal with such "weighty" issues as the
renaming of the ridings of individual MPs, creating associations of former parliamentarians and establishing a national organ donor week.[38]

It wasn't always this way. Between 1867 and 1962, the Standing Orders
of the Canadian House of Commons actually gave precedence to private

members' business on particular days each week. Prior to 1906 a full three days each week were devoted to the consideration of private members' business. This slowly changed over the course of the last century as the government took ever more control. By 1982 actual debate time for private members' business had been reduced to just three hours per week.[39]

Today all important (and for that matter even non-important) legislative issues are decided either by civil servants or the PMO before they ever reach Parliament. The budget Estimates are simply rubber-stamped by House committees and are never scrutinized in a detailed fashion. If they are not passed by committee in a certain period of time, they are simply "deemed to be passed" without any vote ever taking place.

In the spring of 2001 it was most unusual for the House of Commons Defence Committee to issue a series of recommendations to government on defence spending. Naturally, not a comma in the defence budget was changed by the committee, but the committee did recommend unanimously that "the government re-examine its spending plans for the next two fiscal years with a view to increasing the budget for the Department of National Defence."[40]

Of course, the Committee report had no impact on the defence budget, and after the report was issued, the very same defence spending proposals were passed (part of $166 billion in total government spending) by the House of Commons in just seven minutes a few days later. All government MPs on the Defence Committee, who had recommended increased defence spending only a few days before, dutifully voted for the budget as they were obligated to do on pain of expulsion from their party.

For most members of the governing elite, it would be unthinkable to give MPs any serious role in the legislative process. Indeed, the dismal performance of some MPs has at times led me to lean toward a similar conclusion out of simple exasperation. But at least in part, some MPs do not perform seriously because nothing serious is asked of them. They don't have any real responsibilities. The only thing expected of them by their party bosses is that they get positive press or, more usually, that they at least avoid negative press.

Despite the temptation to surrender to elite rule, the fact remains that shutting MPs out shuts out Canadians. If MPs continue to be excluded from real influence, then Canadians themselves are also excluded. The experience in other countries demonstrates that greater legislative responsibility can work. In order to let ordinary Canadians back into the political process, it is necessary to improve the quality of MPs, create the mechanisms to empower them and hold them accountable.

NOTES

1. Eugene Bellemare, *Guide to the Canadian House of Commons* (Ottawa: Library of Parliament Information Service, 2001) pp. 4 and 11. The text provided by the Library Parliament for MPs was used by MPs and then simply "plugged" into their own house-holders, which were then sent to constituents.
2. David Goetz, *Parliamentary Control Over Foreign Policy (Topical Information for Parliamentarians)* (Ottawa: Library of Parliament, December 14, 2000) pp. 1–2.
3. Canada, Department of National Defence. *A Paper Prepared for the Minister of National Defence by Professor Albert Legault Laval University* (Ottawa: Department of National Defence, March 25, 1997) p. 6. Report to the Prime Minister.
4. Ronald Landes, *The Canadian Polity* (Scarborough: Prentice Hall, 1998) pp. 172–173.
5. Jane Taber, "Lincoln Refuses to Vote with Fellow Liberals," *National Post*, February 14, 2001, p. A13.
6. Paul Wells, "Shouting, Heckling — Welcome to the Daily Circus," *National Post*, February 14, 2001, p. A12.
7. Rolf Theen and Frank Wilson, *Comparative Politics* (Scarborough: Prentice Hall, 1996) p. 48.
8. Donald Savoie, *Governing from the Centre: The Concentration of Power in Canadian Politics* (Toronto: University of Toronto Press, 1999) p. 340.
9. Admiral Thomas [interview]. Interviewed by Kitson Vincent and Rob Roy of Stornoway Productions, October 1994.
10. Savoie, pp. 324 and 329.
11. James Allan Evans, "Picking Through the Debris," *Policy Options*, Institute for Research on Public Policy (January/February 2001) p. 30.

12. Jeffrey Simpson, "Canadian Politics and One-Party Government," *Policy Options*, Institute for Research on Public Policy (January–February 2001) pp. 15–20.

13. John Fraser, "Give 'em the Vote," *Saturday Night*, April 1993, p. 10.

14. Jane Taber, "Give These Members a Voice, Turner Says," *National Post*, May 9, 2001, p. A1.

15. Canada. Parliament, House of Commons, *Debates*, Vol. 137, no. 33 (March 21, 2001) p. 2035.

16. House of Commons, *Debates*, Vol. 137, no. 33 (March 21, 2001) p. 2015.

17. House of Commons, *Debates*, Vol. 137, no. 33 (March 21, 2001) p. 2038.

18. House of Commons, *Debates*, Vol. 137, no. 33 (March 21, 2001) p. 2042.

19. House of Commons, *Debates*, Vol. 137, no. 33 (March 21, 2001) p. 1993–1998.

20. Jack Aubry, "Chrétien's Game of Friends," *Ottawa Citizen*, October 21, 2000, p. B1.

21. Ronald Landes, *The Canadian Polity* (Scarborough: Prentice Hall, 1998), p. 168; Robert Fife, "Cabinet's Flunkies," *National Post*, February 16, 2001, p. A13.

22. Robert Jackson and Doreen Jackson, *Politics in Canada*, 5th edition (Toronto: Prentice Hall, 2001) p. 301–302.

23. Richard Van Loon and Michael Whittington, *The Canadian Political System* (Toronto: McGraw Hill-Ryerson, 1987) p. 622.

24. Ted McWhinney [interview]. Interviewed by Robert Roy of Stornoway Productions, October 2001.

25. Canada, Parliament, House of Commons, Standing Committee on Foreign Affairs and International Trade, *Minutes of Proceedings and Evidence* (February 17, 1999). Sections 16:50–17:00.

26. Ambassador Joe Bissett [interview]. Interviewed by Robert Roy of Stornoway Productions, September 2001.

27. Peter Dobell, "Reforming Parliamentary Practice," *Policy Options*, IRPP (December 2000) pp. 13–14.

28. Yves Mény and Andrew Knapp, *Government and Politics in Western Europe* (Oxford: Oxford University Press, 1998) p. 198.

29. The Norwegian constitution also requires special parliamentary majorities for certain measures. Constitutional amendments

require a two-thirds majority, while any measures transferring national power to an international organization require a three-fourths majority.

30. While the Norwegian parliament had great difficulty in establishing viable funding levels in 2001, at least these debates were taking place between elected parliamentarians. John Berg, "Row over Norwegian Cuts," *Jane's Defence Weekly*, July 25, 2001, p. 13.

31. Mény and Knapp, pp. 198 and 201.

32. John Hamre [interview]. Interviewed by Robert Roy of Stornoway Productions, September 2001.

33. Lee Hamilton [interview]. Interviewed by Robert Roy of Stornoway Productions, August, 2001.

34. Paul Hellyer [interview]. Interviewed by Robert Roy of Stornoway Productions, June 2000.

35. House of Commons. *Debates*, Vol. 137, no. 133 (January 28, 2002) p. 8388.

36. Christopher Moore, "Backbencher's Fight Back," *National Post*, February 13, 2001, p. A16.

37. Klaus von Beyme, *Parliamentary Democracy* (New York: St. Martin's Press, 2000) p. 93.

38. Nine private members' bills passed the 35th Parliament (1993–97) and became law and another nine passed in the 36th Parliament (1997–2000). It is probably being charitable to say all generally were of a trivial nature.

39. James Robertson, *The Evolution of Private Members' Business* (Ottawa: Library of Parliament Research Branch, October 11, 1996). Prepared for the House of Commons Sub-Committee on Private Members' Business.

40. Canada, Standing Committee on National Defence and Veterans Affairs, *Report on Plans and Priorities* (June 11, 2001). Report tabled in Parliament.

CONCLUSION

"The Most Serious Place in the Land"

I remember watching Question Period one day in November 1999. Four new members of Parliament, elected in recent by-elections, were being introduced for the first time. In welcoming them to the House, Preston Manning stated, "I would like to add my congratulations to each of the new members and welcome them to the daily circus." A chorus of feigned outrage erupted from the Liberal benches with Mr. Manning's comment. Prime Minister Chrétien responded by saying, "I do not think it is a circus here. I think it is the most serious place in the land."[1]

"The most serious place in the land" is the supposed view of the prime minister. It is a view shared by others. On his election to the House of Commons in 2000, Joe Clark called Parliament "The Big League" of Canadian politics. A scary thought indeed.

Beyond the fact that the interests of ordinary Canadians are today neglected or forgotten in the nation's legislative system, the absence of real democracy at the federal level has implications for the way in which national policies are formulated and the interests they serve. There is a link between the absence of serious democratic oversight in Canada and the policy choices our leaders have been permitted to make for us.

Canada's present political system, with its concentrated power and an irrelevant legislature, has not served the country's international position well. The decline of Canadian influence abroad can be linked, at least in part, to the absence of serious parliamentary oversight. It has prevented any serious consideration of defence and foreign policy issues by Parliament. Because of Parliament's impotence, much of the decline in influence has occurred without Parliament being in the least aware what has happened. This decline in influence and military capability leaves Canada dangerously exposed in the aftermath of the events of September 11. We are a country that is marginalized, irrelevant, vulnerable and, by implication, increasingly dependent on our neighbour to the south.

If Canada is to begin to reverse present trends and ensure some measure of national sovereignty, then we must begin by pursuing real reform of the institution that is supposed to debate our national policies. Parliament must become a place where serious debate really does take place and where MPs become responsible for what they say and do.

Based on my experience, five aspects of reform are essential if serious change is to take place.

1. Change the culture of Parliament.
Presently MPs do not engage in serious oversight because this is not expected of them nor is it permitted by the Canadian parliamentary system. Instead, opposition MPs are expected to taint the government by whatever means necessary, while government MPs are expected to support the government come hell or high water. Artificial partisanship on the Hill deters serious discussion and debate. In this regard there is no more artificial environment than that of Question Period.

As it stands now, Question Period is seen as the central means by which government is held to account. But it is virtually useless for that purpose. About half of a given parliamentary day is soaked up in preparing for Question Period. While most Canadians have probably ceased to take anything that is said during Question Period too seriously, MPs continue to spin their wheels in a daily routine that lulls some of them into a false belief that they are performing an effective oversight role.

Question Period must be reformed, if only to stop it from continuing to bring Parliament into disrepute. Options for reform might include

- limiting Question Period to one longer session every week instead of the existing 45-minute daily sessions;
- devoting more time to individual questions, thus allowing time for better discussion and debate;
- requiring advance notice as to the subject matter of a question, thus reducing the tendency to simply "follow the media," and requiring more substantive responses on the part of ministers to inquiries;
- setting aside one period every week or every month for "prime minister's question time," as exists in Britain on a weekly basis; and
- allowing any MP to ask a question if recognized by the Speaker, instead of the present practice of only permitting those questions that are approved by party whips and House leaders.

While partisanship cannot and should not be eliminated from Question Period entirely, it should nevertheless be possible to encourage more honest debate and minimize the present fake melodrama of the process.

Changing the culture of the Hill also requires gradually altering the expectations that party leaders have with respect to their back-bench MPs. At present there is an expectation, particularly in the traditional parties, that all MPs must sing from the same song sheet. In part this expectation is deeply ingrained on the Hill because it is deeply ingrained in the internal politics of the traditional parties themselves.

Most parties in Canada are used to orchestrating every aspect of their own internal politics, which are too often characterized by fixed nomination races in ridings, conventions that simply rubber-stamp the policies desired by the governing elite and national leadership races that are open to the most blatant, but perfectly legal, corruption.

In many other democracies, the United States and Germany for instance, there are both legal and even constitutional provisions requiring political parties to conduct at least their core electoral activities based on democratic principles. The primary system in the United States, for instance, regulates the way in which presidential candidates are chosen within parties, thus opening candidate selection to direct voter input. Similar legal parameters to govern the core activities of parties in Canada should also be introduced.

2. Bring greater policy expertise to the Hill.

Many, perhaps most, MPs who are elected through our single member constituency system do not have expertise that qualifies them to be policy leaders and departmental managers. At least nominally, constituency MPs are primarily elected to represent the views of their constituents in Ottawa. This is the role that constituency MPs should play in order to inject common sense into the policy process. They need to be empowered to do this. They must have the ability to question whether government spending priorities make sense, to amend legislation that is introduced by government and to advance ideas that their constituents want to see put forward at the federal level. But in order to provide genuine and credible policy leadership, the processes by which MPs are chosen needs to be broadened.

Traditionally, when reforms to increase parliamentary policy expertise have been discussed, it has usually been suggested that staff resources of individual MPs, the leaders' offices and the Library of Parliament need to be increased. But while such reforms are certainly desirable, they will do little to improve the expertise in the House chamber itself.

To accomplish this broader goal, reforms are required in how we select at least some of our MPs. Most European countries maintain at least partial systems of proportional representation (PR) for this purpose. While the constituency system remains vital to maintain a direct link between MPs and the people they represent, introducing a partial PR system (for perhaps 100 of the more than 300 MPs) would allow each party to nominate policy experts for election to Parliament. During the course of an election campaign, perhaps in national issue-specific debates, the public would be able to scrutinize the perspectives and views of the candidates that each party had placed at the top of its nomination list. Introducing a partial PR system should complement, but not replace, the present constituency election system and create a better pool of MPs to draw on for Cabinet and opposition critic positions. It should also improve the quality of parliamentary debates.

Presently, in the Liberal and PC parties, party leaders can directly appoint candidates to run in constituencies. But only rarely, and as an afterthought, do such candidates have specific policy expertise. Instead, such parachute appointments mostly serve to strengthen the control of the party leadership over back-bench constituency MPs. This undermines the control that local communities and constituents have over the representatives they send to Parliament.

There is a need to balance the right of individual constituencies to send their own representatives to Ottawa unfettered by national party machines, and at the same time allow the political parties to nominate people for election who have specific policy expertise. The adoption of a dual PR–single member constituency system could help to facilitate this.

3. Reform parliamentary committees.

Committees are supposed to be the places where the detailed business of the House gets done and where real oversight of government departments, policies and budgets occurs. But committees presently do none of these things.

A first step to making committees relevant is to allow MPs to serve on them for the life of a given Parliament. Party whips should not be able to remove MPs from committees for "insubordination." Chairs and vice-chairs of committees should be elected by secret ballot. However, this change must only be the beginning of a process of reform. It will be even more important to change the culture on committees. In this sense, the independence and freedom of MPs will begin to grow as they serve on committees for the duration of an entire Parliament. Simultaneously, committees must also be provided with larger staffs, instead of the one or two researchers who presently support their activities; and, they should have consistent budgets which the committees themselves, and not the government, control.

Much of the best committee work in Australia is carried out in its Senate committees. Presently the work of the Canadian Senate is largely ignored, in large measure because its members are not elected. The Senate must be elected and legitimized. Making senators ineligible for Cabinet appointment (as was proposed in the Charlottetown Accord of 1992 for instance) would further enhance the independence of Upper House committees by forcing senators to focus exclusively on their legislative responsibilities.

4. Ensure effective oversight over the activities of government.

Many of the reforms discussed above would change the way in which Parliament functions in relation to government. MPs, freed from their present irrelevant roles as either a cheering or booing section for government, could begin to address issues of real importance to Canadians. Parliamentary committees, in particular, might actually begin to function as they are supposed to. Committees of Parliament presently have the ability to subpoena, swear in witnesses and conduct in-depth inquiries. But these powers are never exercised. Were these powers to be activated, the role of parliamentarians would change greatly.

To further enhance the oversight powers of Parliament, both the House of Commons and a reformed Senate should have the ability to scrutinize government appointments. Presently there are virtually no appointments requiring parliamentary hearings or approval. The chief of defence staff is also not required to appear before Parliament when appointed. While Parliament also has no role in the appointment of the auditor general, the auditor general serves a 10-year term and has the mandate to report to Parliament. The simple mandate to report to Parliament has contributed significantly to the frankness and effectiveness of the auditor general's reports. A similar clear mandate for the chief of defence staff or the commissioner of the RCMP might well have a similar impact.

Giving Parliament the ability to review the full range of diplomatic, military and other bureaucratic appointments as a matter of course would enhance quality control in the appointments process. When coupled with the increased control that committees would exercise over departmental budgets, a closer and more direct relationship between government officials and MPs would enhance and improve the frankness of briefings and raise the quality of the information to which MPs are made privy.

5. Make MPs truly responsible to their constituents.

Presently most members of Parliament, especially on the government side, are responsible first and foremost to their party leaders and to their party caucus collectively. This has served to shut Canadians out of the country's national institutions. Changing this will require a government with the political will to surrender some of its power for the purpose of bringing Canadians into the political process in a more direct way.

The possible mechanisms for making parliamentarians responsible to their constituents and to the people of Canada as a whole include

- regularized free voting on most issues;
- the option of MP recall;
- shortened times between elections; and
- citizen-initiated referenda and/or plebiscites.

These suggested reforms may seem radical to some. But there is simply no reason why the will of the prime minister must prevail on every issue or even on most issues that come before Parliament. There is no reason why every budgetary proposal from government must sail through House committees without amendment. And there is no reason why government should be permitted to run the nation's foreign and defence policy as it sees fit without any check being placed on that power by the national legislature. Indeed, there is every reason why these things should not occur.

In Canada elections are held within a maximum of five years. The greater the time between elections, the more insulated parliamentarians are from the electorate — particularly on specific issues. In the United States elections for the House of Representatives are held every two years. In Australia and New Zealand elections take place within three years. A shortened election cycle in Canada, perhaps every three or four years, would serve to increase the responsibility of MPs.

Referenda or plebiscites may, for some, be the most troublesome of the suggested reforms, but such provisions work well in other jurisdictions. New Zealand is an example of a country in the British tradition that permits citizen-initiated plebiscites. In Switzerland, referenda are often used in the realm of foreign and defence policy. In the last several years the Swiss have voted on the abolition of the armed forces (rejected), the entry of Switzerland into the United Nations (rejected in 1986, accepted in 2002) and even the purchase of F-18 fighter aircraft for the air force (accepted).

The recognition of the need for fundamental change to the parliamentary system is reflected in the proposals made by the Quebec government in March 2002 to take the executive in that province right out of the legislature. Instead Quebec has proposed adopting a U.S.-style political system, with the premier elected separately and a Cabinet composed of policy experts from outside the legislature. Whether or not these proposals are realistic or ultimately come to fruition, they reflect a growing realization that the present system is not working well in Canada and is not serving citizens in the way that it should.

Democratization: The Basis for Sound National Policy

Democratization of Canadian politics is not a panacea. Democratization will change the way we do things, and this in itself will create a multitude of new challenges. But democratization will also create checks and balances, and restore to a greater number of Canadians some measure of control over their national government. It will end the concentration of power in Canada and open the system up to broader influences. It will almost certainly make our nation's foreign and defence policy more reflective of the real interests of ordinary Canadians and, hence, more effective.

Democratization may also help create something that Canada has never had before — a national policy consensus that isn't simply based on the views of a few decision makers in the national elite or on stage-managed consultation processes, but rather policies that are grounded in serious discussions which take place among the elected representatives of ordinary Canadians.

Former U.S. deputy defense secretary John Hamre commented that the oversight process seems very cumbersome at times but it has a clear purpose: "Oversight is intense ... You're building a national basis for your program; you're building that national support."[2] That is something that should occur in any democracy worthy of the name.

I have seen back-bench MPs rise above partisanship and come to sensible consensus positions that cross party lines when they have studied an issue in some detail and in a serious manner. Unfortunately, in all these occasions they have simply lacked the power to carry such consensus recommendations forward.

In both 1999 and 2001 the House of Commons Standing Committee on National Defence produced reports calling on the government to respond to the serious crisis confronted by the Canadian Forces and allocate more money to defence. The 1999 report of the Standing Committee on National Defence was supported by the Liberals, the PCs and Reform.

In 2001 the committee recommended a full review of Canadian defence policy, including re-evaluating and increasing the resources allocated to the Canadian Forces. Even though this objective was supported by every MP from every party on the committee and was backed up by the House Finance Committee, the government felt completely free to ignore the report. It ignored a similar report from a Liberal-dominated Senate committee a few months later.

Parliament is ignored because it can be ignored. It is no wonder that after decades of marginalization some MPs either give up and "put in pension time" until retirement or begin to play the political game for all the personal benefit they can get. I believe that giving parliamentarians and committees a greater and more effective voice would produce more realistic policies, introduce oversight for the first time on the expenditure of departmental resources and require those who have until now formulated our nation's foreign policy in virtual isolation to become accountable.

At the present time Parliament is far from being, as referred to by the prime minister, "the most serious place in the land." If national and international issues are actually going to be discussed by the people's representatives in a serious manner, if Canadians are to recover some measure of control over their country's destiny and if the present decline of Canada internationally is to be reversed, then the reform of Parliament is the essential prerequisite.

NOTES

1. Canada, Parliament, House of Commons, *Debates*, Vol. 3 (November 29, 1999) pp. 1865–1866.
2. John Hamre [interview]. Interviewed by Robert Roy of Stornoway Productions, September, 2001.

APPENDIX

Speeches on Kosovo Written for Members of Parliament by Government Bureaucrats Compared with Speeches Actually Delivered in the House of Commons

Speeches Used in the October 7, 1998, Take-Note Debate on Kosovo:

Text of speech written by Foreign Affairs officials for parliamentarians (used by Ms. Aileen Carroll):	Actual speech of Ms. Aileen Carroll (Barrie–Simcoe–Bradford, Liberal), October 7, 1998:
Mr. Speaker, the United Nations secretary general has released a report in which he lays the lion's share of the blame for the current humanitarian crisis in the province of Kosovo in the Federal Republic of Yugoslavia, squarely on the shoulders of the Yugoslav authorities.	Mr. Speaker, the United Nations secretary general has released a report in which he lays the lion's share of the blame for the current humanitarian crisis in the province of Kosovo squarely on the shoulders of the Yugoslav authorities.
The humanitarian situation in Kosovo is disastrous, with hundreds of thousands of displaced people and refugees, some of whom lack shelter and basic necessities. What is most shocking is that many of these problems are due to the actions of the Yugoslav government against its own citizens. In particular, the report points to a clear policy of the Yugoslav authorities to intentionally target civilians with the goal of driving them from their homes and, in many cases, from their own country.	The humanitarian situation in Kosovo is disastrous, with hundreds of thousands of displaced people and refugees, some of whom lack shelter and basic necessities. What is most shocking is that many of these problems are due to the actions of the Yugoslav government against its own citizens. In particular, the report points to a clear policy of the Yugoslav authorities intentionally driving civilians from their homes and in any cases from their own countries.
We call on Yugoslavia, and in particular on President Milosevic as the head of state with the ability to act with decisive authority, to meet its	We call on Yugoslavia, and on President Milosevic as head of state with the ability to act with decisive authority, to meet their obligations

obligations under international law, and lead the way toward a just solution. We hold President Milosevic and all Yugoslav authorities fully accountable for the actions of their security forces, and urge them to co-operate with the International Criminal Tribunal for the former Yugoslavia in this regard. To use disproportionate force, moreover, against civilians will ultimately prove counterproductive in resisting armed separatist forces. The actions of the security forces are exactly what fuels extremism and violence in the Albanian Kosovar population.

The Yugoslav government should instead show leadership by creating the conditions for a meaningful dialogue on a political solution and by fully addressing the humanitarian crisis. This can only be achieved by calling an immediate end to the offensive and repressive activities of the police and of the military, and by offering gestures of good faith to the Albanians of Kosovo, such as a commitment to offer real, meaningful autonomy for Kosovo.

At the same time we also strongly urge the Albanian Kosovars to return to their earlier policy of peaceful engagement to pursue their legitimate goals within the borders of the Federal Republic of Yugoslavia. While Canadians understand the frustration and the anger the Kosovars feel, especially in the light of the scant regard the Yugoslav authorities have paid to legitimate Kosovar grievances and aspirations, violence is not the means to a viable solution to the problems Kosovo and the rest of the region face. Further destabilization through the pursuit of independence by the Albanian Kosovar leadership will not bring any benefits to their people.

under international law, and to lead the way toward a just solution. We hold President Milosevic and all Yugoslav authorities fully accountable for the actions of their security forces and urge them to co-operate with the International Criminal Tribunal for the former Yugoslavia in this regard. The actions of the security forces are exactly what fuels extremism and violence in the Albanian Kosovar population.

The Yugoslav government should instead show leadership by creating the conditions for a meaningful dialogue on a political solution and by fully addressing the humanitarian crisis. This can only be achieved by calling an immediate end to the offensive and repressive activities of the police as well as the military and by offering gestures of good faith to the Albanians of Kosovo, such as a commitment to offer real, meaningful autonomy for Kosovo.

At the same time we also strongly urge the Albanian Kosovars to return to their earlier policy of peaceful engagement to pursue their legitimate goals within the borders of the federal Republic of Yugoslavia. While Canadians understand the frustration and the anger the Kosovars feel, especially in the light of the scant regard the Yugoslav authorities have paid to legitimate Kosovar grievances, violence is not the means to a viable solution to the problems Kosovo and the rest of the region face.

Canada has long supported the diplomatic efforts being pursued to bring about a peaceful solution to the crisis. Minister Axworthy made it clear to the Yugoslav authorities as early as 1996 that any progress in our bilateral relations would depend on Yugoslavia taking positive steps forward in support of human rights, democratization and in addressing the longstanding problems in Kosovo. The Organization for Security and Cooperation has been trying to play a constructive role in Yugoslavia, but has been continually rebuffed. United States Ambassador Hill is continuing in his efforts to broker an autonomy agreement. The international community is working hard to find a solution but we need the co-operation of the combatants to do so.

The problems in Kosovo have recently developed into a major humanitarian crisis in which civilians are the main victims. But this crisis has not occurred in a void. Its current phase is intimately linked to the factors — and individuals — which created the conditions for the violent dissolution of the former Socialist Federal Republic of Yugoslavia, and war in Slovenia, Croatia and Bosnia and Herzegovina, with thousands of lives lost, leaving survivors traumatized in many ways. Irresponsible politicians in the Balkans have for years set neighbour against neighbour with one key goal — the maintenance of power, at any cost — and that cost is, of course, borne by the people. The suffering of their citizens, whether ethnic Albanians, Serbs or otherwise — is rarely uppermost in such "leaders" minds. Ethnic ties are betrayed at whim when it serves the interest of

Canada has long supported the diplomatic efforts being pursued to bring about a peaceful solution to this region. The Organization for Security and Cooperation has been trying to play a constructive role in Yugoslavia, but has been continually rebuffed. United States Ambassador Hill is continuing his efforts to broker an autonomy agreement. The international community is working hard to find a solution but we need the co-operation of the combatants to do so.

Problems in Kosovo have recently developed into a major humanitarian crisis in which civilians are the main victims. But this crisis has not occurred in a void. Its current phase is intimately linked to the factors and to the individuals which created the conditions for the violent dissolution of the former socialist federal Republic of Yugoslavia, and war in Slovenia, Croatia and Bosnia and Herzegovina, with thousands of lives being lost. Irresponsible politicians in the Balkans have for years set neighbour against neighbour with one key goal, the maintenance of power, at any cost — and that cost is borne by their people. The suffering of their citizens, whether ethnic Albanians, Serbs or others, is rarely uppermost in such leaders' minds. Ethnic ties are betrayed at whim when it serves the interest of such politicians. But they find playing off people's fears to be

such politicians, but they find playing off people's fears to be the most convenient and effective tactic to which they frequently resort.

Canadians find such behaviour reprehensible. One's ethnicity makes little difference if one is hungry, cold, terrified and in extreme physical danger. Innocent victims are innocent victims, regardless of religion, language or ethnicity. Simply put, there is no such thing as collective guilt, where individuals are held responsible for the crimes — real or perceived — of their ethnic kin. Recognizing this is key to any lasting solution. Mr. Speaker, Canada has played a constructive role in all the countries of the former Yugoslavia since we first sent peacekeepers there at the beginning of this decade. We have paid high costs, most notably in terms of the 16 soldiers who have lost their lives in the region. Other Canadians have tried, through non-governmental aid organizations or international agencies, to help the people of the western Balkans find their own peaceful, sustainable answers to their many challenges. Canadian taxpayers have been generous in helping the peace process bring tangible benefits to ordinary people. We, in turn, have benefited enormously through immigration from the former Yugoslavia, which provides a bridge between our countries.

We have no agenda to damage anyone's legitimate interests in that region. We have an obligation to make our voices heard when we see tens of thousands suffering people, whose human rights have been callously disregarded and who have in many cases lost all they hold dear. When international humanitarian law and interna-

the most convenient and effective tactic. It is a tactic to which they frequently resort.

Canadians find such behaviour reprehensible. One's ethnicity makes little difference if one is hungry, cold, terrified and in extreme physical danger. Innocent victims are innocent victims, regardless of religion, language or ethnicity. Simply put, there is no such thing as collective guilt, where individuals are held responsible for the crimes, real or perceived, of their ethnic kin. Recognizing this is key to any lasting solutions. Canada has played a constructive role in all the countries of the former Yugoslavia since we first sent peacekeepers there at the beginning of this decade. We have paid high costs, most notably in terms of the 16 soldiers who have lost their lives in the region. Other Canadians have tried, through non-governmental aid organizations or international agencies, to help the people of the western Balkans find their own peaceful, sustainable answers to their many challenges. Canadian taxpayers have been generous in helping the peace process bring tangible benefits to ordinary people. We, in turn, have benefited enormously through immigration from the former Yugoslavia, which provides a bridge between our countries.

We have no agenda to damage anyone's legitimate interests in that region. But we do have an obligation to make our voices heard when we see tens of thousands suffering people, whose human rights have been callously disregarded and who have in many cases lost all they hold dear. When international humanitarian law

tional human rights standards are cast aside in the name of fighting and armed insurgency, in a manner opposed to the letter and spirit of international law, we must not be oblivious to the implications this has for all of us.

Members of the House must therefore condemn in the strongest terms the philosophy which lies behind the actions of the combatants who commit atrocities against civilians in Kosovo. Regardless of who commits such actions, the Serbian security forces or the Kosovar insurgents, such actions will never lead to a just and peaceful solution for all the inhabitants of Kosovo.

We are all deeply concerned with the plight of displaced persons within Kosovo, and of Kosovar refugees fleeing into Albania, the former Yugoslav Republic of Macedonia*, and Bosnia and Herzegovina. Canada has contributed to the efforts of the United Nations High Commission for Refugees, the United Nations Children's Fund and the Red Cross. Canada will continue to do its part, including through the generous donation of individual Canadians.

We are shocked by the use of land mines by Yugoslav authorities and by the Kosovo Liberation Army. These weapons were responsible for the destruction of a vehicle containing two Canadian observers and an interpreter; luckily, no one was seriously hurt. Unfortunately, in two other separate incidents, a doctor working for the Red Cross was killed and two nurses seriously injured, and several Serb police were killed. Canadians condemn such weapons of indiscriminate destruction and

and international human rights standards are cast aside in the name of fighting an armed insurgency, in a manner opposed to the letter and spirit of international law, we must not be oblivious to the implications this has for all of us.

Members of this House must therefore condemn in the strongest terms the philosophy which lies behind the actions of the combatants who commit atrocities against civilians in Kosovo. Regardless of who commits such actions, the Serbian forces or the Kosovar insurgents, such actions will never lead to a just and peaceful solution for all the inhabitants of Kosovo.

We are all deeply concerned with the plight of displaced persons within Kosovo, and of Kosovo refugees fleeing into Albania, Macedonia*, and Bosnia and Herzegovina. Canada has contributed to the efforts of the UN, the UN Children's Fund and the Red Cross, and Canada will continue to do its part.

urge the parties to the conflict to abandon them.

Mr. Speaker,

A stable solution reflecting the best interests of all ethnic groups in Kosovo is what is needed. This is the only source for justice, reconciliation and a lasting peace. While Canada and our partners in the international community do not seek to impose our own solutions, we cannot be neutral to the suffering being experienced and the threat to international peace and security posed by the current crisis. Through the UN and through NATO, we must act to help end the suffering and bring about a lasting answer to these complex problems. Time is running out.

A stable solution reflecting the best interests of all ethnic groups in Kosovo is what is needed. There is only one source for justice, reconciliation and a lasting peace. While Canada and our partners in the international community do not seek to impose our own solutions, we cannot be neutral to the suffering being experienced and the threat to international peace and security posed by the current crisis. Through the United Nations and through NATO, we must act to help end the suffering and bring about a lasting answer to these very complex problems. Time is running out.

Thank you.

Bill Graham (Toronto Centre–Rosedale, Liberal), October 7, 1998:

Mr. Speaker, I would like to thank the member for Barrie-Simcoe-Bradford for her very thoughtful and sensitive appreciation of the situation.

I think she has introduced into the debate tonight an element that we really have not heard from a lot of other members, which is the need for reconciliation because, as we know, violence begets violence ...

Text of speech written by Foreign Affairs officials for parliamentarians (used by Ms. Jean Augustine):	Actual speech of Ms. Jean Augustine (Etobicoke–Lakeshore, Liberal):
[First part of the Foreign Affairs draft is not used in Ms. Augustine's speech]	[Ms. Augustine used her own introduction (247 words).]
These barbarous actions have ramifications which are being felt far beyond Kosovo. The displacement of Kosovo Albanian civilians and the polarization of communities which has resulted from the conflict has direct implications not only for Serbia	These barbarous actions have ramifications that are felt far beyond Kosovo. The displacement of Kosovar Albanian civilians and the polarization of communities which has resulted from this conflict have direct implications not only for Serbia and

and Montenegro but for the neighbouring countries, the former Yugoslav Republic of Macedonia* and Bosnia as well. The consequences of the conflict are reverberating throughout southern Europe.

The campaign of violence and oppression in Kosovo is rapidly leading to a humanitarian crisis of terrible proportions. And agencies tell us that as many as 290,000 people have been displaced as a result of the conflict in Kosovo; 30,000 have become refugees in surrounding countries. The remainder are displaced within the federal Republic of Yugoslavia.

The federal Republic of Yugoslavia, and in particular President Milosevic as the head of state with the ability to act with decisive authority, must meet their obligations under international law and to lead the way to a just solution to the conflict. To use disproportionate force against civilians will ultimately prove counterproductive in resisting armed separatist forces. The actions of the security forces are exactly what fuels extremism and violence in the Albanian Kosovar population.

The Yugoslav government must create the conditions necessary for a dialogue leading to a political solution and must fully address the humanitarian crisis. This can only be achieved by calling an immediate end to the offensive and repressive activities of the police and of the military and by withdrawing these forces.

Montenegro but for the neighbouring countries, the former Yugoslav Republic of Macedonia* and Bosnia. The consequences of the conflict are reverberating throughout southern Europe. My constituents who come from that part of the world know what happens to families and individuals when that reverberation throughout Europe is felt.

The campaign of violence and oppression is going on right now, that humanitarian crisis that is before us calls for our assistance. What can we do as Canadians? Are we to just stand here and speak in this debate? Is this doing something? Is this really my effort to ensure that there is some alleviation of the pain and suffering? I think it is.

It is important that the federal Republic of Yugoslavia, and in particular President Milosevic as the head of state with the ability to act with decisive authority, know that I and others are standing here tonight calling on him to meet his obligations under international law and to lead the way to a just solution to the conflict. To use disproportionate force against civilians will ultimately prove counterproductive in resisting armed separatist forces. The actions of the security forces are exactly what fuels extremism and violence in the Albanian Kosovar population.

We have other places in the world where we have seen the results of such action. The Yugoslav government must know that we have said tonight that it must create the conditions necessary for a dialogue to a political solution and must fully address this crisis. It must know that we have said here tonight that we are calling for an

President Milosevic and all Yugoslav authorities are responsible for the actions of their security forces, and must co-operate with the International Criminal Tribunal for the former Yugoslavia by allowing the tribunal's staff to enter the country and carry out their duties. It is also crucial that the Yugoslav government allow human rights monitors in Kosovo to continue their important work. We commend the efforts made by the Kosovo diplomatic mission over recent months, including the important contribution of our Canadian team.

[Next section in the Foreign Affairs draft on NATO's important role is excluded from Augustine's speech.]

The United Nations and the international community has expressed its concern and outrage over the situation in Kosovo. Two UN Security Council resolutions have been adopted, calling for this conflict to end and for the plight of the displaced to be addressed. A clear will exists on the part of the international community to see this terrible situation resolved as quickly as possible.

Canada has used every means at its disposal to try and bring about a peaceful resolution of this conflict through diplomatic means. In various international fora and bilaterally with numer-

immediate end to the offensive and repressive activities of the police and of the military, and that we have also said here tonight that withdrawing its forces is the thing that should be done immediately.

President Milosevic and all Yugoslav authorities are responsible for the actions of their security forces. They must know that the international community stands in horror at the events that are taking place right now in their country under their command. It is also crucial that they allow human rights managers in Kosovo to continue their important work. We have to commend those individuals who have been on diplomatic missions over these past months, including the work we are doing as Canadians. The individuals who are part of those diplomatic missions, who are part of the human rights missions, must be allowed to do their work and inform the international community of what is happening there. It is important for stability in Europe that this human rights mission be allowed to continue.

The United Nations and the international community has expressed its concern and outrage. It seems to me that is not enough. Two UN Security Council resolutions have been adopted calling for this conflict to end and for the flight of the displaced to be addressed. Who is listening? It is certainly not those with the arms who are using force against the people.

Canada has used every means at its disposal to try and bring about a peaceful resolution of the conflict through diplomatic means. In various international fora and in several

ous friends and allies, Canada has called for strenuous efforts to resolve this crisis. Despite numerous appeals by ourselves and others to the government of Yugoslavia, the plight of thousands of innocent displaced persons in Kosovo continues to worsen.

On the verge of the 21st century, we simply cannot allow a humanitarian catastrophe to materialize in the heart of Europe. To do so would represent a grave affront to international standards of human rights and humanitarian law and to our sense of values as Canadians.

Months have passed since fighting first began in Kosovo. President Milosevic has made and subsequently broke numerous promises to stop the fighting and begin serious negotiations. The time for inaction and for further empty promises has run out. The world must act now. It must act to bring and end to the violence, to demonstrate that a peaceful, negotiated settlement must be found and to ensure that thousands of displaced persons can be accessed by humanitarian organizations and eventually return to their homes. Canada must stand ready to play its role in these important efforts.

places we have with numerous friends and allies tried to resolve the crisis. Despite numerous appeals, despite talks, despite the plight of individuals being put before those in power, the situation continues to worsen. We see it daily.

We are on the verge of a new century. There was a time when there was a glimmer and a window of hope that there would be peace in this world. There was a time when we saw a tunnel where we thought there was some light, that there would be peace and that leaders and the people who were in the positions of making decisions would make the kind of decisions for their people that would see this world at peace. Whatever needs to be done at this point in time, I am urging that Canada stand with the rest of the international community, with NATO and with others to ensure that we do what is necessary to bring the horrible and horrendous daily slaughtering of people that we see on our screens to an end.

Question by Gurmant Grewal (Surrey Central, Reform):

Mr. Speaker, I listened to the hon. member very carefully. We are talking about a humanitarian issue here.

It is a very important issue but there is another issue attached to this, that if we are planning to take any military action or if we are committing our military support to NATO, that means we are committing men and women of the Canadian Forces.

The question arises here of whether we are well equipped. Are our brave men and women well equipped with the materials they need?

I would also like to know from the member how much it will cost us. For how long are we going to commit our military forces? Can the member throw some light on that?

Ms. Jean Augustine:

Mr. Speaker, when I stood I did not stand as an accountant, not as someone who is looking at the bottom line. I stood because, as most Canadians, we are moved by the slaughter of human beings.

I think Canada has a responsibility to stand and be counted, not in terms of dollars, not in terms of what it will cost economically. I think there is a moral situation here. That decision has to be one whereby we join with others. We use whatever resources we have.

When the minister of defence spoke earlier I think I heard him say the number of aircraft we have, the men and women we have in that part of the world at this point and our capability at this point. I do not think that Canada will be marching off on its own but that Canada will be playing a role, supportive and otherwise, to ensure a quick resolution.

It is not an accounting job here. It is not looking for the bottom line but it is looking at human beings who are caught in a very horrendous situation.

Speeches Used in the February 17, 1999, Take-Note Debate on Kosovo:

Speech drafted by officials in the Department of National Defence for parliamentarians:	Actual speech of David Pratt, Liberal member for Nepean–Carleton, February 17, 1999:
Mr. Speaker, renewed fighting in Kosovo has once again fixed the eyes of the world on the Balkans. Yet as we debate this issue in the House tonight, we do so with real hope that a solution can be found. I would like to direct my remarks to this aspect of the motion we have before us.	Mr. Speaker, renewed fighting in Kosovo has once again fixed the eyes of the world on the Balkans and as we debate this issue in the House tonight, we do so with a real hope that a solution can be found. I direct my remarks to this aspect of the motion we have before us.
The contact group–sponsored talks between Belgrade and Kosovo Liberation Army in Rambouillet, France, offer for the first time the possibility of a solution to this struggle. We earnestly hope that the parties can come to an agreement and that the difference between them can be resolved.	The contact group–sponsored talks between the Serbs and the Kosovar Albanians in Rambouillet, France, offer for the first time the possibility of a solution to this struggle. We earnestly hope the parties can come to an agreement and that the differences between them can be resolved.

In my view, Canada must be prepared to participate in any potential peace agreement that emerges from the Rambouillet process. Just as we were ready to participate in NATO's Implementation Force upon confirmation of success at the Dayton peace process, we must be prepared to react should these talks also succeed.

As a member of the international community, as a member of the NATO alliance, and as a nation that values peace and democracy, we have a moral obligation to participate in a NATO-led peace operation in Kosovo should such action be deemed necessary. Peace and security in the Balkans have been under threat for nearly a decade now, and Canada has joined the international community from the beginning to respond to those threats.

Mr. Speaker, as I conceive it, there are four key reasons why we should favourably consider a role in any NATO-led operation in Kosovo.

First, let me remind you of Canada's proud multilateral history. As a major trading nation, this country thrives in a stable international system where we protect our interests by working with others. While Canada faces no immediate direct military threat, we are directly affected by instability elsewhere. Our security and prosperity depends on global peace and stability.

Our willingness to play a meaningful role in international relations is a Canadian tradition. We went to Europe to fight for peace in 1914 and returned to do so again in 1939. After the end of the Second World War we fought for those same ideals in Korea. In addition, we have done so for many

Canada must be prepared to participate in any potential peace agreement emerging from the Rambouillet process. Just as we were ready to participate in NATO's implementation force upon confirmation of success at the Dayton peace process, we must be prepared to react should these talks also succeed.

As a member of the international community, as a member of the NATO alliance and as a nation that values peace and democracy, we have a moral obligation to participate in a NATO-led peace operation in Kosovo should such action be deemed necessary. Peace and security in the Balkans have been under threat for nearly a decade now and Canada has joined the international community from the beginning to respond to those threats.

As I conceive it there are four key reasons why we should favourably consider a role in any NATO-led operation in Kosovo.

First, let me remind members that Canada has a proud multilateral history. As a major trading nation, this country thrives in a stable international system where we protect our interests by working with others. While Canada faces no immediate direct military threat, we are directly affected by instability elsewhere. Our security and prosperity depend on global peace and stability.

Our willingness to play a meaningful role in international relations is a Canadian tradition. We went to Europe to fight for peace in 1914 and returned to do so again in 1939. After the end of the Second World War we fought for those same ideals in Korea. In addition, we have done so for many years through our commitment to peacekeeping — over the last 50 years more than 100,000 Canadian men and women have served in peacekeeping missions around the world.

We must continue this tradition. Canadians are internationalists and not isolationist by nature, and we are proud of our heritage of service abroad. Our multilateralism is an expression of Canadian values at work in the world. We care about the course of events abroad and so we are willing to work with other countries to maintain international peace and stability.

Second, our desire to contribute to international security has made us active partners in the North Atlantic Treaty Organization. The North Atlantic community is one of Canada's most important and enduring international links. We are fully committed to collective defence and see the alliance as a force for stability, deterrence and rapid reaction to emergency. Canadians have kept faith with NATO and those ideals for five decades now. We have always been ready to join our allies in opposing threats to stability and peace. Mr. Speaker, today we face another such situation. If NATO becomes involved in a peace support mission in Kosovo, then we should be there to play our part. Canadian participation in a NATO peace mission to Kosovo is in every way consistent with our commitment to peace and security in the transatlantic region and our commitment the North Atlantic alliance.

Third, the Balkan region is highly volatile and represents a serious threat to international peace and security. Should the situation in Kosovo worsen,

years through our commitments to peacekeeping. Over the last 50 years over 100,000 Canadian men and women have served in peacekeeping missions around the world.

We must continue this tradition. Canadians are internationalists and not isolationists by nature. We are proud of our heritage of service abroad. Our multilateralism is an expression of Canadian values at work in the world. We care about the course of events abroad and so we are willing to work with other countries to maintain peace and stability.

Second, our desire to contribute to international security has made us active partners in the North Atlantic Treaty alliance. The North Atlantic community is one of Canada's most important and enduring international links. We are fully committed to collective defence and see the alliance as a force for stability, deterrence and rapid reaction to emergency. Canadians have kept faith with NATO and these ideals for five decades now. We have always been ready to join our allies in opposing threats to stability and peace. Today we face another such situation. If NATO becomes involved in a peace support mission in Kosovo, then we should be there to play our part. Canadian participation in a NATO peace mission to Kosovo is in every way consistent with our commitment to peace and security in the transatlantic region and our commitment to the North Atlantic alliance.

Third, the Balkan region is highly volatile and represents a serious threat to international peace and security. Should the situation in Kosovo worsen, the risk of neighbouring states getting drawn into the conflict would also rise. Albania, the former Yugoslav Republic of Macedonia and Bulgaria, as well as Greece and Turkey or even more distant powers such as Russia and Iran could conceivably become involved.

Mr. Speaker, twice this century brushfire wars in the Balkans have grown to engulf Europe in war. Canadians are not blind to the lessons of history. While the chance of another global war is highly remote, in the Balkans and elsewhere we must persevere with our efforts to maintain international peace and security through the reinforcement of regional stability.

This brings me to my fourth reason for continuing a Canadian presence in this troubled region, Mr. Speaker. We have been an active player in the Balkans since war first broke out in 1991, and so long as we can make a meaningful contribution to improving the situation there we should continue to do so.

When the warring factions agreed to a cease-fire in the former Republic of Yugoslavia in September 1991, we were among the first participants in the European Community Monitoring Mission that was set up to verify the settlement, contributing up to 15 of the mission's 350 civilian and military observers.

In 1992 the UN Security Council established the United Nations Protection Force in Yugoslavia, or UNPROFOR, as an arrangement to facilitate a negotiated settlement in an atmosphere of peace and security. Canada contributed two major units, a logistics battalion and personnel for various headquarters positions.

the risk of neighbouring states getting drawn into the conflict would also rise. Albania, the former Yugoslav Republic of Macedonia and Bulgaria, as well as Greece, Turkey or even more distant powers such as Russia and Iran could conceivably become involved.

Twice in this century brush fires in the Balkans have resulted in war in Europe. Canadians are not blind to the lessons of history. While the chance of another major war seems remote, in the Balkans and elsewhere we must persevere with our efforts to maintain international peace and security through the reinforcement of regional stability.

This brings me to my fourth reason for continuing a Canadian presence in this troubled region. We have been an active player in the Balkans since war first broke out in 1991. So long as we can make a meaningful contribution to improving the situation there we should continue to do so.

When the warring factions agreed to a cease-fire in the former Republic of Yugoslavia in September 1991, we were among the first participants in the European Community Monitoring Mission that was set up to verify the settlement, contributing up to 15 of the mission's 350 civilian and military observers.

In 1992 the UN security council established the United Nations Protection Force in Yugoslavia, UNPROFOR, as an arrangement to facilitate a negotiated settlement in an atmosphere of peace and security. Canada contributed two major units, a logistics battalion and personnel for various headquarters positions.

UNPROFOR's mandate included the protection and demilitarization of the three UN protected areas, the implementation of various cease-fire agreements in Croatia and Bosnia-Herzegovina, the delivery of humanitarian aid and the protection and the monitoring of the "no-fly" zones and UN "safe areas."

NATO's Implementation Force, or IFOR, was the next significant step to establishing peace and stability in the Balkan region. The purpose of IFOR was to enforce compliance by the warring parties in the former Yugoslavia with the Dayton Peace Accord. Canada contributed more than 1,000 personnel, including a brigade headquarters, an infantry company, an armoured squadron, an engineer squadron, a military police platoon and support personnel.

Building on IFOR's successes was NATO's Stabilization Force, or SFOR. Responding to a UN Security Council resolution, the North Atlantic council authorized in late 1996 a NATO operation to support the further implementation of the Dayton peace agreement. SFOR's mission — still being carried out today — is to provide a continued military presence to deter renewed hostilities and to stabilize and consolidate peace in Bosnia-Herzegovina. There are currently about 1,300 troops deployed with SFOR. The Canadian contingent, deployed throughout an area roughly the size of Prince Edward Island, includes a mechanized infantry battalion group, national support and command elements and an engineer design and works team. Canada also provides personnel to various multinational staff positions in the SFOR

UNPROFOR's mandate included the protection and demilitarization of the three UN protected areas, the implementation of various cease-fire agreements in Croatia and Bosnia-Herzegovina, the delivery of humanitarian aid and the protection and monitoring of the "no-fly" zones and the UN "safe areas."

NATO's Implementation force, or IFOR, was the next significant step to establishing peace and stability in the Balkan region. The purpose of IFOR was to enforce compliance by the warring parties in the former Yugoslavia with the Dayton peace accord. Canada contributed more than 1,000 personnel, including a brigade headquarters, an infantry company, an armoured squadron, an engineer squadron, a military police platoon and support personnel.

Building on IFOR successes was NATO's Stabilization Force, or SFOR. Responding to a UN Security Council resolution, the North Atlantic council authorized in late 1996 a NATO operation to support the further implementation of the Dayton peace agreement. SFOR's mission — still being carried out today — is to provide a continued military presence to deter renewed hostilities and to stabilize and consolidate peace in Bosnia-Herzegovina. There are currently about 1,300 Canadian troops deployed with SFOR. Our contingent, deployed throughout an area roughly the size of Prince Edward Island, includes a mechanized infantry battalion group, national support and command elements and an engineer design and works team. Canada also provides personnel to various multinational staff positions in SFOR headquarters. Our

headquarters. Other operations in the Balkans that Canadian Forces have or are participating in include a NATO-led operation enforcing the compliance of the no-fly zone over Bosnia-Herzegovina, the enforcement of a United Nations embargo on the former Yugoslavia, the United Nations mission of observers in Prevlaka, and the UN preventative deployment force in the former Yugoslav Republic of Macedonia. In addition, we have also been actively contributing to a variety of multinational operations in Kosovo.

We currently have 23 troops deployed with the OSCE Kosovo Verification Mission, established to verify compliance by all parties to the October 1998 Holbrooke-Milosevic agreement.

The Canadian Forces contribute 60 personnel and six CF-18s to the NATO Extraction Force. The force exists to remove the OSCE verifiers and other designated persons from Kosovo should it prove necessary. Our CF-18s also stand prepared to participate in any NATO air campaign against military targets in the federal Republic of Yugoslavia. This task force, which is supported further by 130 Canadian Forces personnel, also supports the SFOR mission.

Mr. Speaker, the many operations and missions I have just outlined are illustrative of Canada's strong and continued commitment to maintaining peace in the Balkan region. More than 20,000 Canadian Forces personnel have rotated in and out of that theatre. We clearly have invested significant personnel and resources in order to promote peace and security there, and have made a genuine and meaningful

other operations in the Balkans that Canadian Forces personnel have or are participating in include a NATO led operation enforcing compliance of the no-fly zone over Bosnia-Herzegovina, the enforcement of a United Nations embargo of the former Yugoslavia, the United Nations mission of observers in Prevlaka and the UN preventive deployment force in the former Yugoslav Republic of Macedonia. We have also been contributing to a variety of multinational operations in Kosovo.

We currently have 23 troops deployed with the OSCE Kosovo verification mission, established to verify compliance by all parties to the October 1998 Holbrooke-Milosevic agreement.

Our contributions to current NATO operations in Kosovo include 60 personnel with the Extraction Force ready to remove OSCE verifiers and other designated persons from Kosovo should it prove necessary, eight Canadian forces personnel deployed as headquarters staff with the Kosovo air verification mission, and 130 personnel and 6 CF-18s with operation echo, ready to participate in any NATO operations.

The many operations and missions I have just outlined are illustrative of Canada's strong and continued commitment to maintaining peace in the Balkan region. More than 20,000 Canadian Forces personnel have rotated in and out of that theatre. We clearly have invested significant personnel and resources in order to promote peace and security there and have made a genuine and meaningful difference. We should maintain that investment because more remains to be done, as events of the past few weeks have clearly shown. Large refugee flows, political struggles between various ethnic groups, continued human rights abuses and the ever-present danger of widespread war are all illustrative of just how much more work the international community needs to do. With the right kind of agreement out of the negotiations in Rambouillet, we can and should once again shoulder our share of international efforts in the region.

Speech written by DND officials for parliamentarians:

Mr. Speaker, it is a pleasure to speak to the motion calling on this House to take note of possible Canadian peacekeeping activities in Kosovo and possible changes in the peacekeeping activities in the Central African Republic.

I would like to address some of the issues relating to the situation in the Central African Republic, beginning with the background to the current situation we are facing.

The past several years have been enormously difficult ones in that country. In November and December of last year, free and fair elections were held. These were the first tentative steps toward the restoration of national institutions since dire political and economic conditions swept the country in 1993.

difference. We should maintain that investment because more remains to be done, as events of the past few weeks have clearly shown. Large refugee flows, political struggles between various ethnic groups, continued human rights abuses and the ever-present danger of widespread war are all illustrative of just how much more work the international community needs to do. With the right kind of agreement out of the negotiations in Rambouillet, we can and should once again shoulder our share of the international efforts in the region.

Actual speech by Paul Szabo, Liberal Member for Mississauga South, February, 17, 1999:

Mr. Speaker, it is a pleasure to speak to the motion calling on the House to take note of possible Canadian peacekeeping activities in Kosovo and possible changes to our peacekeeping activities in the Central African Republic.

First I would like to address some comments to the issues relating to the situation in the Central African Republic, beginning with the background to the current situation that we are facing.

The past several years have been enormously difficult ones in that country. In November and December of last year, free and fair legislative elections were held. These were the first tentative steps toward the restoration of national institutions since dire political and economic conditions swept the country in 1993.

In recent years, unpaid soldiers mutinied on three separate occasions and French troops were brought in to quash the uprisings. In January of 1997, the rebel soldiers and those forces still loyal to President Patassé signed the Bangui accords, which addressed measures necessary to bring peace back to the country. This agreement also established the Mission Interafricaine de Surveillance de l'Application des Accords de Bangui, or MISAB.

This mission, made up of military and civilian personnel from France and six African countries, was created in order to maintain peace and security and monitor the implementation of the Bangui accords. In June 1997 MISAB was forced to put down another mutiny against the government. Meanwhile, conditions in the country continued to deteriorate.

By early 1998 MISAB's mandate was coming to an end, and French troops had begun to withdraw. It was apparent, however, that further international assistance was required if the Central African Republic was to remain free of violence. In March of last year, therefore, the UN Security Council unanimously adopted Resolution 1159, establishing a UN peacekeeping operation to replace MISAB. The initial three-month mandate of the Mission des Nations unies en Republique centrafricaine, or MINURCA, began with 1,350 troops from six African countries, France and Canada.

As the parliamentary secretary to the minister of national defence has outlined, MINURCA was given a variety of roles, including maintaining

In recent years, unpaid soldiers mutinied on three separate occasions and French troops were brought in to quash the uprisings. In January 1997 the rebel soldiers and those forces still loyal to President Patassé signed the Bangui accords, which addressed measures necessary to bring peace back to that country. This agreement also established the Mission Interafricaine de Surveillance de l'Application des Accords de Bangui, or commonly referred to as MISAB.

This mission, made up of military and civilian personnel from France and six African countries, was created in order to maintain peace and security and to monitor the implementation of the Bangui accords. In June 1997 MISAB was forced to put down another mutiny against the government. Meanwhile, conditions in the country continued to deteriorate.

By early 1998 MISAB's mandate was coming to an end and French troops had begun their withdrawal. It was apparent, however, that further international assistance was required if the Central African Republic was to remain free of violence. In March of last year the UN Security Council unanimously adopted resolution 1159 establishing, a UN peacekeeping operation to replace MISAB. The initial three-month mandate of this new mission, the Mission des Nations unies en Republique centrafricaine, or MINURCA, began with 1,350 troops from six African countries, France and Canada.

As was previously outlined in the debate, MINURCA was given a variety of roles including maintaining security in and around the capital of security in and around the capital of Bangui, training civilian police and ensuring the security and freedom of movement of UN personnel. This mandate was extended in July of 1998 and again in the following October.

The UN secretary general recognized this progress in his December 1998 report to the Security Council suggesting that MINURCA was a success story so far. The UN's involvement has allowed the CAR to become, as he said, "an island of relative stability in an otherwise war-torn region." He reported that the mission had played an important role in the legislative elections held just a couple of months ago, and had been instrumental in helping the government prepare plans for restructuring the army and civilian police force. As we know, the UN presence also launched a human rights awareness campaign and provided medical and humanitarian assistance in and around Bangui. In addition, the stabilization of the country has led to some economic recovery.

Nevertheless, the secretary general also noted that peace remains fragile and that the political climate is still permeated by division and distrust. He concluded that a continued MINURCA presence is required at least until the fall 1999 presidential elections. Mr. Annan is recommending that MINURCA's mandate should be extended and that the force structure should remain essentially the same.

Mr. Speaker, the current mandate will expire at the end of this month. MINURCA still has a very important role in the slow but steady recovery of

Bangui, training civilian police and ensuring the security and freedom of movement of UN personnel. This mandate was extended in July 1998 and again the following October.

The UN secretary general recognized the progress that had been made in his December 1998 report to the Security Council suggesting that MINURCA was a success story so far. UN involvement has allowed the Central African Republic to become, as he said, "an island of relative stability in an otherwise war-torn region." He reported that the mission had played an important role in the legislative elections just a couple of months ago and had been instrumental in helping the government prepare plans for restructuring the army and civilian police force. As we also know, the UN presence launched a human rights awareness campaign and provided medical and humanitarian assistance in and around Bangui. In addition, the stabilization of the country has led to some economic recovery.

Nevertheless, the secretary general also noted that peace remains fragile and that the political climate is still permeated by division and distrust. He concluded that continued MINURCA presence is required at least until the fall of 1999 when there will be presidential elections. The UN secretary general, Mr. Annan, is recommending that MINURCA's mandate should be extended and that the force structure should remain essentially the same.

The current mandate will expire at the end of this month. MINURCA still has a very important role to play in a slow but steady recovery of the

the Central African Republic. It is important to seize this opportunity to build on our success to date. Canadian participation is vital in this regard as our Forces are providing the communications framework for the multinational force.

At a joint Defence and Foreign Affairs Committee meeting last April, members of Parliament recognized the importance of this contribution and unanimously resolved that Canada should participate in MINURCA. Today, Mr. Speaker, there are compelling reasons to support both the extension of MINURCA as well as our continued participation.

The extension would allow MINURCA forces to continue to foster a secure and stable environment so that the presidential elections scheduled for later this year can take place in a free and fair way. It would also continue to foster the process of reconciliation and reconstruction in the Central African Republic.

The key considerations in this matter are clear enough. First, given our past involvement in this region and our record of leadership in peacekeeping and peace support operations, it is only natural that the UN would look to us to stay the course. We are in a position to share our valuable experience and work with Africans to help them find lasting solutions to the complex challenges they face. Through MINURCA and other operations, through our membership in La Francophonie and through our membership in an ad hoc UN group known as the "Friends of the Central African Republic," Canada has already made a meaningful contribution to international

Central African Republic. It is important to seize that opportunity to build on our success to date. Canadian participation is vital in this regard as our forces are providing the communications framework for the multinational force.

At the joint Defence and Foreign Affairs Committee meeting last April, members of Parliament recognized the importance of this contribution and unanimously resolved that Canada should participate in MINURCA. Today there are compelling reasons to support both the extension of MINURCA as well as our continued participation.

The extension would allow MINURCA forces to continue to foster a secure and stable environment so that the presidential elections scheduled for later this year can take place in a free and fair way. It would also continue to foster the process of reconciliation and reconstruction in the Central African Republic.

The key considerations in this matter are clear. First, given our past involvement in the region and our record of leadership in peacekeeping and peace support operations, it is only natural that the UN would look on us to stay the course. We are in a position to share our valuable experience and to work with the Africans to help them to find lasting solutions to the complex challenges they face. Through MINURCA and other operations, through our memberships in La Francophonie and through our membership in an ad hoc UN group known as the "Friends of the Central African Republic," Canada has already made meaningful contributions to international efforts to maintain stability efforts to maintain stability in Africa. The UN is looking to us to help by continuing this effort.

Second, we are in a privileged position during our two-year membership on the UN's Security Council — and during our presidency on this body this month — to make an especially meaningful difference to international efforts to improve the situation in the Central African Republic. Our continued participation in MINURCA is a natural way to making the most of our opportunities in this sphere.

Finally, the skills and professionalism of our troops would clearly be of enormous benefit to our colleagues in MINURCA. As is well known, Canada has contributed to almost all UN peacekeeping missions — and along the way developed a wealth of experience. This experience and our ability to work in English and French make Canadian soldiers perfectly suited to work along the other military contingents of MINURCA.

In the Central African Republic we have a chance to continue to help foster stability in a troubled and fragile place. We have the opportunity to demonstrate once again our continued ability and willingness to promote international peace and security. Finally, we have another chance to reflect the wishes of Canadians, who have told us that they want Canada to work toward a stable global order. From my vantage point, if the right security and other assurances can be provided, these are compelling reasons for us to continue our efforts to make a difference in the Central African Republic.

in Africa. The UN is looking to us for help by continuing in this effort.

Second, we are in privileged during our two-year membership on the UN Security Council — and during our presidency of the body this month — to make an especially meaningful difference to efforts to improve the situation in the Central African Republic. Our continued participation in MINURCA is a natural way of making the most of our opportunities in this sphere.

Finally, the skills and professionalism of our troops would clearly be of enormous benefit to our colleagues in MINURCA. As is well known, Canada has contributed to almost all UN peacekeeping missions, and along the way has developed a wealth of experience. This experience and our ability to work in English and in French make Canadian soldiers perfectly suited to work alongside other military contingents of MINURCA.

In the Central African Republic we have a chance to continue to help foster stability in a troubled and fragile place. We have the opportunity to demonstrate once again our continued ability and willingness to promote international peace and security. Finally, we have another chance to reflect the wishes of Canadians who have told us that they want Canada to continue to work toward a stable global order. In my view, if the right security and other assurances can be provided, these alone are compelling reasons for us to continue our efforts to make a difference in the Central African Republic.

In the final moments I have I would like to briefly comment with regard to our position in Kosovo. Earlier this day I listened carefully to the minister of foreign affairs and to the minister of national defence. All parliamentarians appreciated their words of praise for our troops and about the need for Canada's continued participation, particularly in Kosovo.

The minister of foreign affairs said something that I thought was very relevant, very simple but straightforward. He referred to our participation not just as a peacekeeping contingent but for civil peace building. This aspect of peace building is extremely important. Canada has developed an international reputation as peacekeepers as well as peace builders. It is that reputation, that skill and that ability, that we can bring to the situation in Kosovo.

The minister also referred to the human rights situation, the fact that young children are being drawn into military conflict and that Canada as an internationally recognized champion of human rights around the world is well suited. It is important for us to play a role there. I wanted to highlight that.

As the minister concluded his speech he finally asked parliamentarians to put on record their views on this matter. I am pleased to have participated in this debate and I am pleased to support the minister's call for parliamentarians to support our participation in Kosovo as well as in the Central African Republic.

Speeches Written and Delivered in Take-Note Debate on Kosovo, April 12–13, 1999:

Speech written for parliamentarians by officials in the Department of National Defence:	Actual speech delivered by Hec Clouthier, Liberal MP for Refrew–Nipissing–Pembroke, in the House of Commons, April 12, 1999:
	Mr. Speaker, it is a privilege for me to split my time with the hon. member for Haldimand–Norfolk–Brant. In times of peace and prosperity, countries and individuals alike follow higher standards because they are not being forced into a situation in which they must do something they do not want to do. But war is a stern teacher. In depriving them of the power of easily satisfying their daily wants, it brings most people's minds down to the level of their actual circumstances. The circumstance that is uppermost in the minds of people today is the worsening human crisis in Kosovo.
With the worsening humanitarian crisis in Kosovo uppermost in our minds today, our thoughts rightly turn to a range of important questions. What is the current situation in and around Kosovo? What is the status of NATO's efforts to reduce Slobodan Milosevic's ability to further harm Kosovo's inhabitants? What does this conflict mean for us as Canadians and for Canada as a member of the North Atlantic alliance? What is the nature of our interests and obligations, be they strategic, political or moral?	Our thoughts rightly turn to a range of important questions. What is the current situation in and around Kosovo? What is the status of NATO's efforts to reduce Slobodan Milosevic's ability to further harm Kosovo's inhabitants? What does this conflict mean for us as Canadians and for Canada as a member of the North Atlantic alliance? What is the nature of our interests and obligations, be they strategic, political or moral?
As we debate these and other issues today, it is clear to me that our perspectives on some of these questions, perhaps those that come closest to home, are largely influenced by our respective views of Canada's tradi-	As we debate these and other issues today, it is clear to me that our perspectives on some of these questions, and perhaps those that come closest to home, are largely influenced by our respective views on Canada's

tions. I join this debate today to say a number of things, but first and foremost to speak my mind on what I think has developed in the course of this century into a proud Canadian tradition of helping others.

It is only fair to begin by saying that Canadians have not always been sufficiently concerned about the course of events abroad. We have had occasion to regret this in the past. But it is also fair to say that, for many years now, Canadians have shown a very real appreciation for the significance of events occurring far from home, and that this awareness has had an important influence on government decision making.

When they see that the international situation demands it, Canadians have supported sending the Canadian Forces into harm's way in order to make a tangible contribution to the cause of international peace and security. This willingness to involve ourselves in the world has become traditional for us, and it is a tradition that we can all be proud of.

It is a tradition rooted in culture and commitment — and is an expression of our values and interests abroad. Canada has longstanding links to the broader international community through culture, economy and family. As a major trading nation, we thrive in a stable international system and we are directly affected by instability elsewhere. Our security depends on global peace and stability, and we protect our interests by working with others.

traditions. I join this debate to say a number of things, but first and foremost to speak my mind on what I believe has developed in the course of this century into a proud Canadian tradition of helping others.

Canadians have shown a very real appreciation for the significance of events occurring far from home, and this awareness has had an important influence on the government's decision making.

When they see that the international situation demands it, Canadians have supported sending the Canadian Forces into harm's way in order to make a tangible contribution to the cause of international peace and security. This willingness to involve ourselves in the world has become traditional for us, and it is a tradition that we all can be proud of. It is a tradition rooted in culture and commitment. It is an expression of our values and interests abroad.

Canada has longstanding links to the broader international community through culture, economy and family. As a major trading nation, we thrive in a stable and international system and we are directly affected by instability elsewhere. Our security depends on global peace and stability, and we protect our interests by working with others.

That is why we are founding members of the North Atlantic Treaty Organization, the United Nations, and why we have committed ourselves to a host of other international institutions. It is also why we went to Europe to fight for peace in 1914 and returned to do so again in 1939. After the Second World War we fought for those same ideals in Korea.

Since then we have become the world's pre-eminent peacekeeper: well intentioned, well equipped and well trained. Over the last 50 years more than 100,000 Canadian men and women have served in peacekeeping missions around the world. When the Nobel Prize was awarded to the United Nations for peacekeeping operations, Canada was singled out for its contributions and honoured by the international community.

The concept of peacekeeping, which Prime Minister Lester B. Pearson gave the world over 40 years ago, was a simple yet powerful idea. And history shows this idea caught on.

Prime Minister Pearson's perspective on international security also provided two of the fundamental pillars of our foreign and defence policies. The first is that the promotion of international peace and stability is of paramount importance to Canada. The second is that the promotion of this stability is best undertaken collectively because it clearly demonstrates the will of the international community.

Mr. Speaker, for these reasons Canada may be required from time to time to commit our military resources to protect deeply held Canadian interests and values.

That is why we are founding members of the North Atlantic Treaty Organization and the United Nations, and why we have committed ourselves to a host of other international institutions. It is why we went to Europe to fight for peace in 1914 and returned to do so again in 1939. After the second world war we fought for those same ideals in Korea.

Since then we have become the world's pre-eminent peacemaker: well intentioned, well equipped and well trained. Over the last 50 years more than 100,000 Canadian men and women have served in peacekeeping missions around the world. When the Nobel prize was awarded to the United Nations for peacekeeping operations, Canada was singled out for its contributions and honoured by the international community.

The concept of peacekeeping, which Prime Minister Lester B. Pearson gave the world over 40 years ago, was a simple yet powerful idea. And, as history shows, this idea caught on.

Prime Minister Pearson's perspective on international security also provided two of the fundamental pillars of our foreign and defence policies. The first is that the promotion of international peace and stability is of paramount importance to Canada. The second is that promotion of this stability is best undertaken collectively because it clearly demonstrates the will of the international community.

For these reasons Canada may be required from time to time to commit our military resources to protect deeply held Canadian interests and values.

We must also remember that Prime Minister Lester B. Pearson's concept of peacekeeping was not limited to providing troops when the fighting had stopped. He clearly understood that military forces sometimes had to be employed not merely to monitor peace, but to *create the conditions in which it can be established*. In 1997 United Nations Secretary General Kofi Annan echoed Lester Pearson's vision, stating that "you can do a lot more with diplomacy when it is backed up with firmness and force."

Our country has a well-deserved reputation as a peacekeeper, but that reputation and the events that created it are also elements of a wider tradition. That tradition is one of international engagement on a range of issues, peace and security being among them. To understand that tradition we must not forget that we have never and will never shy away from stronger means if that is what the pursuit of peace requires. Canada, of course, always prefers a diplomatic solution. Our tradition has always been to appeal to the powers of reason and try to achieve peace without the use or even the threat of force.

Sometimes, however, diplomatic action is not enough. Diplomatic efforts sometimes fail to produce the desired result and that leaves governments with a choice. They have the option of walking away, but where the interests are real the international community is left with little choice but to take action against those who refuse to adhere to international standards of conduct. This is a reality of international relations.

This decade alone has given us examples of such circumstances. When

We must also remember that Prime Minister Lester B. Pearson's concept of peacemaking was not limited to providing troops when fighting had stopped. He clearly understood that military forces sometimes had to be employed not merely to monitor peace, but to create the conditions in which it can be established. In 1997 United Nations Secretary General Kofi Annan echoed Lester Pearson's vision, stating that "you can do a lot more with diplomacy when it is backed up with firmness and force."

Our country has a well-deserved reputation as a peacekeeper, but that reputation and the events that created it are also elements of a wider tradition. That tradition is one of international engagement on a range of issues, peace and security being among them. To understand that tradition we must not forget that we have never and will never shy away from stronger means if that is what the pursuit of peace requires. Canada, of course, always prefers a diplomatic solution. Our tradition has always been to appeal to the powers of reason and try to achieve peace without the use or even the threat of force.

Sometimes, however, diplomatic action is not enough. Diplomatic efforts sometimes fail to produce the desired result and that leaves governments with a choice. They have the option of walking away, but where the interests are real the international community is left with little choice but to take action against those who refuse to adhere to international standards of conduct. This is a reality of international relations.

This decade alone has given us examples of such circumstances. When

Saddam Hussein invaded Kuwait, the international community had to employ its military resources. In Bosnia NATO has had to use selective force to bring about the conditions for peace and stability. On both occasions Canada was there with our allies.

Last year we returned to the Gulf to pressure Iraq to comply with United Nations weapons inspections. And of course this year we returned to the Balkans to ease the humanitarian suffering in Kosovo.... Over the years thousands of Canadian Forces personnel have made Canada's presence felt. Our present involvement in NATO operations, then, is only the most recent form of our longstanding commitment to security in this region.

There are those who will argue that the use of force against Slobodan Milosevic's efforts in Kosovo is not in line with multilateralism or with Canada's traditions. I think these people are wrong, and that Canadian participation with our allies in Kosovo is in every way consistent with our traditional approach to international security threats and the protection of human rights ...

Saddam Hussein invaded Kuwait, the international community had to employ its military resources. In Bosnia NATO had to use selective force to bring about the conditions for peace and stability. On both occasions Canada was there with our allies.

Last year we returned to the Gulf to pressure Iraq to comply with the United Nations weapons inspections. This year we returned to the Balkans to ease the humanitarian suffering in Kosovo. Over the years thousands of Canadian Forces personnel have made Canada's presence felt.

In my riding we are privileged to have one of the largest military bases in Canada, CFB Petawawa. I am proud to say that the troops of Base Petawawa have discharged their duty with diligence, dedication and devotion to securing peace throughout the world. Our present involvement in NATO operations is only the most recent form of our longstanding commitment to security.

There are those who will argue that the use of force against Milosevic's efforts in Kosovo is not in line with multilateralism or with Canada's traditions. I believe these people are wrong.

In conclusion I would like to paraphrase John Donne. No person is an island entire of itself. Every person is a part of the whole. Any person's death diminishes me because I am involved in mankind. Therefore, never ask for whom the bell tolls; the bell tolls for thee.

Right now the bell is tolling loud and clear that Canada must defend the defenceless of the world, the hundreds of thousands of refugees in Kosovo who have fled from the destruction of their homes and the murder and rape of their relatives. We cannot and will not stand for this kind of evil ethnic cleansing, this genocide, this destruction of humanity, because when the oppressed of the world call, Canada answers the bell.

I am so proud that ordinary Canadians from such places as Arnprior, Barry's Bay, Calabogie, Douglas, Eganville, Renfrew, Petawawa, Pembroke, Deep River, Stonecliffe, Deux-Rivières and thousands and thousands in my great riding of Renfrew-Nipissing-Pembroke are committed to helping the refugees and committed to Canada's intervention in the Kosovo crisis.

Mr. Speaker, when words cannot protect the innocent, Canada cannot stand idly by. We must move forward with out allies to end Mr. Milosevic's brutal campaign. Thank you.

When words and hope cannot protect the innocent, Canada cannot stand idly by. We must move forward with resolute resolve to end Milosevic's brutal campaign so that one day the bell will toll no longer, so that one day all mankind will live in peace, security and prosperity.

Speech written for parliamentarians by officials in the Department of National Defence:

Actual speech delivered by Raymonde Folco, MP for Laval West, April 12, 1999: [Speech begins in French, then continues in English]

... Mr. Speaker should bear in mind that before Mr. Milosevic rose to power, Kosovo — made up principally of ethnic Albanians — had constitutional autonomy within Yugoslavia. This right was stripped away by Mr. Milosevic in 1989. From that point forward he has deliberately implemented a plan to impoverish and

We should bear in mind that before Mr. Milosevic rose to power, Kosovo was made up principally of ethnic Albanians and had constitutional autonomy. That right was stripped away by Mr. Milosevic in 1989. From that point forward he has deliberately implemented a plan to impoverish and oppress the Kosovars. Early last

oppress the Kosovars. Early last year his security forces mounted a campaign against innocent civilians similar to the ethnic atrocities we witnessed in both Croatia and Bosnia. Villages have been attached and destroyed ...

In the end the Kosovars agreed, exercised that courage and signed the agreement. Mr. Speaker, Mr. Milosevic did not have this courage. The Yugoslavs had no intention of negotiating or signing an agreement. The diplomatic track had run its course. Our patience and our commitment to leave no diplomatic stone unturned was once again rewarded by Mr. Milosevic's unwillingness to stand by agreements he had made, or to seek a peaceful solution. In fact, they continued their force build-up during the Rambouillet process.

We have no quarrel with the people of Yugoslavia — it is Mr. Milosevic and his government which bear responsibility for this human tragedy. Now we have been forced to turn to a measure of last resort — military force. This was not an easy decision nor a hasty one. But the interests we seek to preserve and protect in this region are significant. Peace and stability in Europe has always been a pillar of Canadian security policy. Our interest in restoring and maintaining that stability is as great today as in the past ...

year his security forces mounted a campaign against innocent civilians similar to the ethnic atrocities we witnessed in both Croatia and Bosnia ... [speech switches back to French, then again in English]

In the end the Kosovars showed the courage to sign the agreement. However, Mr. Milosevic was only interested in gaining precious time. The diplomatic track has run its course. Our vision and our commitment to leave no diplomatic stone unturned were once again rewarded by Mr. Milosevic's unwillingness to stand by the agreements he had made or to seek a peaceful solution. In fact, he continued the build up of his forces during the Rambouillet process.

Let us be clear about one thing. We have no quarrel with the people of Yugoslavia. It is Mr. Milosevic and his government which bear responsibility for this human tragedy. Now we have been forced to turn to a measure of last resort, military force. This was not an easy decision nor a hasty one. But the interests we seek to preserve and protect in this region are significant. Peace and stability in Europe has always been a pillar of Canadian security policy. Our interest in restoring and maintaining that stability is as great today as it was in the past ... [continues in French to the end]

INDEX

Page numbers in *Italics* refer to illustrations